WAGON OF FOOLS

& Other Parables

Samuel Benjamin Gray

ISBN 0-9824749-0-3
EAN13: 9780982474907
Library of Congress Control Number: 2009928812

Visit www.booksurge.com, www.amazon.com or
www.thewildolivepress.com to order more copies.

To the God of Abraham, Isaac, and Jacob;
and to his children—may they have ears to hear and eyes to see.

Acknowledgements

No work of fiction is solely from one mind, and certainly never from only one heart. Ideas, thoughts, events and people provide the seeds which germinate and grow into a story. Too, if the author is wise, he or she will ask a number of respected individuals to prune the garden prior to its harvest. Many such people have provided creative inspiration, encouragement, or technical assistance so that these stories could be set before you, and it is in this spirit that the author wishes to acknowledge:

✿ His wife, who provided inspiration and encouragement beyond words, and carried so many burdens so that these stories might come to fruition. Some of these stories are hers as well; God knows the tears she's shed reading them come from too many hard memories.

✿ His mother, who infused in him a fierce desire to read and write well (if you find any mistakes, no need to contact the publisher — she'll have already seen him drawn and quartered).

✿ His father, who taught him the meaning of mercy and the importance of humility, perseverance, and gratefulness.

✿ Michael and Judy Phillips, for their technical assistance. They spent an enormous amount of time in the midst of many other pressing engagements reading and editing the manuscript. Thank you both for your wonderful kindness and superb technical review. The remaining mistakes are mine alone.

✿ Chris Streinz and his family, for their reading and comment.

✿ Kilburn and Danielle, for inspiration and friendship, good advice about shooting, and the world's best lemon bars.

✿ The Salisbury family, for their encouragement and for the time they took to read a few of the original stories: we still ride to the top of the hill and pray for you, friends.

✡   Mr. Mark Helprin and his short story, *Jacob Beyer and the Telephone*, which served as the inspirational diving board for *Return to Koidanyev*.

✡   Mr. Peter Schwartz, for early inspiration.

To Messrs Helprin and Schwartz, and to those others of their clan who also move in "much bigger circles", the author extends advice given by Berel Jastrow to his brother Aaron:

Lekh lekha

Disclaimer

These parables are works of fiction. With the exception of historic figures, the characters are fictitious, and any resemblance of the imaginary characters to actual persons living or dead is unintended and fortuitous. Michelangelo, Pascal, Generals Pavlov and von Kluge, and Hitler were real people; the noted author Helprin is a real person. *Return to Koidanyev* was inspired by the short story *Jacob Beyer and the Telephone*, by Mark Helprin. Gustav Krupp von Bohlen und Halbach did at one time own the Krupp steel company in Germany. Oświęcim (Auschwitz) and Chelmno nad nerem (Chelmno) were real locations. Przebrno and Krynica Morska were real places. The Einsatzgruppen were real. In some stories, events similar to those depicted did in fact occur at or near the locations described.

Contents

STORY BEFORE A PATROL

My father was a good man but a strange Jew. I know he was a good man because I lived with him until the day of my fifteenth birthday. I know he was a strange Jew because everyone in our village said so.

I wonder about this now. I am in the woods, in Lithuania, with the partisans. I have been here since the Germans invaded Poland. What is happening here and what I think now about my father and the kind of Jew he was is itself a strange story. You should know about it, so…I will write it out. I have some time before the next patrol.

My father was an orthodox Jew from Poland—and from Poland you don't get more orthodox. He wore the tzitzit and the tallit and the kippah even in the fields, and he always kept kosher. I learned to cook a kosher Shabbat meal by the time I was five. My father read and studied Torah like all good Jews, and I am pretty sure he read more than most; no, I am positive. Our one room besides the kitchen on the ground floor of our house was lined with books which my father and mother treated as respected friends, treasured companions. He and my mother read more than anyone else in the village—this I am sure of, too.

I remember Flaxman, the tailor, once said to my father, "Yaacov, you look like a Jew, you walk like a Jew, you even shrug like a Jew…" and he wagged his fingers and tapped the side of his head, "but from the way you talk, you don't *think* like a Jew." I didn't know what he meant then. We

1

Jews read a lot…we are, after all, supposed to be the People of the Book. Yet my father would actually read the book when most of the people in our village simply listened to the Rebbe tell them what other men thought or said *about* the book. I think this is what made my father unlike the others in our village.

There was something else also that made my father strange. He believed everything in life was ordered and structured by God. He would tell me when I was young that he believed God was sovereign. To a boy this word was difficult, but my father taught me its meaning every day of his life. Many others in the village said they believed this too, but you could see that my father believed this truth by what he did and how he behaved. He was truly content with whatever life brought him. He approved of the order and structure that he found in life. He truly believed that whatever happened, it was the right thing. I used to think this was a wonderful thing as a boy, to have a father who was content to such a degree that nothing bothered him; nothing shook his faith in the God of Torah. He would consider everything that happened as the right thing, that God sees everything and knows about everything and is fashioning every thread of every life in every land to conform to His will. I sit in the woods now and listen to stories from Jews who have escaped from places like Oświęcim and Chelmno nad nerem, and I see the horror and the blankness and the realization in their eyes that they will live a life of terror from this day until the day they die, and it makes me think of my father and wonder that he could believe such things.

He would sit in the synagogue, before the Germans came, with his best white shirt and his black vest, with the tallit under the shirt and his kippah tilted back and listen with wide eyes as the Rebbe would speak of the Torah and how God's wisdom could be applied in any situation life could deliver. The Rebbe would talk about how God was sovereign over all life and every day and how much He loved us and was working to do His best for us, and the men would listen and then they would go back to the farms and complain about the harvest, about the goats not giving enough milk, about their wives, about their children, about politics, about the Germans and what they would do if they came to Poland, about the government. I would wonder about this because I never heard my father complain...and he had enough to complain about.

We lived in a very small farming village just north of Modlin. Maybe there were thirty families in the village, and we were all Jews. We had cows and goats and chickens and my father was a butcher. My mother would make the most wonderful blankets with lace trim that she sold to others in the village, and once every summer we would hitch the horse to the wagon and drive to the great city of Warsaw to sell what she made during the winter, when the snows came up so high against the little house that we could not see out of the windows on the ground floor for months. My room was in a small upper story, a small bedroom, but it had a window that looked out over our small front yard and I could see the road north that led from Modlin up into the rolling green hills of East Prussia. Our farm looked out over this road; we were the closest house in the village to this road. On winter days I would stare out the window and wonder about what adventures I might have if I traveled up that road. It is when I remember my daydreaming that I come closest to believing that God has a dark sense of humor.

When I was five my brother Arele was born. My mother, always frail, died giving Arele life. My father shed tears, I know, and he was deeply grieved, because he loved my mother. Yet he did not ever complain—this I also know. The one thing that struck me, and I still remember it to this day, was after the Rebbe and the other men came to take away my mother's body in the wagon, I ran behind the barn, not wanting others to see me cry, and there was my father, on his knees in the dirt, with his hands lifted up to heaven. I stopped short, my hand on the rough wood of the barn, the smell of cut grass sharp and clear, the sound of bees in my ears, and I heard my father thanking God for taking his beloved. I was only five and could not understand how a person could thank God with tears in his eyes and the pain of loss still in his heart, but there was my father, thanking the Almighty God of Abraham, Isaac, and Jacob for taking his wife to keep her safe from things to come. More than any other thing, this picture in my memory of my father on his knees thanking God upon such an occasion has served to keep solid what little faith I have. Raskowicz laughs at me all the time, but if my father could believe such things…if my father could kneel in the straw and with an honest heart lift up his hand in thanks for the passing of his wife, who is Raskowicz to say he's wrong? And I wonder maybe that my father knew then—or maybe God told him—such things about the Germans that we are only now finding out; maybe he knew that something worse would happen to my mother. I have heard the stories; it makes me respect my father a little more because of what maybe he knew.

Things were fine for a year or two, with my father and me, and we both worked hard to raise Arele and take care of the farm. One day my father came to me in the barn while I was forking hay to the cow and said, "Moshe, come, sit with me for a minute." I threw the last flake into the pile and sat down in the dirt at his feet. He sat on an old wooden stump that we used to split kindling and butcher the occasional chicken. Whenever he would sit on the butchering stump, I knew that he wanted to talk about something important.

"Moshe, we should talk about Arele."

"Yes, Poppa."

"Moshe, there is something I think that makes Arele a little different."

"Yes, Poppa."

"Do you notice anything different about Arele?"

"Yes, Poppa. He doesn't make the noises that Mendelsohn's baby makes. He just stares and stares. I wonder sometimes, Poppa—"

"Yes, Moshe, I wonder too. But I think God knows what He is doing, my boy. There must be something that God has for Arele to do that he can only do if he is like the way he is. So we must wait and see what it might be, and we should be patient. Is this okay with you?"

"Yes, Poppa. I can help care for him."

"Thank you, Moshe. I will need you to be a good brother to Arele. To have such a child, that has a job which only he and God know about…well, it is a big and important thing and we cannot interfere. We must not keep the boy from what he is supposed to do by being cruel, or treating him like the other boys in the village treat their brothers. We must be to him as we would wish others to be to us."

"No, Poppa, I wouldn't be mean to Arele."

My father put a rough hand over my head and caressed my cheek. "No, Moshe…no, you wouldn't, I know this." He smiled—my father was always smiling, which is another reason the people in the village thought he was a strange Jew—and said, "Now, Moshe, finish up moving the hay and then let us see what we can do about the fences, hey?"

Things at home were steady after this, although sometimes Arele would do things that would confound us. One day when he was eight Arele came down from our room—he was sharing mine—and walked directly to the barn. It was in the spring. He walked into the barn while my father and I were moving manure. We had a work horse at the time, a large Belgian draft named Paul, which my father thought a great joke, but a joke no one in the village understood. I myself never understood it either until I read a New Testament we were given by a little tailor from Modlin—a Christian, I am pretty sure—that was in a bundle of food and blankets he left for us in the woods. He was killed later by the Germans for hiding two Jews in his cellar. Jews would cross to the other side of the street before they would risk touching a New Testament, but I read it because I wanted to see what words could possibly move a person to give up their life for a Jew. I saw that Paul was a prominent writer of many books in the New Testament. This was something else that made my father strange—I realize now from the many things he said when he was alive that he must have read this Gentile book, and as I read it through, it helped me better understand my father and what he thought. I began to wonder if the influence of this strange Gentile book is what made my father appear to the men in the village to be so strange. But then I recalled that Paul himself was a Jew, who wrote to the Gentiles that they should not disdain the Jew. This carpenter who the Gentiles say is the Messiah was also himself a Jew. It is confusing.

And so that day Arele walked into the barn and began to scuff his toe in the dirt floor. I looked over and got back to work, but my father paused.

Arele continued to kick at the ground, and I saw that he was scuffing a line in the dirt—an uncommonly straight line. Then I saw that Arele was scratching along the outline of a small door in the floor—a door I'd never seen. But Arele was like a dog on the trail of a strong scent, and he scuffed and scratched in a spastic sort of way—he was never very coordinated and he could not even hold a glass of water to drink because his hands shook so badly. He kicked and scuffed and attacked the ground until at last there appeared very clearly a door of wood, buried under the dirt floor of the barn.

"Arele," my father said, quietly.

Now what happened next was strange, because usually Arele never responded to anything anyone said to him. Perhaps it was just the quiet, numinous quality in my father's voice that made Arele look up. He looked directly at my father, straight into his eyes, and said quietly in Polish, "This is my job."

At first I thought Arele wanted something to do—here we are, my father and I, both working hard, and he wants to help. He looked away from my father then, bent down and with shaking hands, shoved his fingers into the crevasse between the dirt floor and the wooden boards and gave a yank. Nothing moved at first—he wasn't very strong—but he pulled and pulled, and eventually the door came up, shedding dust and straw and clumps of manure. Dust hung in the sunlight streaming through the barn door, and Paul blew out his nostrils.

There was a wooden box in the ground. With surprising strength, strength I would never have suspected from my small brother, he lifted the box up out of its resting place, opened the lid, and pulled out a rifle.

"Arele," my father said, again, "please…be careful." But my father stood there leaning on his fork and made no move to stop my brother.

Arele gave no sign that he had heard my father—this was normal. The rifle, however, was not—it was as if Arele had known about a Norwegian buried in the barn. My father told me later that this was the first time he had ever seen the gun.

Arele looked at the rifle and turned it this way and that. I am not sure he even knew what it was, or what one should do with it, but after a few moments, he put the rifle back in the box and shakily closed the lid. He put the box back in the hole in the barn floor and, with shaking hands, dropped the lid down over the hole. It did not fit. He looked at me, and then looked at my father, and said, "This is my job. This is what I am supposed to do." They were more words than I had or ever would hear him speak, and I believe that my father did not remove the rifle immediately because of Arele's conviction that it had something to do with his calling in life.

There was something else, another time, more recently, when Arele did something strange. My father and I were cleaning out the cow's stall and after a long winter, there was much to clean. We would fork out the stall, throw the old straw and manure into a cart, and then together push the cart behind the barn to pile the manure into a compost pile. It was my father's habit to put the compost pile near the garden, which was on the side of the barn opposite to the front of the house.

It was a hot day in September just after the Germans had passed our village on their way to Warsaw when my father and I wheeled out the first cart load and we were pushing it toward the other side of the house when we heard a long, keening moan. My father and I looked up, startled, sweat dripping already from our faces, and saw Arele standing on the doorstep to the house, lifting up his head, moaning, with a long, wailing, "ooooooo" sound, and pointing at us.

We knew from experience that this noise he made meant "no" for some reason. As with most things, though, this eruption from Arele was hard to understand. We turned from considering him and began to push the cart again, but Arele ran down from the house toward us and then angled off just behind us to a spot not ten feet away. He picked up a stick and began to pound the dirt. My father stood up and watched Arele pounding the ground. He wiped a trickle of moisture from his forehead and asked, gently, "What is it, Arele?"

Arele paused and again looked straight at my father and pounded the ground again with his stick, with a long "eeeeeee" sound. My father kept his eyes fixed on Arele and said in a quiet, urgent tone of voice, "Moshe, get a pitchfork."

I pulled the pitchfork from the top of the manure in the cart and held it out to him. "It is right here, Poppa."

For some reason my father was speaking very softly. "Yes, so it is. Moshe, I want you to put a pitchfork of manure where Arele is pounding."

I looked up at him, questioning.

"Go ahead, do it, Moshe."

I lifted a small amount of manure from the cart and walked over to where Arele was pounding the stick, still crying out, making his "eeeeeee" noise. I dropped the pile where his stick was hitting the dirt, and he stopped, then looked at my father again, and said, again in what my father would tell me later was perfect Yeshiva Hebrew, "This is my job." Then he ran back inside.

My father took out a handkerchief and sat down with his back against the barn. "Moshe, "he said, "it appears Arele wants the manure pile here instead of on the other side of the house."

I looked up at my father. "Why would that be, Poppa?" I asked, shaking my head.

My father shrugged. "It's his job," he replied. "If it's his job, who are we to say that it's not?" And so my father and I lugged the manure from the stall and piled it where Arele had pounded the dirt until the pile was eight feet high and ten feet around. I did not understand this habit my father had of just accepting things. I was almost fifteen that day and like any other young adolescent believed that I had almost completely gathered all knowledge encompassed within the universe and didn't need any advice from others. But I did listen to my father that day, and helped him, though I did not understand why we needed to put the compost pile on that side of the barn. It would make things difficult when we had to carry it all back again to the garden.

❊ ❊ ❊

I remember that it was after the curiosity with the manure that we began to hear from our community about the Germans doing strange things to the Jews in Poland, and we began to wonder what would happen to our village.

There is another part to this story. I get this part from a German prisoner we captured just north of Modlin, near our village I think, and he told us a story that makes me wonder about my father and that maybe perhaps he wasn't so strange.

The German prisoner, a Freidrich Schturm, was a corporal in the German army. He came from a village near Pomerania, in northern Germany, and was assigned to Army Group North, he said—the Fourth Army under General von Kluge. He was just a driver, assigned to drive a lieutenant. We partisans do not know many things but we have learned that mere lieutenants in the Wermacht do not have drivers, and so when he said this we were going to just shoot him outright, but he held up his hands with wide eyes and stuttered in a fearful, rapid-fire northern German accent that he was telling the truth. I do not know why but Raskowicz put up a hand to the rest of us, and we lowered our rifles, although Pinkelson did jab the man in the ribs with his bayonet so hard that it went through the German's greatcoat and made him wince and grab his side. Raskowicz growled but did not bite at Pinkelson because Raskowicz knows what the Germans did to Pinkelson's parents and sisters. Like Raskowicz would say, not everything in life is fair…so the German got to tell his story.

Schturm was just a corporal when the Fourth Army moved across the corridor for the invasion of Poland. The whole world believed Hitler's lies. I would sometimes ask my father why it was that evil people could tell the most convincing lies so powerfully that everyone would believe the lies and not believe the truth. My father, without even a nod or a shrug, would smile sadly and say, "Moshe, remember, God has reserved the evil in the world for a day of destruction."

And I would ask him, in all the frustration of my adolescent impatience, "But what does that mean, Poppa?"

"It means, Moshe, that the Creator of all life knows what He is doing, and if you see someone who is evil you can know two things." He held up a finger as if he was lecturing in some great college hall in Warsaw. "First, you can know that God is doing His best for that person—yes, even that evil person. God does not want any person to forego the pleasures of a relationship with Him." He held up a second finger. "And second, you can know that if that person does not stop being evil, God has a fate planned such that the working out of that fate will bring about God's perfect will."

This detour into logic and theology I completely ignored; I only knew what I'd been hearing about the Germans. "When will this day of destruction come, Poppa…will it come before the Germans get here?"

My father paused then and said that there was coming a day when the whole world would know that God was God, but he thought that before that day God's own people would have to learn that they were His people and that they had an obligation to obey Him. I got the sense from him that he felt we Jews had much to account for.

"You watch, Moshe," he said to me one day when we heard the first of the stories; it was as if he'd expected them. "The cleaver will fall hardest upon the most religious Jews…oh yes, make no mistake. We Polish Jews are more orthodox, more traditional, more attentive to keeping the law than any Jews you could find in the world…and what will it get us? It will get us the great hammer of God down upon our heads for our hardhearted ignorance of the *spirit* behind the law, that's what it will get us. To whom much is given, much is required. And do you think we will figure this out? Do you think we will turn to Him in sorrow and tears and…" He did not go on; he could not. He would be crying by then.

My father believed that before this last day when all evil would be destroyed, the Jews would be once again restored to their land in Palestine and there God would deal with them so dreadfully that what remnant remained would finally recognize who He was and what He wanted of His people. He said that a great and horrible but necessary thing would first happen to the Jews, something so horrible that the world would be compelled to restore us to our homeland one last time—compelled as a sheepdog compels the sheep. "God steers the nations as a man steers a horse in the field, Moshe," he would say. "And the nations will rage and the heathen imagine a vain thing, but God will have them in derision and His will shall be accomplished. But it will not be the worst, Moshe... what is coming over the near horizon is nothing compared to what your grandchildren will see." This frightened me, and I did not understand it, for I had yet to see even the horror on the near horizon.

His eyes would darken and when he would talk about such things the men in the village would scoff and wonder out loud when Yaacov the butcher began to rate so highly that God Himself would have talks with him. They would wonder out loud why all of a sudden Yaacov the butcher knows what the God of All Creation is thinking. "Grow old in Poland," they would say, "and don't worry about it."

Unlike the people in the village—even the Rebbe—my father thought that one could talk with God like a man talks with his friend. After warning them about their hearts (this they would laugh at), my father would shrug (this they recognized) and shake his head (this also they would recognize) and he would say that they should just wait and watch and be careful, and maybe we should all think about going to America if they didn't want to know what he was talking about. This completely unexpected reference to some mythical land of golden streets and strange, tall people who spoke a barbarian language would throw the village elders into utter confusion. They would throw up their hands and begin to talk so loudly that I could not understand any more. My father would just raise his eyebrows a little and lift his shoulders just so, as if to say that maybe he wasn't so smart after all, but maybe just the same they should wait and see. It is remarkable what a man can say with just some eyebrows and a couple of shoulders. It is a shame no one listened.

So I am going to tell you about what the German corporal said; time is short.

He was sitting in the dirt near our fire and telling us his story. He was a driver in the Fourth Army under von Kluge, assigned to drive a young lieutenant. This lieutenant grew up in Danzig, the son of a prominent university professor. Schturm knows all this because the young officer would talk incessantly to another officer. Schturm said this officer's name was Groothausen, or Grauthessen, or something. He was a major in the SS. Schturm was terrified of the SS, and did not know why a young lieutenant was being dragged around the Wermacht by an SS major. When he hears this, Pinkelson wants to shoot the German corporal again, because such things were just not done. Pinkelson thinks the corporal is lying, but the corporal said that he could explain why such a thing was so, so Raskowicz tells Pinkelson to sit down and be quiet. Raskowicz is always looking for intelligence. Pinkelson sits down but he holds his machine pistol leveled at the German. Veershciem sneers at the corporal to show the German that we are just waiting for the end of the story before we kill him.

The corporal tells us that this lieutenant was apparently some kind of wunderkind—a child prodigy, a genius. But, he said, he was not just any kind of genius. "This boy amazed even the most intelligent professors at the university when he was only eight or nine years old. This boy mastered every field of mathematics, biology, and chemistry by the age of ten. He would publish papers and the best minds in Europe would come to see which professor authored them, only to discover that the author was some ten-year old! They would be shocked."

Well, Schturm tells us, this boy's head would be on the chopping block in Hitler's Germany, because Hitler hated academics and intellectuals, but one day somehow this young German wunderkind attended a meeting of the Hitler youth and from that day forward demanded that his parents take him to every meeting. The boy became a fanatical worshipper of Hitler.

As the boy grew, his intellect grew, but so did his hatred of everything that Hitler hated—which, we did not need reminding from Herr Corporal Schturm, meant that the genius boy's hatred of Jews grew until it was white hot. The boy made a small name for himself in Danzig by walking around the streets in a Wermacht uniform his parents had made for him (there were collaborators even then) and throwing rocks through the windows of stores owned by Jews. But the reason that the Germans put an SS major with him, Schturm says, was to guard him.

"Guard him for what?" Raskowicz asks.

"Well, to guard him and his papers," Schturm says.

"What papers?" Veershciem asks, cutting in.

"The papers he would always carry around in a satchel, about this big," the German says, holding out his hands. "The boy would talk constantly about his plans to kill every living Jew. Some kind of wonder virus, he said. He said that the professors at his university hated him because he was so much smarter than they were, and he was glad that the Nazis were giving him a chance to use his mind. He said he was the salvation of the Reich and that he could give Herr Hitler everything he ever dreamed of. He was not right in the head."

Raskowicz ignores the corporal's speculation.

"How did the SS get involved?"

"The university tested him," Schturm replied. "They asked him to make a virus that would kill only one kind of rat or something. He did so; they were amazed. Then some German professors from Berlin came and brought in some people from different countries—some Poles, a few Lithuanians, even Spaniards and Italians, and each group had a few Jews. The boy asked them some questions, wrote in a notebook, did some calculations, and then went into his laboratory. He came out with a vial of some liquid and told them all to drink it. He said it was a test serum to prepare them for further examinations. They believed him and drank it; they all drank from the same vial. Only the Jews died. The professors asked the kid about how this virus spreads. The kid told them that he can put it in water, in the air, anywhere, and in about three weeks eliminate the Jewish race from the earth."

When he says this Raskowicz sits back in horror. Pinkelson's face turns white as he sits beyond the fire. Veershciem's mouth opens and he looks as though he will be sick.

"So the professors ask the kid for the formula, and the wunderkind shakes his head back and forth, pats the satchel he carried, and says, 'What was in that vial was all that has been made. I will give the formula only to the Fuehrer in Berlin.' The professors are about to argue with the boy but the boy holds up a hand and says, 'Best, Herr Professors, that you check with Berlin before you respond. So the professors do, and the word comes back from Berlin that they want to see the young genius right away, and they were instructed to give the boy anything he wants."

Raskowicz is still shocked, and Pinkelson is trembling. Schturm continues.

"'I want a commission in the Wermacht as well,' says the boy wonder on the phone, and they give him a commission as a lieutenant—right there over the phone. This is not the old Army, I can tell you. My old lieutenant was thirty-eight, with ten years in the ranks and three years of combat service, before they promoted him."

"Get on with the story," Raskowicz says, thinking the German is trying to delay the inevitable. The corporal shakes himself and complains a little, but keeps talking.

"The boy also told them about his experiments with something like heavy water and the production of something called uranium, whatever that is, but I didn't understand much of what he said. He had plans for some strange weapon that could destroy an entire city with one bomb; he was definitely not stable, I can tell you. But Berlin was very interested in this. I think this is when they decided to send out the SS major. The major and I pick up the boy in Danzig. I remember one professor turning to another when the boy got into the car, and I heard the whispering and saw their fear. They were saying that he was not quite human; he wasn't natural. They were afraid. I saw it. I know.

"On the way back to Berlin we get caught up in Army Group North's invasion of Poland and get rerouted toward Modlin by some idiot sergeant at a roadblock. The SS major is screaming and yelling and waving his papers, blowing on about his high clearance to get back to Berlin, but the boy is okay with the detour because he wants to go kill…he wants to go kill people, and he wants to go to the front." We all realize that Schturm was going to say that the boy wonder wanted to kill Jews but thought better of it, surrounded as he was by several Jews holding guns pointed at him. He went on.

"After the major foams at the mouth for a while, the boy tells him to sit down and shut up and let me drive him to the front. Let me tell you, the major wasn't accustomed to anyone talking to him like that, much less some wet-behind-the-ears Wermacht lieutenant. I saw him in the mirror; he got very red in the face and was about to rake this boy over the coals when the boy turned and looked directly at him.

"My God, my blood ran cold, and the little bastard wasn't even looking at me. The major turns white, shuts his mouth, sits back, waves a hand toward me and tells me in a weak voice to press on to the front. Two miles later he tells me to pull over, gets out of the car, and vomits. The wunderkind just looks out the window.

"From Danzig we cross the corridor with von Kluge at the beginning of September and cut into East Prussia and then down south into Poland. Most of the time we would ride along behind one of the Panzer columns, but one day the lieutenant decides that he wants to make a raid on his own. Well, he issues this order to the major, who I can see doesn't like being ordered around by a lieutenant, but will die before he says anything. He swallows his pride and makes the request of the Commanding Officer of the nearest panzer battalion. Apparently word had been passed from Berlin to give the young lieutenant what he wants as long as his satchel gets down to Berlin safely.

"So the Commanding Officer detaches three tanks, and the tanks along with our Kubelwagon begin a drive down to some small village just north of Modlin, well behind the front. The major is riding in the front with me; no more riding in the back with the kid for him. The kid is in the back by himself with his satchel. We pass an overturned Polish armored car and before I can drive by, the boy shouts at me to stop—he was always ordering me around—and I stop. He jumps out and rummages around the wreckage for a while, until the major leans out and suggests that perhaps he should get back in the car. Then a strange thing happens.

"The kid was rummaging around in the wreckage, and he suddenly just stopped, and I swear, the whole world held its breath. Everything got quiet; the birds stopped making noise, the fire in the armored car stopped crackling, the wind calmed; there was no other sound. It was like some giant blanket fell down over the world. We were maybe three kilometers from the village. There had been a little breeze, but the wind suddenly stopped. Some farmers were burning leaves in the distance and I remember the smoke rising straight up into the sky like exhaust from a furnace while they stood and stared at us with their rakes in their hands. And the other thing; I became terribly cold, though I didn't know why.

"The lieutenant comes out of the wreckage of the armored car with a pistol in his hand—they had given him a sidearm—and walks up to the Kubelwagon and lifts the pistol and points it at the SS major and says, 'If you ever talk to me again in such fashion I will see that you are shot. Do you understand me?'"

Pinkelson does not interrupt because this is so strange that no one can imagine the German making any of this up. Veershciem begins to look worried. The corporal continues.

"The major is as shocked as I am to hear a lieutenant in the Wermacht speaking in such a way to a major, even if he is in the SS. The major opens his mouth to object. I guess the lieutenant thought he was going to say something, so the lieutenant shoots him."

Raskowicz' head jerks back and he blinks hard, and Pinkelson and Veershciem and I all gasp. This is too much to believe, but too strange to discount.

"He shot him? In cold blood?" Raskowicz is stunned.

The German's eyes were distant now, and full of fear—not of us, but of the memory of what he'd seen. "There was something not right about this man," he said quietly, afraid that he might be heard by...someone or something. "This boy...I was watching his eyes as he stared at the major and...and...there was just nothing...just two black holes. No one was inside. I...I have never seen such darkness."

"You are lying," Pinkelson yells and leaps up. We know he is frightened because we all are as well. "This doesn't happen!"

The German turned to him with a look that made Pinkelson's heart stick in his throat. "You can kill me if you wish, boy, but he was not human," he said quietly, shaking his head, staring into the fire. "He was not human."

None of us argued with the corporal at this point, since many of us had heard stories by then; stories of other things. We will believe until the day we die that many men in that place and in that time did things which could not be explained by any reference to humanity.

"Go on," Raskowicz says quietly.

The German shakes himself slightly and continues. "So this kid shoots the major square between the eyes. The major's head jerks back and his brains spatter all over me. 'Do you have a problem, Corporal?' the lieutenant asks, switching the pistol until the little black hole is staring directly at me. 'No Mein Herr,' I reply, and put both my hands on the wheel and look forward. It was one of the hardest things I've ever had to do in my life. So he goes back to the wrecked vehicle and finally pulls out two cans of gasoline and jogs back to the car. 'We can have some fun with these, don't you think, Corporal?' he asks, giggling like some demented child. 'Yes, Mein Herr,' I reply. 'Let's find some Jews to burn,' he says. He puts the two cans of fuel in the back next to his satchel and climbs back into the Kubelwagon."

Pinkelson growls at this, and Veershciem looks down at his rifle, but no one says anything else. Raskowicz is blinking rapidly.

I should now write and tell of what happened on the day my father and brother died, and then you can decide if my father was strange.

I was behind the barn trying to catch a chicken for the noon meal when I heard the rumbling sound made by military vehicles. There were not so many—even then I could tell the difference—but I did hear the unmistakable clinking sound of tank treads turning over bogey wheels. This was not a good sign. I walked around to the front of the barn, which had a cleared area that faced the front of the house and the road north. I could see dust clouds. Then I saw a short blue bolt burst from the door—my brother Arele in a blue shirt raced past me through the open barn door and into the dark shade within the barn itself. I stood still, looking at him and then looking back at the dust clouds. I ran round to the back of the barn. My father was driving Paul, harrowing the oat field. I yelled until I got his attention and he seemed to sense my urgency. He came around the barn just in time to see tanks trundling up the road toward the house. It was then that we both saw Arele run back into the house, carrying something. My father and I realized at the same moment what it was—the rifle from the box in the barn.

"Arele!" my father cried, and then bolted for the house. Just as suddenly he stopped, looked at me, hard, and said, "Stay here, and watch those tanks." My father got to the door and was just yanking it open when I heard the flat crack of a rifle. I remember that my first thought was, "How could Arele have loaded the thing?" Before I could finish the thought, there came another crack. I began to walk slowly toward the house when I heard a dull report, then a ripping shriek. I saw smoke in the distance, near the tanks, and then most of my house exploded. The concussion blew me almost the entire length of the yard toward the barn, where, if I'd landed on the ground, I would have died. But instead I landed in the large compost pile.

* * *

"We were driving toward this one farm house north of Modlin," Schturm was saying, "and the next thing I know, there is a kind of 'clunk' or plunk sound, and then the lieutenant begins to look around, wondering what is happening. There is a hole in one of the gas cans and it is spouting fuel all over the back of the Kubelwagon. I can smell it. I stop the car and look back and he is bent over, looking at the hole, wondering how it got there, and then I hear the same sound again, this time more clearly. I recognized it then, since I fought in the Great War; it was the sound of a Karabiner 98. Someone was shooting at us. Anyway, I was looking at the lieutenant while he is running his fingers over the hole with gas pouring out of the cans after the first shot. I heard a second shot, and a red hole appears where his right eye was and his head explodes. The round that kills him hits the back of an iron stanchion in the vehicle and ricochets around. It must have caused a spark because the next thing I know the two fuel cans explode and blow me out of the front seat onto the ground. I sit up in time to see the entire back end of the Kubelwagon go up in flames. The lieutenant's body and his satchel, with his precious papers, are burning furiously.

"They have good people in the panzer corps, you know, and they quickly figure out that we are taking fire from the farm house. The lead panzer turns its main gun toward the house and destroys it completely.

"Apparently the tank commander recognizes that he is going to be in deep trouble for letting the lieutenant get killed, so he takes his tanks immediately back to the battalion to report, leaving me in the dirt by the side of the road next to the dead lieutenant and the burning Kubelwagon. I walk back that night and get to my unit the next day."

* * *

I have always wondered what my father would have said about this story. I always thought that God had made a mistake, making Arele the way he did, but after hearing Schturm, I am not so sure. I do not know how Arele could have hit the lieutenant and the gas cans from three hundred yards— but clearly he did. Perhaps no one will know why a Wermacht lieutenant and his satchel were of such importance that the Creator needed to create a young boy whose one and only task in life was to shoot a Karabiner 98 rifle and kill a lieutenant and burn up some papers. I wonder if perhaps my brother didn't save all the Jews in the world from a fate even worse than which we see happening to us now, and as I think this, the voice of my father comes to me.

"Now, Moshe," he says quietly, with a sad smile, "is it the tool or the craftsman that accomplishes the work? Is it Arele, or the God who made Arele, that you should thank for such deliverance?"

I wonder that my father would think there could be a fate worse than what is happening to us Jews now. I wonder about why God would see to it that a German with knowledge about how to eliminate every Jew on the face of the earth would be killed—it is the only reason I can see for my brother's life; it was the one thing he did—yet Hitler, a German far more powerful than a young Wermacht lieutenant but as yet incapable of killing us all, is permitted to live. What is God doing with us? What does he want? If He wanted us all dead, why have Arele kill the lieutenant? I wonder about these things, especially when we get escapees from the camps who tell us of the horrors and the terror and the inhumanities that are happening to us because we are Jews. Again I hear my father's voice.

"Moshe, God knows what He is doing."

Veershciem is saying that it is time to go.

Pinkelson asks what we should do with the German. Raskowicz says that we cannot afford to keep prisoners, and it was his bad luck to get caught, so he tells Pinkelson to "do what you wish" and waves his hand in the air and walks away. Pinkelson stands there with his machine pistol leveled at the German and stares at him for almost a minute, trembling, but he cannot pull the trigger, so he turns around and walks away with me to go on patrol.

MACUSHLA

Once there was a little girl who lived with her father and mother and older sisters in the Irish section of town, in a red brick house with white shutters. The older sisters were very pretty and, as such things naturally follow, so was the little girl—or at least, so she would be. For some reason, her beauty for a time rested beneath a plain visage in the way that storm clouds, emptied of their fury, yet hold back the sun. Perhaps God wanted the emergence of her outward appearance to be timed with the development and emergence of a more transcendent inner beauty. For whatever reason, this delay in transformation resulted in a situation in which the little girl, comparing herself to the surface beauty displayed by her sisters, did not think of herself as pretty. She thought of herself instead as plain, homely, and dull, while she saw her sisters as exciting, vibrant, glamorous, and far beyond herself in grace and comportment. And so it was that she fell into the habit in thought and action of relating to them more as a servant than a sister. Her sisters, not being her equal, responded according to their natures, and thought of her and thereby treated her as a servant.

The little girl was called Macushla. Her father, an Irish immigrant, could not resist the joy that overwashed him upon her birth, and spontaneously decided to call her "Darling" in Gaelic. Her mother disapproved of such sentimentalism, but for once was overridden, and the blessed daughter came into the world thus heralded. In their little circle of the world that was an Irish tenement, the name was natural and sweet, a garland about her head, testifying to her father's love whenever she emerged to walk about the town to see what she might do for others. Her habit of service could not be constrained in display only toward her sisters. Such a thing by its very nature pushes itself outward until it swallows up and embraces everything in a fragrant consumption of self, as when a fire consumes frankincense and myrrh. In such a way did she come to be especially cherished in the little knot of hard-working Irish families.

Life was hard then; everyone worked at the refinery in town—the only place of employment for the Irish, since the bakery and butcher and the vegetable markets were run by the Italians. Truth be told, many Irish were glad that it was so—prosciutto was an unknown delight in Ireland, and better by far than boiled corned beef to many a Celtic palate. The country was blossoming, burgeoning, growing big shoulders. Oil and the products that spewed forth from oil would transport the nation and its immigrant people to a position of power and security and luxury. The streets would be paved with gold and trees that grew money would grow in every back yard, springing from seeds of hard work, sweat, and luck. The Irish families in that little town had their share of such seeds.

One day when Macushla was five she went out to see what could be done for Mrs. O'Brian. Mrs. O'Brian had been ill, and Macushla thought that perhaps she wanted a biscuit. In Macushla's home there was a plate eternally replenished with biscuits on the counter next to the stove, and it reminded Macushla of the stories her father would read to her on Sundays, of that man who took a few loaves of bread and a few fish and made them just keep coming out of a basket. Just so did this plate keep producing biscuits, no matter how many the little girl would consume. So Macushla wrapped a biscuit in a napkin and went forth to conquer the dragons that persecuted Mrs. O'Brian.

On the way, she came upon the one true terror of her life—the Macready's dog. Or, truth to tell, 'twas the other way round—the dog came upon her. It was either the scent of the biscuit or the work of the devil, I cannot say, but the dog came trotting round the corner of the street, eyes alight with the joy of discovering one so small in his power. It was a mean dog, like its owners; small-minded, consumptive with greed, begrudging other men kindness due as though kindness was coin they could ill afford to freely dispense.

The dog smelled the biscuit, Macushla saw the dog, and the dog smelled the fear all at once. Macushla bolted back up the street. She did not scream; she was too frightened. The dog darted after her, tongue lolling, eyeing the biscuit clutched in the little white fist.

A small boy of seven was walking on the other side of the street, sent by his mother to the grocer for kosher salt, when Macushla came running breathlessly around the corner. In this town it was not uncommon to see children running, yet children seem to know instinctively the difference between a run for joy and a run from terror. The small boy took in the dog, the girl, and the biscuit, and recognizing the town's four-legged bully, grasped the situation in a moment. He took up a slat from a broken vegetable crate and darted in front of the dog and gave it a whack on the head that stopped it in its tracks. The dog in turn grabbed the boy by the lower leg and worried him dreadfully. The boy smacked the dog repeatedly, enduring the pain manfully, and broke the slat over the dog's head. The dog, weary of the sport, regretting the biscuit but not willing to bear the treatment required to obtain it, retreated.

There was much blood on the ground when Macushla, who had watched the fight, ran back to help. The boy still had half of the slat in his hand and was growing quite pale.

"Are you all right?" she asked, partially in awe, still trembling. She began to cry when it broke in upon her heart that the blood on the ground—the boy's blood—had been spilled on her account.

The boy grimaced in pain and tried to sit up. He had black hair and very striking blue eyes, and she could see that he was taller than she was, even lying down. "Has...is the dog gone?" he asked weakly. Macushla could only nod, her heart in her throat. "My mother is going to be upset about this," were his next words, "they were my good pants." Then he fainted.

With great presence of mind, Macushla darted into the grocer's shop, pulled Mr. Mastrontonio out by the hand into the street, and when the squat little grocer saw the boy and the blood and the broken slat and heard the little girl go on about the dog—well-known predator was this dog—he took the situation in hand, picked up the boy gently, brought him into his shop, and sent his assistant to run for the parents while he cleansed his wounds. The long and the short of this little story is that after the passage of a few weeks the boy was up and about again, none the worse for wear. The grocer had the constable round. In these days when children were more valued than the animals who preyed upon them, there was no wringing of hands over what to do. The constable found the dog one day in an alley, took his revolver, and shot the foul mauler in the head. The Macready clan moved to Chicago.

Throughout that year and into those following, the little girl and the boy, Arthur, were inseparable. He was her knight in shining armor. For his part, she was to be protected, and as he came to know her better, the sweetness of her nature, her courage, and her inclination to care for others before herself endeared her to him in the soft and gentle way that only bonds in childhood can be forged—the purest bonding process known upon the earth, and the one that fades last from memory.

* * *

When Macushla was ten and Arthur twelve, they were visiting Mrs. O'Brian (aye, the same poor soul) who was again down among the thorns of malady. Macushla would sit and read to the old woman while Arthur cut the lawn, trimmed the hedges, and repainted the steps. In return the woman O'Brian would have nothing but to get up from her sickbed and produce a wondrous pitcher of lemonade which would have made angels cry, ah, the taste of it. Arthur sat there on the bricks next to the steps (which were still wet with paint), sweat beaded upon his kingly brow, his shirt dark in splotches. It was a hot day in summer.

"The steps look nice, Arthur," Macushla observed, holding her own glass of godly nectar.

"They're coming along…the first coat should be dry soon in this heat." He looked over at her. "What are you reading to Mrs. O'Brian?"

"Och, it's a grand story about a prince that makes his way across the sea to find adventures, and he rescues a farm girl and they live happily ever after."

Arthur nodded slowly, looking up at the house across the street. Mrs. Gilletto was shaking out a bedspread from the upstairs window.

"Morning, Mrs. Gilletto," Arthur said, lifting his glass.

Mrs. Gilletto stared down at the two children at the O'Brian house. "You two aren't bothering that poor woman, are you?" she yelled, in English with a trace of an Italian accent.

"Oh, Mrs. Gilletto, we're just readin' her a wee story, is all," said Macushla, face upturned to Mrs. Gilletto and the summer sun all at once, "and she likes it, or I'm a toad."

"Well, you youngsters take care not to put her out, d'ye hear me?" Mrs. Gilletto went on shaking the bedspread and then disappeared back into the window suddenly, like a turtle retreating hastily into its shell.

"So the prince rescues the farm girl," Arthur went on. "You know, in all those stories, they end up living happily ever after. I wonder what that means, to live happily ever after?"

Macushla sat there on the bricks, her legs dangling down, barefoot, with a glass of lemonade in her hand, smiling up at the hot sun, and wondered too about what such a thing could mean. "I suppose," she said thoughtfully, "it means that they grow up and they like what happens to them."

Arthur pondered this assertion, took a sip of lemonade, and nodded. "Probably," he said, "and probably they never live in Chicago."

"Why not Chicago?" Macushla asked pugnaciously, turning to stare at Arthur. She had nothing particularly against Chicago.

Arthur looked inscrutable and wiggled his eyebrows darkly: "Because Macready's new dog is in Chicago."

They both laughed heartily. Macushla's heels pattered against the brick facing, feet giggling, and they finished their nectar. Arthur finished the steps, Macushla finished the story, and life went on in the rich and fertile summers of their childhood.

When Macushla was eleven, Arthur thirteen, they were messing about in a boat Arthur's father had made, rowing out upon a great rushing river that flowed around ancient castles until it came to a waterfall that dropped thousands of feet into a enchanted land of fairies and dragons—but which, truthfully, was only a small stream just deep enough to bear a boat with two small children and Arthur's unlucky border collie, captured and stowed away for the express purpose of defending against sea serpents. By now Macushla was just at the very glimmering edge of showing the beauty of form that would emerge as she grew. Her hair, a bright shiny red in her youth, was darkening to a rich copper-tinged auburn; her eyes, green, flashed ever brighter. She was thin and lithe, quite athletic, at ease on land or sea or tree, with or without shoes.

And too she was discovering a growing interest in that man about whom her father occasionally spoke. Her father alleged that this man was also God. He read her stories about him, when their mother was out and about on some errand or other. She enjoyed these times of closeness with her father. His eyes would brighten and his entire being would seem energized and alive as he read and spoke about this man who went about healing and causing no end of trouble with the religious authorities.

Arthur followed her closely in these matters; they spoke of everything freely. Though such stories had not broached the threshold of his home—his parents were Jewish—he knew that of all things Macushla was honest and true, and would not be interested in something that even hinted at untruth, calumny, or forced sincerity. If she believed a thing to be true, he would bet his life that it would be true. It was only when he actually framed these words to himself (and because he was a boy who loved the truth) that he realized the depth and level of regard he was developing for this young girl...and it seemed to be the most natural thing in the world.

"My Daddy was reading the other day about that man, Jesus, who went out in a boat and talked to lots of people. Why do you think he did that?"

Macushla asked, petting Solomon, Arthur's dog, who, if he had to be at sea, was content only in her arms.

Arthur pulled manfully at the oars, negotiating skillfully around a protruding tire. "Probably because when you get on water your voice carries farther."

Macushla laughed. "No, silly...why didn't he just walk out without the boat; he could have, you know. My Daddy says that he walked on water. So why did he get in a boat?"

Arthur pulled at the oars for a while, and thought, and pulled some more, putting his back into it, and they moved at a good pace against the current. His exertion caused him to breathe harder. "Well," he said thoughtfully, "if I was to guess...it might be that...he didn't want to make a spectacle...of himself. I mean...would you pay close attention...to a story I was reading if...I got out of this boat and was walking on the water... while I read to you? He probably...just wanted people to pay attention... to what...he was saying."

Macushla, whose little servant heart understood this completely, nodded. "That would make sense, Arthur. I think you're right."

They went a little further upstream, no waterfall or castles or dragons yet in sight.

"But Arthur...how did you come up with that notion?"

"Well, Macushla Dearie..." Arthur replied, still pulling hard, and imitating the local Irish, "you said that he wanted people to pay attention to things his father wanted the people to know about. It wouldn't make sense to draw attention to himself then, would it? I mean, if you wanted Mrs. O'Brian to pay attention to doctor's orders you brought, well then, you wouldn't tell her while floating three feet in the air, turning yourself all kinds of dazzling colors now, would you?"

Macushla laughed again and ran her hand in the water slowly, cupping it to give Solomon a drink, which he took, gratefully, from her palm. "I understand that part, Arthur. He must have cared more for putting his father's message out among the people, but...but *how* did you come to know that? That's what I'm curious about. Did the explanation just pop into your head?"

Arthur stopped rowing then, and leaned on the oars and stared at Macushla, as if seeing her for the first time. She looked up from watching Solomon drink and saw the summer sun, now low on the horizon, halo the dark hair around Arthur's head, and he became almost luminescent. He smiled suddenly, for he really hadn't known the answer to her question until just this moment, when it struck him like a flash of light that pierced to his very heart.

"And what's so funny?" she asked, her own eyes smiling, tossing her head so unselfconsciously that Arthur felt his soul would break loose from its pins. "Seriously, how did this come to you? I mean, it sounds right, it feels right...it...it completes a picture in my mind. I suppose that's what the storybooks call wisdom—understanding why things happen to people, and *why* people do things. You're right—absolutely, completely, without a doubt. But how did you *know*?"

Arthur's smile changed then. In later years she would come to remember just that time when his smile changed, although she didn't recognize it then. He smiled in a different way, a deeper and more respectful way it seemed to her at the time, and she saw his normally dark complexion become even darker, redder, and he said, very quietly, "I've seen it before," and then didn't say any more. He picked up the oars, and in the way that friends have of recognizing that silence is the better part of speech, they didn't say anything during the rest of that boat ride. Yet it was then that Macushla, with deep surprise and the awakenings of joy, realized that things had changed between them—changed like a nuanced shift in a breeze that would yet not bend a broken reed. It was borne in upon her without a doubt that Arthur loved her, and she knew without question, as an article of faith, as certainly as there had been that man who walked on water, that there was no other boy or man she would ever love. There in the boat on that summer day with Solomon in her lap, Macushla discovered the joy that comes when the human heart is joined to the one for whom it was made, and she saw stretched out before her just how she might live happily ever after. This knowledge, this trust, this confidence that she would live happily ever after was the closest thing to joy that she had ever known.

When Macushla was thirteen and Arthur fifteen, Macushla's father got a promotion. It would take him out of the refinery, which was in truth becoming dangerous—ten men had died in the spring of that year when part of the plant exploded and buried them and their hopes under fifteen tons of brick and pipe and crude. But alas, the promotion meant a move to another city, light years from their little Irish community. When she first heard of her father's good fortune, Macushla reacted immediately and typically with joy for another's happiness. Her sisters were less forthcoming with their exuberance, since they each had concerns which mainly revolved around the issue of leaving numbers of young men who worshipped them for their beauty.

"'Tis truly a hard thing,' the mother said, twisting the knife of guilt with a velvet hand, "taking children from their schooling and friends at such tender ages." She of course referred to the older sisters, who would be required to leave the local high school. This place possessed a poor academic reputation but excelled in the ability to stoke the fires of selfishness in a furnace of proms and dances and games and boys and frills and foppishness. The sisters reveled in that which fed their natural inclinations and were loathe to leave, no matter that this new course in life was safer for their father—they didn't think of him much, actually. Their school was an insipid institution that sucked truth and life and wisdom and beauty out from the very bodies and souls of children. This kind of schooling was fast becoming the quintessential American experience for millions of teenagers—an adolescent gauntlet, essential to the formulation of that which would come to be considered normal—and suitable ground wherein wicked Academe would plant her seed.

There might be some who would also be so unkind as to assert that the mother would rather have preferred the husband remain at risk in an exploding factory (where, it must be mentioned, he made good money... and he *did* have insurance) so as to keep her older daughters in that place where they could freely absorb the frippery that passed for culture in this sad land. I for one would refrain from making such a bold statement—I would simply mention the possibility that it might have been, and leave dogs to sleep with dogs.

Macushla, even at such a young age, was so unaccustomed to considering her own needs that it was not until that evening as she lay in bed did she realize that to leave their town meant leaving Arthur—and she sat bolt upright when this thought struck. Her heart began to beat wildly; it was the first time in her young life that the true meaning of tragedy made itself known. From an upright sitting position she melted in agony back onto the bed—a collapse of the soul, accompanied by a single groan from the depths of her heart. She could not imagine life without him. What would they do? *How* would they live happily ever after if they lived light years distant from each other? He would meet someone else; he would never wait for her to find her way back to him. He would grow up and thousands of young girls would throw themselves at him in haste, and he would pick one and that girl, not she, would grow up and live happily ever after with him, with their children, and Solomon, and Solomon's puppies. It was the worst night of her life—a night in which she learned what tortures can truly come with even a tiny fraction of focus upon self. It is a remarkably heavy blow to bear, experiencing such a thing so late in life. Her sisters, inured to the condition of considering self above all other things, would not have thought twice about it, and would have slept the sleep of the just. In fact, they did this very thing. The sisters would leave many broken-hearted admirers strewn about their little community when they moved, but they gave the young men nary a thought. They were asleep the minute their pretty heads descended like butterflies upon their frilled, Irish-laced, rose-scented pillows.

Macushla drenched her cotton rag of a pillowcase with tears, and she would think ever afterward that the night before the news of her father's promotion was the last happy night of her life. And from that night forward, she did indeed descend into a darkness that shook her worse than Macready's dog.

And so the day soon came when Arthur stood in the middle of the street and watched as the mother and the father and the sisters drove away, bearing Macushla in the back of the car, staring soulfully out the window, hand raised in agony. He stood there for forty-seven minutes in the heat, stunned, wondering what would happen to his life now that its light was removed. A constable moved him from the center of the street and noted with compassion and wisdom that something was truly wrong with a young, broad-shouldered boy of fifteen who would stand in the middle of a street with tears running down his face, looking as if the burden of the world had descended upon his shoulders. Policemen have an eye for such things. His mother and father eventually had to come and lead him home. He slept for two days, and walked about in a fog for three more.

* * *

When Macushla was twenty-two, Arthur twenty-four, she completed her graduate degree in Literature. She'd taken extra classes and worked very hard to graduate high in her class. She obtained her Master's degree with high marks and set her eye on a teaching position at a nearby college. Her older sisters had each long ago been married, not one attaining the age of twenty-one before claiming innumerous tortured, heart-pounding, sweaty-palmed proposals from many suitors. They each adroitly selected from the herd the bull of choice, making each bull feel as though they themselves had done the choosing. Each wedding was picture postcard perfect, the mother ensuring that not a jot or a tittle was out of place. Each sister was now ensconced as the reigning monarch in her own miniature domestic kingdom, sharing with the mother on a daily basis the progress of the campaigns to conquer the other domestic potentate. The father, more gray-haired, aging unnaturally as the new position took its toll, was content to cruise like a submarine underneath the surface of the family, avoiding the shells that would be fired should he have the temerity to surface and voice an opinion. He would only open his heart with Macushla, and only when they were alone, but sadly these times were all too infrequent.

Macushla too, upon losing her hope that summer day so long ago, had become withdrawn and slightly morose. She would catch herself, though, and try to jolly herself out of the pit of despair. By the time she was fifteen, she had surmounted the worst of the blow and could avoid the numbing remembrance of the pain for a few hours at a time by immersing herself in the needs of others. But such a bond—a bond forged between two souls— does not break easily or without scars. Macushla began to be worried about her behavior. She recognized that she was still worrying too much and thinking too much about herself. With renewed passion and vigor she embraced activities that would, she hoped, drive away the last dregs of these wretched, heartbreaking mental ruminations.

It was during this time that she came to hate the self, and to hate that thing in her human heart that would lead her to build castles for her life in her dreams, only to see them dashed. She began to focus on just living in the day, on trying to do what she knew to be right *that day*, without worrying about what it might mean for her future, for her welfare, or for her happiness.

In such a way she worked through the remainder of her teen years and into her early twenties. She found herself with a diploma, a good academic record, and an offer to teach at a small college on the outskirts of a large city. It was the only offer she had, it was from a reputable college, they would help her with her doctorate, and it was close enough to allow her visits to her family on holidays. And so off she went into the world, her father driving her to the station, the mother being too busy addressing the aftermath of damage done by a recent skirmish in the kingdom of one of the sisters.

Her father walked slowly with her along the platform, carrying her case to the place where they would part. Macushla was surprised to see that her father's face was wet with tears, and as she realized that she would be leaving home, possibly not to return under their roof, that she would not be able to nod and wink and escape with her father out to the backyard for a word with the only sane person she'd known and loved for the last several years, the only one who knew her heart and loved her—the only person besides...besides Arthur—it broke the dam holding back her own flood of sorrow, and she turned to him. He took her in his arms without a word and they sobbed upon each other's shoulder: he for the loss of his darling and that sweet and precious tenderness that only a father can know from, and have for, a loving daughter; and she for the love of a father who had set for her, in the midst of riotous selfishness, a guiding beacon of wisdom, light, selflessness, and love. She so cherished her father that she thought her heart would break there on the concrete pad of the train station. There that day on the concrete pad of the train station, her father's heart did break, and he would never be the same after his darling Macushla left his care.

The whistle blew, the man in the Charlie Chaplin suit shouted, steam blossomed, her case was handed over to her, and the train took her down the tracks to the next part of her life. Her father, broken-hearted, walked back slowly to what was left of his own.

When Macushla was twenty-three, Arthur twenty-five, she went to dinner at her favorite restaurant near the campus. The storm clouds of youth and adolescence had passed and the sunshine of her beauty shone forth in dazzling display. She came into the bloom of her life, with shiny auburn hair, exquisitely-refined features, form and figure still of a young girl yet with a grown woman's grace. She had just ordered when a party, obviously businessmen on a business trip, took the table next to hers. She could not help overhearing their conversation, recognizing them as business travelers and speculating about their occupation. When one of the men, a sandy-haired, handsome fellow of about thirty asked if he could borrow her desert menu, she smiled and handed it to him. He took the menu and sat down boldly at her table. With just the right amount of calculated charm he asked if he could order desert for her.

She looked at him for a moment, thinking. Time stood on a knife's edge. Angels held their breath, tears in their eyes.

"Nothing with fruit or alcohol," she said after some small hesitation. She wasn't a teetotaler; she had an important research meeting with her advisor the next morning and wanted to be fresh. Nor did she wish to appear rude, and truth to tell, she appreciated the company.

"Chocolate," he said confidently, knowing that all women love chocolate. Macushla smiled in acknowledgement. There are some truths too banal to be stated.

"I'm Robert," he said, reaching out a hand, "Robert Tennyson."

"Macushla," she replied.

Robert was a businessman from a faraway place. The talk at the friends' table diminished markedly upon him settling at hers—either he was the mainspring of their discourse, or they were hoping now to eavesdrop upon her conversation with him. He struck her as a leader, someone to whom others would defer. She was not far wrong.

"Mac...can I call you Mac? I'm thinking you're a student here?"

"I teach, but yes, I'm going for my doctorate."

"Wow...you're going to be a professor?"

"I hope to be...at least, I think that's what I want. Not quite sure, you know." She looked down into her cup and stirred the remains of her tea.

"What will you teach?"

"Literature, I think. At least that's my area of specialty at the moment."

"Books...hmmm....the bane of man's existence." He arched one sandy eyebrow. "I suppose you'll be the type who whips students to read Shakespeare and Milton and then rips their heads off when they fail to grasp the 'deeper meanings'." He said the words 'deeper meanings' with disdain, and out of some sense of misguided need to be polite, Macushla ignored the little red flag that appeared in her heart while she stared at the little silver teaspoon on the saucer. She looked up and smiled, but found herself beginning to weary.

"No...I don't...I don't think so. We each take...well, different things from good literature, though I agree that there are common themes."

"Such as?" he asked directly; nothing like a businessman for the direct approach, she thought. And he remained blithely unaware of the poor impression his denseness had made.

"Well, there's life, and love, and tragedy, and romance and heartbreak, and truth and beauty, to start."

She felt the conversation flow along, but there was no spark, no lift under the heart, only the effort to be pleasant to a man obviously trying to find his way through a conversational minefield. She wondered if he was intimidated. She'd encountered it before in shallow men put off by her intelligence. But then he began to speak of books—books that she'd read, actually—and some of his theories on education, which happened to align a bit with her own, and soon they'd made it through the obstacle course of introductory small talk, devoured jointly the murderous chocolate confection—a twelve-inch high, eight-layered double chocolate cake drenched in chocolate sauce with chocolate chips as garnish—and were succeeding in their initial attempts to get to know one another.

Macushla ended the evening by trading phone numbers and went away still unmoved but nonetheless grateful for at least one evening of pleasant (though perhaps slightly insipid) conversation unmarred by solitude.

In the days to come Robert phoned occasionally, and they picked up their conversation where it had ended, discussing interesting theories, books, movies, and the events of the day. He was persistent—sometimes unabashedly so, she thought, in the absence of any significant encouragement on her part—and things would have continued along in this vein for perhaps forever, but something happened which shook Macushla to the core of her soul.

When Macushla was twenty-six, Arthur twenty-eight, her father died. He passed away one morning and no one could discern how or why. He died there in his bed while the mother was brushing her teeth. The mother was in full throat that morning. She was continuously transmitting, rarely stopping to take input, and was preparing for a visit to one of the sisters who was dealing with still another attempted domestic coup. The mother was beginning to wonder if perhaps the sisters had not selected their husbands with the requisite degree of attention to the quality of subservience in a man's character. After all, there were no questions about who ran *her* kingdom. Just prior to these ruminations, she had directed the father to bring the car round to the front of the house. He did not respond, which was normal. He was, according to her lights, proceeding to do what she asked.

She sailed out of the bathroom and through the bedroom, not even presuming to glance at the spot whereupon her husband of many decades had departed for greener pastures, leaving simply an earthly shell of flesh-framed dust. The more self-absorbed one becomes, the more easily one ignores those who are not—and thence the harder it is to see the meaning of death when it comes. She went to the kitchen to make her breakfast.

It was a Saturday, and, she thought, the husband would be about the lawn, or the yard, or whatever such things men did on Saturdays. She, on the other hand, would be embarked upon *serious* business. She finished her toast and tea and banana, collected her things, and stepped through the front door out to the home's curved driveway. With surprise she noted that the car was not presented, the footman not in evidence. She pursed her lips; a firm, forbidding line formed across her face. She marched back through the house, calling his name in a tone the house had learned meant mild displeasure, soon to be followed by an outright eruption of righteous anger. The lips were the dead giveaway. But the father was beyond all such concerns at the moment, and the mother ranged through the house, becoming increasingly piqued, until she came to the bedroom where she saw his form, in frustratingly peaceful repose upon the bed.

"Get up," she said, snappishly. She found herself perversely irritated at his seemingly peaceful posture in the face of her inconvenienced state. "I've been calling for you these last ten minutes. What do you think you're doing?"

It was only later that she paused to wonder why, in his final repose, there was painted upon his worn and aged face a blissful and beatific smile.

The death of her father shook Macushla harder than anything had since she'd lost Arthur. After the initial period of grief, upon some reflection, she recognized from the magnitude of this shock that she had drawn about her a cocoon and built a wall between herself and others, and while her father's death grieved her, this realization frightened her to the depths of her shoes. She did not know who she was becoming any longer, and began to fear greatly what dark path she might unknowingly pursue. Service to others was the very touchstone of her character, and to have unknowingly set aside such an intrinsic portion of her nature for so long—and not to have realized it—was too much to bear. Life had to go on. She realized that she did not want to be the person she'd become. She did not yet know what she wanted to be, or what kind of person she should be, but this is common among the young. The pity is that they take such permanent steps in such unknowing blindness.

It was at this time that Robert began to sense that perhaps his suit was warming, or, as some ungracious souls might allege, he sensed a turn of events which might prove to his advantage. He targeted the emerging vulnerability like a guided missile. He asked no questions about the deeper currents of her heart; his vanity sufficed to meet any need he might have had to immerse himself in another. Macushla, or "Mac" as she now called herself in deference to Robert, offered no explanations, for she was beginning to forget what questions to ask.

* * *

When Macushla was twenty-six, she and Robert were married. Her initial impressions were correct; Robert was very successful in business. He was clear-eyed, very intelligent, could drive to the heart of a matter, was extremely personable, and was developing a reputation as a rainmaker for his employers. He was promoted to Vice President in a defense contracting firm by the time their first child arrived—a boy.

One night before the child was born they were discussing the name, and instinctively Macushla spoke up, expressing her hope that they would name the child after her father, whom she had loved so deeply. Robert pursed his lips in the thoughtful, pensive way he had (it frightened her sometimes how much it reminded her of her mother, and it frightened her even more that she hadn't noticed it during their all-too-brief courtship) and said slowly, "Yes...yes, that might be a good thought...but Mac, truly, I was hoping that there would be a Robert junior, you know? Would that bother you too much? I mean..." and he let the question hang.

The old Macushla, without blatant announcement or trumpets heralding her return to the stage of Mac's life, said immediately, "Why yes, certainly Robert, that would be nice...no problem at all." She put her hand on her large belly, as if communicating to the child somehow her apology for the loss of initiative in his naming, saying an unspoken goodbye to the child who might have borne a resemblance to her father's nature. "Maybe we could make his middle name my father's?" she said, softly, wistfully.

Robert grimaced to express polite disagreement, but in a way which is intended to convey sadness that there is such discord. "Well, Mac, it was my hope that Robert junior would...well, you know, that he would have my mother's maiden name. It's kind of a tradition you know...it would be...well, I don't think it would be right to break the line. We could name the next after your Dad, sure thing. Would that be acceptable?" And in that easy and compelling manner he had, he awoke the old Macushla as sure as the last trumpet will wake the dead, and she realized that here at last was an opportunity to throw that thing called self off a cliff and embark fully upon the service of another. She squared her chin, looked up at her husband faithfully, and said, "Sure, Rob...that's just fine. He'll bear the name proudly."

Robert patted her on the head and kissed her. "Great. I wonder, Mac, could you put up a case for me? I've got seventeen reports to write and no time to pack. Be a dear, would you? Thanks." And Robert went off to the study to write, and Macushla heaved herself off the bed and packed the suitcase for his trip.

When Macushla was twenty-six (still), Robert Fitzhume Tennyson the Third was born. Robert Hennings Tennyson the Second was away in Seattle at a corporate off-site, meeting with a number of production department heads, planning the production of an incredibly complex and therefore incredibly expensive new technological marvel.

Macushla pushed and breathed and screamed and pushed harder and harder and screamed louder and there was the water and the blood and then the baby and then blessed relief, and then a small, furry-haired, dark-eyed creature in swaddling clothes upon her breast, and she lay back and let just one small tear peek out from her eye. Her hand caressed her son; her heart spoke silently—*Arthur, I'm sorry.*

The young lord of the manor was treated to all sorts of blessings by the Tennyson clan. Sadly (or perhaps not), Robert's new home was quite far away from Macushla's mother and the sisters, and so they only sent cards. Robert's mother, the Matron Fitzhume, however, encamped like Alexander in Afghanistan. Macushla was feted to some small degree, grudgingly, yet it was a strange and not very comfortable sensation. This beneficence lasted but a day or two and no one regretted its passing. Robert was all pride and smiles and encouragement—he'd earned another promotion, the technologically marvelous program was progressing, and he'd gotten a son upon his wife. Life could be no better.

The young lord was soon followed by two girls—twins—and twice lost was the thought of naming a child for her father. Somehow, in a turn of events which Mac could not recall, the Matron Fitzhume garnered the privilege of naming the two peas in a pod. Macushla was sufficiently surrendered—or perhaps the word might be humiliated—at this point that the intrusion did not stir the pot of her emotions. Robert was becoming increasingly successful at work, which meant in the emerging American society of business that he was spending more and more time away from home. The Matron would occasionally appear to grace the children with her presence and dispense pearls of character from her nature, and disappear upon the advent of the children's true natures—which, all being human, were naturally deplorable.

Macushla exerted herself like Athena, like Hercules, like Hector, to stem this massively overpowering stench of selfishness, but she could not fight what she could not understand, and so lost the battle. The children, with the encouragement of the occasionally-appearing Matron and the even less frequently-appearing husband, were riotous even in repose. When the tyrants became ambulatory, the house could only with kindness be called bedlam.

Macushla began to gain weight, neglected her appearance, did not put on makeup for her husband's increasingly later arrivals from the office, completely forgot her lingerie drawer, and lost all interest in reading or even thinking about reading in her former academic discipline. When hope dies, self-discipline carries out the casket. What use to read, or even try to think about reading, when there were children to chase, diapers to empty and clean, food to prepare, rooms and floors and windows and tables and chairs and ceilings and walls and toilets and tubs to clean? Why think about wisdom and truth and beauty when squirming bipedal creatures requiring the application of wet cloths at both ends seemed to be the sum and substance of all existence? Why even live with no hope of love?

When Mac was twenty-eight, she lost her fourth child at eight months in her pregnancy. She felt things were different suddenly in the afternoon, and when she began to bleed, she called Robert, who was fortunately at the office in town that week. His secretary answered and indicated that he could not be disturbed; he was actually briefing the company's President (truly, 'twas himself in the flesh) on the progress of the technological marvel. Macushla would have demurred in typical fashion but felt it was important—she did not know how long she would be functional, and so asked the secretary to intervene, indicating that there was an emergency at home.

There came a longish sigh, freighted with the professional woman's disdain for an incompetent, stay-at-home female who could not even handle a problem which in all probability simply required the application of a band-aid. "If you insist," she said, professionally of course, absolving herself of all responsibility—as if interrupting the President of the company might result in crucifixion. There was a pause and then Robert appeared on the line, with a voice that Macushla immediately recognized as one of irritation—scathing, boiling irritation—at being removed from the Presence. He was barely concealing righteous anger at being summoned away from the throne at the very moment of his potential triumph. Yet in the professional world one must not be *seen* to be callous toward one's family. "What is it?" he hissed, trying to reach through the phone and smack her into some semblance of awareness regarding the relative importance of his work and the obligations of professional conduct in general.

It was, regrettably, at this time that the twins began to wail and lament the state of the world, and in so doing awoke the young lord of the manor. This young miscreant, with incredible misfortune, with a chubby, wayward arm flung about in the throes of awakening, knocked over the bedroom phone. He was sleeping in the master bedroom, which is where he insisted upon sleeping at all times, disdaining his own lavish suite. The dislodged phone resulted in a remarkable stereophonic cacophony from two open lines in the house of bedlam. Robert, graciously, took this as simply an unmistakable sign of complete and utter incompetence on the part of his wife as opposed to crediting this blasphemous interruption to pure malice. He hissed each word separately and distinctly—as though speaking to a child—even more imperiously into the phone: *"What...is...the...problem?"*

"Robert..." and the pains were beginning now, "I...I'm not feeling well...I need you to...I need you to come home..." At least this is what she said; we do not know what Robert heard above the din raised by three screaming children. And so Robert did what any good professional would do—thinking on his feet, he hung up the phone, as it was impossible to hear anything, and directed his secretary to call his wife in ten minutes to see if everything was okay. His secretary smiled with admiration at the care and concern he showed toward the little woman at home—what a sensitive, caring man, she thought, and beamed admiration from her meticulously made-up visage. Robert went back to ascend again into the rarefied and beatific Presence, there to beam forth admiration for those pearls of wisdom which might drip from the throne.

And so it was that Macushla packed three adrenalin-laced lemurs into the back seat and drove herself to the hospital, doubled over in pain. Fortunately she had the presence of mind to drive to the emergency entrance of the hospital. As she arrived there came a gush of blood and very soon thereafter she collapsed over the steering wheel, efficiently stopping the car by ramming it against one of the sturdy brick pillars just to the side of the entrance way. Hospital attendants, not unfamiliar with such strange goings-on when dealing with expectant mothers, rapidly picked her out of the car, others relieved the car of the children, one noted the great amount of blood on the front seat of the very expensive luxury vehicle, and the ensemble made its way through the sea of triage patients and directly into a treatment room.

Macushla awoke a number of hours later and instantly, with an epiphany that she could only later credit to God, in less time than it took for her to open her eyes, realized two things. She had no life in her, and she had no Life in her.

After an eternity to dwell upon these two bitter pills, she moaned slightly, and there appeared in her line of vision a harried, gray-haired, kindly-faced lady in a pink sweater. "Welcome back to the world, Dearie," the woman said.

"What...what happened?"

The nurse, sadly too experienced in such moments, knew that the most compassionate policy was to swing hard, swing fast, and swing for the fence to get it over with. "I'm sorry...but you lost your baby."

This Macushla had already known and ruminated upon in the eternity between her epiphany and the opening of her eyes. But one thing she did not know. "What...what was it?"

The nurse, expecting the question, was neither confused nor unfeeling. "A boy, Dearie," she said, gently touching Macushla's hand on the coverlet of the bed. "He was a fine boy. Now, you rest...you rest."

Macushla closed her eyes again and realized with another flash of insight that this child would have born her father's name—and then she wondered why it sometimes required pain and blood and loss for these flashes of insight to penetrate the human consciousness. It was then, with the memory of her father so clearly brought to her tender mind, that she realized she had forgotten, lo these many years, to even once recall to mind the man about whom her father spoke—Jesus, yes, that was His name— who would do marvelous things and heal people; who actually claimed to be God, walking around on earth, who claimed full, outright, complete, unstinting obedience from those who would venture to call themselves His children. When was it, she asked herself, that she had last heard or thought of or spoken that name? When *was* it...*yes*, of course, now she remembered…it was that night when she learned of her father's promotion, and realized too that with it would come the loss of Arthur. Yes, now she remembered…she had fallen asleep that night calling out Jesus' name. And in the dark remainder of her life after the breakage of that bond, she had never once thought to call that name or that Life to remembrance.

When this truth was opened to her, when she admitted to herself with no scruples or rationalizing that she had let go the lifeline to Life, to Light, to Truth, and to Beauty (for so her father had painted this man, and she believed her father to be utterly truthful), that she had forgotten the One who had the best claim to her obedience because He Loved her best, there came over her such a sorrow, such an agony, such a sense of loss and mourning, that tears gushed up from the well of her essence and the pain welled up from her soul into her physical body such that her back arched once in a rictus of agony and heartbreak. In another second her soul had collapsed into the fetal position and from her parched throat came the sound of a soul breaking: you will know it when you hear it only if you have uttered it yourself. And upon the heels of this flensing, consuming agony came something she would never, ever forget even past the end of her days.

There was a vision, like a picture or a movie that formed before her— not in her mind, not a dream, but something she actually saw. She saw that thing she knew to be her self, her soul, in striking, stark clarity, just as God saw it, with all its imperfections—but with those imperfections as perceived by Perfection Himself. This picture of how and what she was, in such close proximity to the Ancient of Days, the Light of the World, Perfection itself, was so utterly damning, so filthy, so crushing, that she hid her face in abject horror and humiliation at what she was and how offensive she could now perceive herself to be. The contrast was burned into the very fiber of her mind and soul in that brief instant; it would last a lifetime. When one day much later she read Isaiah's lament that he was "a man of unclean lips", the words needed no explanation.

Yet upon the burning fringe of this vision came a tiny but nonetheless tangible feeling of a fluttering within her, as if she'd swallowed a butterfly, a feeling not unlike the first movement of a baby in the womb, but which incongruously she knew without a doubt to be that birth of true Life within her, a strange but certain gift given to her at this moment, testifying beyond doubt that this man her father had read and spoken to her about was Light and Life and Truth and Beauty itself, and that His Spirit had actually at that instant come to make His abode within her, though she did not know the details nor would she have been able to frame a description of it. He had shown her clearly who she had been, enabling her to admit to herself the utter hopelessness of attaining anything righteous or holy on her own merit, and then in Spirit taken up residence in that shell which she had hitherto known as her body. This man, God himself, had a complete right to His new abode, she realized—and to her obedience. With the finality and weight that comes with the descent of truth also came the awareness that she now knew to whom she should, and would surrender—she now knew with complete certainty that here was a Life, and Life itself, in which she could live as a true person, one in which she could comfortably be without the self, and yet be filled and complete and content. The explanation and justification to eradicate the self was now (literally) within her... Light and Life and Truth and Beauty, so magnificent, so overwhelming, so overpowering, so deserving, that to consider one's self as in any way able to take precedence over such as He would be the height of folly—like esteeming garbage above gold. The knowledge Macushla gained in that short period of time transcended religion or tradition the way an ocean transcends dishwater.

It was at this point that some might say Macushla did a very foolish thing; others might disagree. From the very depths of her heart, in the newness and fresh rushing awareness of His life in her, she spoke out to this new Presence and asked, "God, please, make me like that man my father read to me about. Make me like Jesus. I remember my Daddy telling me that is why you sent him—so that we could know how to live. So please, make me like Jesus." Little did she, or anyone who prays such prayer, realize the implications of such a request. The very logical method whereby anyone becomes like another in thought, word, and deed, is usually to go through the same experiences as did the object of one's prayer. And so this request, so blithely voiced in prayer and song throughout Christendom, is a great danger should God take the supplicant seriously, for if He does, the petitioner risks experiencing rejection by those they love, scorn from those whom they raised and nurtured from childhood, ridicule from colleagues out of fear or jealousy, and very likely physical suffering as well, inflicted by those very people who one is literally keeping alive. God has no rule set; the supplicant may experience some, none, or all of such things, but it is a fact that when God sets out to make a person like His Son, He does so usually by taking that person through experiences which result in that person feeling the things His Son felt, learning the things His Son learned, and doing the things His Son did. Most Christians know that this is what is meant by the religious term 'the cross': it is a shame so few choose it.

Before she fell off to sleep, thinking finally of her little boy, she wondered why it was that there must be times when the only course open to Wisdom requires the taking of life to create Life.

Macushla returned home that evening to an overturned anthill. The Matron Fitzhume had only herself just arrived after being phoned by the secretary who, unable to reach the incompetent Mrs. Tennyson after several tries, took a late lunch, handled several tasks for lesser luminaries, then phoned the Matron Tennyson, since that was the only other contact number she possessed. As he passed her in the hall, she happened to mention to Robert that she was unable to reach his wife but had contacted his mother. "I'm sure everything is okay," she said.

"Thanks very much, Mickie," Robert replied, smiling, hurrying to another meeting; "extremely thoughtful of you to call my mother—very efficient."

"It was nothing, Mr. Tennyson," she said smoothly, efficiently, professionally; "my pleasure."

Macushla had no heart for recrimination when Robert eventually returned home at ten that evening. She was still wrestling with the stark picture of her own sin, burned into her soul like the flash of light imprints upon one's retina only the most visible images. It had burned away any desire to find fault with another. The pain and agony and utter world-shaking experience of seeing that thing she knew as self for what it truly was had left her breathless, and she felt that she would be completely unable to issue a word of recrimination to another soul for the rest of her days.

For a seed to grow into a plant, the seed first dies and then becomes something completely different. When a person's soul dies, crucified on the cross of Mercy, the new nature will become something which in no way resembles what it was. To become so, typically, it must be nurtured in much the same way as a new plant is nourished. There is usually water, and sun, and protection from the wind and predators, and good soil. And yet, the Master Gardner may withhold such nurturing for a greater or more stringent purpose.

* * *

When Macushla was twenty-nine, Robert took a two-week vacation with members of the company to go hunting at a lodge in Montana. Robert was no hunter, but 'twas himself the Corporate President (that greatest of men), who sure and required his attendance, and thus he went. Macushla packed plaid shirts in which lumberjacks would die happily. She packed pants, the pockets of each capable of containing enough gear to supply a regiment, and boots hardy enough to walk across Antarctica. When Robert left and the lemurs went into hibernation for the evening, Macushla stepped out to the porch in the cool of the evening and reflected upon her life.

By then she knew that what had happened to her in the hospital when she lost her second son was what Christians termed a conversion experience, though slightly more painful than simply walking down an aisle. She had met the risen Christ—He about whom her father had spoken of so often in her childhood—in brokenness and blood and abject poverty of spirit. She had become, as the culture termed it, "a born-again Christian" (as if there were many different Christian species instead of only the one to which the Founder referred). She also had learned not to speak of what happened to her or what she experienced to others. This was simply because not many had such experiences; not many had come to be truly broken. Most of those Christians with whom she spoke had undergone the typical sincere walk down the aisle, with someone close by encouraging them to 'ask Jesus into their heart', or attended Vacation Bible School and 'made a commitment'. There was just as typically the assumption of life as before, but now with one's 'Get out of Hell Free' card tucked safely between the pages of their unopened Bible. Such experiences like the painful realization in pictorial, visionary form of her own sin, of how she appeared to God, and of the experiential event of solidly realizing that He had come to take up residence in her spirit were roundly denounced and held in suspicion. Macushla was not an overly demonstrative woman, nor given to dwelling in or depending upon emotion—she found she could not bear the insincerity and shallowness of relations built primarily on emotion—but she could not deny what had happened to her. And truly what had happened to her had as little to do with emotion as did the power which parted the Red Sea had to do with how Moses felt at the time.

Due to some unknowable instinct, she had not, even a year later, shared with Robert what had happened to her that night in the hospital. Perhaps she knew he would suffuse her with ridicule. He could not, however, help but notice that she was even meeker than normal, that she now had taken up the strange and somewhat unseemly habit of reading the Bible ("Everything in its place and time, you understand," he'd admonished with professional disapproval), and was becoming increasingly concerned over her desire to be with others who also demonstrated these socially unbecoming proclivities. He made it very clear that there was to be no discussion of such extremist literature in front of the children (but he was away much of the day and she could not help but speak about Him to the children). He was even more strident when insisting that the words "born-again" were not to be used whenever she was in the presence of his professional colleagues. But he made an effort—a pained, demonstrative, complaining, laborious effort—to adjust to her descent into what he could only believe was some sort of "crutch" or dependency, as if it were a malady to which incompetent housewives were especially prone.

"The loss of the baby changed her," he confided in solemn tones to Jennifer at lunch one day, one of the corporate rising stars, a young twenty-six year old who'd become a Partner with one of the top six consulting firms after her graduation from a prestigious Ivy League university, a stint clerking for a Supreme Court Justice, a summer internship with a modeling agency, flying solo around the world in an open-cockpit biplane, and a year spent coaching the U.S. Olympic swim team (she'd won a gold medal earlier). Jennifer listened sagely, brightly, compassionately, with svelte legs crossed, skirt three inches above the knee, six-inch black stiletto heels planted firmly in corporate reality. Paint would have been less revealing than her blouse.

"I don't really know what's come over her," Robert continued, commiserating. "Sometimes...sometimes it makes me..." and he let the sentence drift off into the lake of their conversation like a fully-baited hook, which the worldly-wise young woman was too professional to snap at too abruptly, but which was instead filed away for use in such time as Mr. Tennyson should ever be in a position to ratchet her career upward.

It is also important to understand that as Macushla stood there on the porch that evening, she was in the midst of that segment of time in a believer's life when the heavens seem like brass, the skies like rubber as prayers rebound without reply. It seems during these times as though God Himself has taken a holiday. There is dryness; a sense that one's relationship with God, up until then having been a river filled with evidence of His vibrant and easily-seen Presence is now a cracked, parched, barren desert wadi. This is intentional, Macushla would have known, had she been privileged to associate with true Christians. This occurs so that young believers can begin to develop an ability to seek Him out on their own, much like a young chicken must peck its way out of its shell on its own so as to develop the strength it will need to survive the coming days. It may seem heartless to those foolish enough to question the Creator. Nonetheless, Macushla was at the very bottom of the pit of despair that evening. The Matron was due in, and every visit undid what little progress Macushla made in disciplining the children. Robert was growing ever more distant and cross. In a flash of honesty she admitted that there was little or no real relationship between them. This caused her less pain than she expected, once the admission was out of the closet of her heart and placed in the light of day. She decided to soldier on nonetheless; there were the children, after all. She had not thought of Arthur for many years, and she did not think of him then either, directly—only indirectly, as some sort of vague reminiscence like a marker or buoy in the foggy sea of time, when occasionally the faint hope surfaced that life might be perfect, or at least sweet at times, or just once in a while less crushing than it truly was.

Macushla was therefore well along the path of brokenness, with its attendant inclination to be more sensitive to hearing from God, when she snapped on the radio to dull her aching loneliness. The dial twisted and she recognized the voice of a Bible teacher from one of the new churches that were becoming popular.

"I want to talk to all you women out there tonight," the casual voice began, and Macushla sat quietly, rocking back and forth, descending into that calm bowl of solitude where she turned her heart to what God might be saying to her.

"Do you sense that your husband is losing interest?" This line caught Macushla's attention; she dared hope that perhaps God was going to speak to her tonight—perhaps the brass sky had cracked and He was going to pour out some living water.

"Do you find that he's got no time for anything but work? That he's just not home as much anymore? Do you wonder about that? Does he let you handle the children most of the time? Why is that, do you think?"

She had stopped rocking by now and was trying to breathe, praying that the children would remain asleep so she could listen to the wisdom emanating from God's lips through this man's teaching to her ears.

"Well, let me ask you a question. How's your hair?" The question took her aback; perhaps she hadn't heard the man correctly. But the radio voice continued: "I mean, right now, how's your hair?" Macushla's hand darted upward. "Are you wearing make-up? When was the last time you met your husband at the door in something more alluring than jeans and a sweatshirt?" Sadly, Macushla was wearing jeans and a thick and baggy sweatshirt which had become her uniform since...well, since before she could remember. The unjust barb flew home.

"Don't you realize your husbands are interacting with some of the world's most beautiful women every day, ten or twelve hours a day, at their offices? These women get up at the crack of dawn, spend an hour or two on their make-up and hair, and then drive in to carve out a ten or twelve-hour workday right alongside your husbands. And those husbands come home to...to what? Seriously...I realize the children are a hassle and the kitchen floors need scrubbing, but really, what's more important?"

It was at this point in the teaching that Macushla felt herself descend again into a valley of bitter remorse, only it was very different from that time in the hospital. Then, there was a piercing, cleansing, painful sweetness about the process. Now she only felt dirty, and shamed, and incompetent, as if she couldn't do anything right. These feelings were being confirmed by this man who (sadly) had the imprimatur of God himself. On the porch, she cringed before God, ashamed of herself, and waited for that rebounding, uplifting surge of hope and forgiveness and...and Life.

Nothing came. She waited...and waited. Still there was nothing. The teaching went on, with further detailed admonishments, damning faint praise, and juvenile efforts on the part of the radio preacher to be a stand-up comedian as well as a spiritual instructor. When the saccharine-toned music began to play in the background indicating that the teaching was coming to an end, she fell out of the chair onto her knees and begged God to forgive her for her laziness and dilatory approach to being a wife and mother. She swore to Him that if He would only be patient with her, she would *fix* things. She would *do better*. Alas that any Christian should utter such sentiments.

* * *

When Macushla was thirty she began to fix things. The very morning after she heard the alleged but nonetheless fateful words on the radio, she began to diet. Once shed of a few pounds, she bought a pair of sneakers (a slim and athletic female saleswoman referred to them as running shoes), availed herself of the local day care center, enduring staunchly in faith the heart-rending agonies of abandoned children, and took up running. She would fix things. By year's end she'd lost twenty-eight pounds and had returned to her lithe and athletic form. She made a little ceremony of burning the old sweatshirt and jeans in the back yard, neither of which fit any longer. She smiled then…the first smile she'd permitted herself since listening to the teaching during that dark night on the porch. It was a grim, determined, steely smile…it was not a smile Arthur would have recognized.

One evening, delving into new-found reservoirs of assertiveness, she prevailed upon the Matron to endure the children for an evening. She acquired Robert's favorite cut of beef from the grocer (who was very different from Mr. Mastrontonio, but Mac did not remark upon the fact). She baked a potato and, throwing caution to the winds, secured sour cream, bacon bits, and chives. It was a Friday evening, typically that day of the week whereupon he would come home relatively early—at least before eight in the evening. She boldly put two candles along with her cards on the table, setting only two places. She would fix things. She wore a new dress, procured for the occasion. Hope served in addition to meticulously applied make-up, brightening her eyes from within while shadow and liner served as external drapery.

The lord of the manor appeared within the expected time frame. Car noises ceased from the garage, the door opened, the briefcase slid into its place by his office entrance in the hallway, he walked into the living room, and stopped. There he saw Mac, newly attired, newly slimmed, killer table set, intentions clearly stated. Only a pudding-headed fool would have failed to grasp the situation, and Robert's head was certainly not filled with pudding. He smiled—a thin, weak smile which did not conceal a sense of burden and perceived imposition.

Macushla thought later that it was the smile that extinguished her last smoldering wick of hope. Had he thrown a javelin through her chest, he could not have pierced her more cruelly. So many words can be expressed by the human features upon that screen to the soul, the face. He smiled with his mouth, not his eyes; she saw this right away. And in his face she saw the expression which he strived to hide but could not; it was as if an overwhelming burden descended upon him, knowing that he had to try to generate romantic or emotional feeling for a woman about whom he clearly thought of as, well, not quite up to par. In a flash of insight she knew he was comparing her to the Jennifers and Madelines and Mickies and Ashleys and Margos that populated his world at work. She instinctively conducted a running assessment: she reviewed her hair, her face, the facility of the dress to highlight her feminine form, but then caught herself when the truth struck her. Nothing she could (or, she realized, wanted to) do would help her compare favorably with those fictional feminine forms. As she saw the results of his comparison slowly emerge—she saw this by his attempt to hide it—her heart sank. She realized with awful finality that there was nothing she could do to elevate her status in his eyes. She could meet him at the door wrapped in cellophane and he would ask distractedly about dinner. His comparing her to other women did not hurt as much as the now-obvious fact that he clearly despised her. Being despised by another is hard to bear; it is almost impossible to bear when the one who despises you is that one to whom you have been bonded—at least to some degree—intimately. And it is even more devastating to be despised and rejected by someone for whom you have worked and suffered and sacrificed so that they could prosper and succeed and have a chance to attain what they thought might bring them joy. It is the ultimate rejection.

It is said that courage is defined as doing something brave even when one is afraid; dogged determination, then, might have much to do with courage. Macushla, emotionally shattered, ruinously and abominably rejected, would have had every right to throw up her hands, declare the game over, throw a tantrum, retreat to a cold boudoir, and seek redress in divorce court. To her credit, as her heart split, instead she made a Herculean effort just to breath, smiled sweetly, served the meal, and went on with the evening as if she'd seen nothing. Robert conducted himself as if nothing had transpired, congratulating himself on his ability to bear his 'cross' at home. One part of her prayer had been answered.

Macushla was thirty-one when Robert presented the news to her, in a rather official, business-like, and logical manner that he was no longer in love with her. He would be divorcing her. Macushla was on her knees in the kitchen at the time, cleaning yet another liquid disaster caused by the young lord of the manor (she was in sweat shirt and jeans, ironically, though these were much smaller in size). Moreover, her illogical and potentially harmful behavior, Robert continued, was such that he would be compelled to seek full physical and legal custody of the children. The Matron Fitzhume would back him in this, Macushla was informed, and would supply an abundance of damning testimony regarding excessive appeals to unknown spirits, illogical attachments to fantasy creatures, and an obsession with reading an ancient, fictional, and somewhat dated piece of hate-literature—referring to her by now well-worn Bible.

He'd retained the most famous and expensive divorce lawyer possible; his company was backing him fully, and he'd even discussed it with the President (they were becoming confidantes by then). If she knew what was reasonable she would realize that causing a messy fight or scandal would only make it more difficult. She should simply agree to his eminently reasonable conditions. It just made sense.

This was a hard blow; no mother surrenders her children easily. Yet the plain facts were such that things could not be otherwise. Her acceptance of this was eased in bitter fashion as the young lord of the manor, now approaching the princely age of five, marched over after his father's speech, looked down his nose at her (as he'd seen his father do), sneered, and kicked her bucket over. He marched back to his father, who said nothing, but just patted the boy on the back and pursed his lips (looking like her mother), shaking his head slowly, as if to say, 'What a pathetic excuse for a woman you've become.'

Macushla was thirty-three before the razor-like pain caused by the severance from her children, with her children's unstinting and enthusiastic agreement, became bearable.

Since Robert had the children, she received no child support. Since Robert had played golf every Saturday with the judge who happened to be assigned to their case, things were such that he paid no alimony. When Robert divorced her, he was directed to supply her funds for two weeks, designated as 'relocation assistance'. Robert's attorney called it a gracious severance package. The judge could not help but snicker behind his gavel. Macushla, numb and tearless from nights wherein she did nothing but cry, wandered through the proceedings like a stunned ox led to slaughter. In court she was made to feel fortunate the judge did not fine her for being a bumbling incompetent who'd wasted the best years in the life of such a fine, outstanding young man. When it was brought out that she was a religious fanatic (according to the court's definition), she was made to feel as if she'd been granted a stay of execution when she wasn't fined for contempt and locked up in prison. Dark and dire were Robert's attorney's proclamations as to the deleterious effects such disfiguring philosophies might have upon the priceless progeny.

Divorce is one of the most crushing and humiliating experiences any human being can suffer; at least, if they are fortunate. Macushla was indeed fortunate in her divorce, and another prayer was answered. It tossed her into the muck and mire of failure, not only suffering from the shame and embarrassment such a thing wrought, but enduring the double agony of the loss of her children. When she awoke from the shock, she knew with unsurpassed certainty that she would feel the pain from the loss of her children for the rest of her life, no matter what God might do from this point forward. Nothing heals this wound.

And from behind this cloud of understanding there dawned a brighter lining. She comprehended now, to just the tiniest, most infinitesimal fraction of a degree, how God feels when a human being chooses to turn away from Him, rejecting Him, accepting the world, disdaining and scorning His love.

She felt just a little of what it must have been like (sure, what it must *be* like) for Him to endure the agony of losing his children…children for whom He labored, sweated, sacrificed, bled, and died. To Macushla, it was not just a loss, as if they'd fallen off a cliff inadvertently, or died. No, it was more than a loss, just as a divorce is more painful than a death in that it is a voluntary rejection, a pushing away, a flat, utter, painful refusal of relationship. It was the intentional severing of a bond. It was a spear in the side.

Suddenly she recalled—actually, God recalled it to her mind—that fateful prayer she had sent forth the night she lost her second son. She'd asked to become more like Him, and she realized that in order to bring that about, God was putting her through experiences in life that created in her those same feelings which His Son experienced, only to a degree that she as a small human could endure. The realization that He was doing this so that she could become more like Him actually began to heal the rent made by the spear.

O how careful we should be in what we request, should the request be granted! To her credit, she did not balk at this realization. On the contrary, knowing the *reason* why these things were happening to her was an enormous relief to her battered, bruised, and bloody heart. It was as if her soul, floating in a raft for weeks on a vast, trackless ocean, saw the knowledge that God was indeed still working in her life as a ship on the horizon, steaming straight for her little raft, blowing its whistle—only the whistle sounded like the soft murmurings of a dove.

After this comforting awareness of God's presence still in her life, things slowly began to get better. Contrary to all expectations she obtained a position teaching at a local elementary school near a university. She rented a one-room walk-up. She had one suitcase, no furniture, and three boxes of books she'd kept safe from the bipedal, rotary-clawed paper rippers that roamed at will in the house of her previous life.

She taught first grade. The children called her Miss Macushla. No one at that school ever did know or hear her former last name, which she despised like an ever-present stain that she could not scrub clean.

Eventually Macushla earned her doctorate in literature, and after a hard and daunting search found a position teaching at a small northern college. The first-graders were sad to see her go, and they gave her a party. A few of them cried when they handed her their cards, and she recalled from her own childhood the smell of white paste that always reminded her of elementary school, innocence, summer, and freedom from pain.

She barely made it to her little one-room apartment before completely breaking down in great wracking sobs after enduring the experience of having other people's children mourn her passing while her own would not even call. The tirade on the dangers of her religious inclinations by her former husband's prominent attorney had a dramatic effect on the judge, and he had so ordered that no contact be made until the children reached their majority so as to avoid any untoward influence. The children she had carried in her body, for whom she had bled to give life and given up her own, had forgotten her as if she'd never existed. On her last night in that little single bed with the steel-spring mattress, she lay curled up from a pain that no one who has not been rejected by their own children can ever know. It is as if there is one long unceasing swirl of pain that wells up from what you know is the center of your soul and, having nowhere to go, unleashes itself like a hurricane trapped in a tent, contorting that tent of a soul into a tight little ball while the storm rages within. Extra tear bottles were called for that night in heaven.

* * *

When Macushla was thirty-five, after a bracing drive across the country, she stepped directly but warily down the main walkway of the campus. She was reporting in December to begin in the winter semester, and snow covered the trees as if they had been advised that the photographer from the Saturday Evening Post was going to arrive, and had requested of God suitable raiment. She marveled at how the tiniest accumulations of snow on the tiniest of branches combined to create a majestic, complex yet elegantly simple effect, and it reminded her of how God took the tiniest, most elemental events in a person's life and in simple elegance, with a complexity unimagined, crafted the most dazzling, the most breathtaking pictures of each life imaginable (she was, as you can see, beginning to heal). There was *so much*, she marveled…so much to get from even the smallest thing in nature. She walked on thus, hands buried in the pockets of her thin coat, dark auburn hair speckled with snowflakes draped over her shoulders, and felt at peace. She no longer needed the dramatic, the spectacular, or the flash of blatant evidence to reveal what she had come to know was a supreme and cosmically unchangeable fact—that God loved her, that God was doing His best for her every day, and that He would not rest until she was what He wanted to make of her. It was a marvelous prospect that stretched out into eternity. The fires of refinement—difficulties, sorrows, hardships, pain, and persecution—are to our lives as pressure is to diamonds; our God is after all a consuming fire. The middle-aged woman who walked the snowy lane that day had come to the point where she was willing to again say to God, *do whatever you wish to do with me*, and mean it. Such a prayer now meant worlds more than it had at first, because now she knew what it meant. It is one thing to ask God to do something when you don't know what it means, being ignorant of how God might reply. It is another thing altogether to offer Him everything that is your life—offer it up to be burned, shamed, broken, or cast down—with a more informed, experiential knowledge of what His response could be. To have had the experience of being passed through the fire and yet to retain the willingness for Him to do so again… this is what the ancients knew as trust.

When Macushla was thirty-eight, she felt well-settled at the university. Her classes were going well and she was demonstrating a mature and appreciated talent to make literature come alive for those students desiring to learn. For the others, she could make them at least laugh at their own foolishness. She had been truly humbled, and therefore could not find it in her character to think herself better than those who either did not appreciate what she did, did not understand what she did, or did not believe as she did.

Of course the disdain for Christianity was flourishing within academia, and it was just becoming fashionable then to disparage—in academically acceptable form, complete with footnotes and the references and consultations of other like-minded sages—the utter impossibility of miracles, the foolishness of a faith which one could not accord with the principles of science, or the slavish submission to a fire-breathing, savagely vengeful, white-bearded Hebraic figurehead who commanded full and utter obedience. Here began Macushla's phase of life wherein she learned to do battle. Sometimes there were skirmishes conducted in gentle whispers with students enduring crushed and broken hearts, or heartbreaking engagements with those whose hearts were already seared. She would struggle and fight on the high mountains for the drunk, drugged, or pregnant and abandoned, wondering how on earth they would be able to survive another hour. And sometimes the fight would be in the trenches, slugging it out in the spiritual mud with professors whose arrogance would have left the Pharisees agog. They slashed in ridicule at one assumed (but fatally inaccurate) Christian tenet after another. She would sometimes parry with a line of argument she'd read in a most wonderful fantasy story: she would tell them that if God was truly as they supposed him to be, it would be the right thing *not* to believe in Him. This riposte took many of them up short—the honest ones, at least. The bitter, angry wolves among them—the ones who knew the truth but sought to bury it (and her) nonetheless—would not be dissuaded, and continued to sharpen their knives and look for ways to confound her at least, or to have her dismissed at best.

There were no men for Macushla. She would awaken each morning in her (slightly better, slightly furnished) apartment, eat a spare breakfast, walk to her classes, conduct her research, meet with her doctoral students, and take a bit of exercise in the afternoons, all in an easy rhythm that took each day as a unique and separate opportunity to do what God asked her to do—just that day. She did not look to the next day, or the next week. Being human, though, she would get lonely. Sometimes this loneliness would result in the pain of her lost children welling up—nothing seemed to dim that. The tears would come and, while the pain was still as agonizing as ever, she began to sense that perhaps she might, just *might*, possibly bear it.

She began to ache to catch even just a glimpse of a dove as she walked the campus grounds. It seemed to her, though it was purely her imagination, she was sure, that every time this pain resurfaced, she would catch sight of a dove just afterward, and the Doctor of Literature took this as a sign that the Doctor of the Universe was there, with His spirit, comforting her. The thought of developing a bond with a man, of embarking upon a relationship again, was like planning a leap to the Pleiades soon after learning to walk across the play pen.

When Macushla was forty, her hair began to streak with silver. She needed glasses to read. Her form, still lithe and trim, remained athletic and, more importantly, her heart and soul were continually growing toward eternity. She attended a small church close to the university, frequented mostly by manual laborers in town—the janitors, the merchants, the farmers, the factory workers. She was the only professor. At times students would come, more out of curiosity than any desire to know Who was being talked about. She most enjoyed the evening Bible studies, where those serious about enriching themselves with the Word of God would gather. They were a group of like-minded believers seeking simply to learn at the feet of their Lord, and He would never fail to teach them. Macushla did not say much during these evenings; she simply soaked in the wisdom that flowed like spring water from old janitors; from old, rough-handed cleaning women with hair still in their kerchiefs after cleaning rich people's floors that day; from older men in factory coveralls with pain-filled eyes, gentle nonetheless, who spoke of heaven as though they had just returned from a walk on golden streets.

One day the Comparative Religion faculty sponsored a lecture by a famous writer. This was a great coup. The writer rode the cusp of one of the most divisive arguments occurring then in the nation, and it was rare for anything associated with the discipline of comparative religion to excite the debating juices of the nation at large. Since the Literature department had always maintained a fairly tolerant attitude toward the Comparative Religion department at the University—rather broad-minded of them, if they did think so themselves—there was a flyer posted in the literature faculty lounge, and Macushla decided to attend. It was the same night as her Bible study, but the event would be held early enough so that she could just leave the one to attend the other.

It seems that a writer, whose name was Shlomo Hakelev (she'd heard of him, but hadn't read any of his books), a Jew, was taking to task his fellow Jews for completely and utterly abandoning their faith and heritage. It appeared from his writings that Hakelev was actually inferring that the Holocaust was God's judgment on the Jews. In the country, outside of academia, anti-Semitism was still extremely unacceptable, the Holocaust still remaining somewhat fresh in peoples' memories since the recent end of the war. Anyone demonstrating the least tendency toward such a philosophy would be drawn and quartered. In academia, however, things were different. The roots of American education had been planted by those whose philosophy compelled them to drive out of the academic temple with whips anything that smacked of the Judeo-Christian culture or ethic. Where such soil exists, the weed of anti-Semitism will always flourish.

The Comparative Religion department was quite confounded. On one hand, here was a Jew taking to task his fellow Jews. This was in complete accord with their pernicious though as-yet unmentionable anti-Semitic inclinations, but to have a Jew bash Jews was just the thing to feed the anti-Semitic baby without appearing to hold the bottle. On the other hand, the man was one of those extremely irritating religious types who advocated that Christians were to love and honor and cherish the natural olive tree that was Israel—and the Jews themselves, too (confound things to damnation). This apparent dichotomy served to thoroughly confute these robed disciples of Rousseau, but there is nothing they liked better than an apparent contradiction in terms. They perceived such a situation in the same way that Goliath considered David. There was no possible way in their minds that the truth which might emerge from the encounter would be other than that which would accord with their preconceived ideas, and therefore they looked forward to having the controversial Jew—who some said was a survivor from the concentration camps—in for a good round of debate. "All the better to consider the truth," they would grumble and harrumph. "Let's see what the young fellow has to say for himself."

In order that they might let the irritating man dig his own grave, they scheduled him for a debate. What was more natural than a civilized debate in the hallowed and pacific halls of academe? Let every man have his say, they said...as long as what was said was approved, they thought.

On the night of the debate, Macushla found herself enduring a wretched cold. Her throat was raw, her sinuses blocked, and she coughed and hacked her way through the cold and windy night to the auditorium. She slid into a seat near the back of the auditorium, which was, for a comparative religion debate, rather packed. Two students sitting in the row in front of her speculated to themselves that perhaps it was because of Hakelev's background. "They say he survived Auschwitz. He escaped just before they closed the place."

The debate was to take place on a raised platform. She could see two tables facing each other upon the stage. At one there was a single chair placed next to a small tabletop microphone. At the other were three chairs and three microphones.

Macushla could see a knot of men standing to the left of the stage, preparing to mount the steps, engaged in what was apparently quite an animated conversation. Arms were waving, fingers pointing toward chests and then toward the heavens, hands patting shoulders, heads nodding, smiling, and then tossed back in laughter. A very large, very portly man in a black beard, a black silk suit, and a brilliant white shirt was gesturing with ornate confidence. She could tell from the picture in the program that his was Herr Doktor Itzhak Eckstein, the Rabbi on the faculty. His biographical paragraph said that he had three doctorates—in Hebrew, Comparative Religion, and Psychology. He had, before 'retiring' to teach, been the Rabbi of the largest orthodox temple in New York City. He had written resoundingly popular articles flaying David Ben Gurion, Chaim Weisman, and that Meyerson woman for even considering the establishment of a State of Israel without the approval of the international community. And, he would go on to say, what about those true Zionists who said that the Messiah must first return to rebuild the temple before there would be a Jewish nation again? This nugget in the pudding delighted his comparative religion colleagues; anything to confute those arrogant sons of Abraham. "Quite solid scholarship, really," they would say to themselves, "first rate." He had even made a pilgrimage to the Holy Land to join the Hasidic communities protesting the creation of the State of Israel.

There was Matarashi Swami Omi, a distinguished guest from the Comparative Religion department at the University of Berkeley. "Swami" as he was affectionately named in the program, had recently been on a hunger strike, protesting one situation or another, for the past three years. He had eaten nothing but one slice of bread each month, and that only to commemorate those who were suffering. He had walked from the West Coast all the way to the campus for this debate, they said, because he was concerned that taking any form of automated transport might harm the environment, or that the conveyance might kill a small furry animal in the road, or smash a bug against the windscreen, and he refused to be a party to the murder of any living thing. It was said that he was convinced that he had been a worm in a previous life: like Eckstein, he was greatly respected by the staff at the University.

The third visitor was a tall, white-haired, very distinguished looking gentleman. Macushla did not need the program to recognize the Midwest's most prominent radio churchman, the Right Reverend Wally Joe Woolkins. She had heard, and the program testified, that he was syndicated on almost twenty radio shows around the country, and his preaching was 'lighting the fires of revival' in every nook and cranny of America's heartland—or so the radio tagline, faithfully represented in the program, indicated. 'Woolly Wally Joe', as he was known, was a self-proclaimed, fire-breathing, stomp-down, latter-day prophet who preached profit to all God's children. He alleged that those who had the courage to "dig down, dig deep, and dig big" when it came to think about giving, would be mightily rewarded by God. The silk suit, shoes, rings, coiffure, and cufflinks need hardly be described. Macushla could see them from where she sat in the back of the room. It was her first experience seeing a radio preacher in the flesh. She had no love for the breed since her experience on the porch so long ago, and she beheld the vision of the presence warily.

These august giants of the faith were rapt in conversation, engaged in effortlessly impressing the dean of the Comparative Religion department. They conversationally circled each other, watching to detect any dust of neglect or the debris of 'old time religion', looking for any opportunity to slay anyone or each other with the swords of their own precious philosophies. The little white-haired Dean of the department stood, one hand in his jacket pocket (elbows patched, mind), the other clutching his pipe, smiling with diabolical calculation, subtly anticipating a slaying of altogether another sort while outwardly conveying the very picture of an academic—affable, diminutive, and slightly confused.

While these great goings-on were occurring, a tall man emerged from a door on the right side of the auditorium, and with no ado at all made his way down the aisle toward the steps. He mounted them laboriously, leaning on a stout walking stick, tapping it as he went, and sat down at the table with one chair. He was clean-shaven, with very close-cropped hair. He appeared to Macushla, even from where she sat, to be almost skeletal. He wore a black blazer, threadbare and shiny at the elbows, khaki slacks, and a pale, dusty-looking shirt. He carried a thick black book, which Macushla took to be a Bible, and set it down next to him at his elbow. He then folded his hands, composed himself, and looked up toward the sound of the conflagration on the other side of the auditorium. She took this to be Mr. Hakelev.

Few people had noticed him entering, but strangely, as the Dean was nodding his head, rapturously engrossed, his eye happened to stray from beholding the presences and apparently the worn man interrupted his line of vision. Startled, the Dean began tagging the elbows of the august gentlemen and indicating that perhaps it was time, if they had all finished the expression of their assuredly profound thoughts, for them all to ascend to further glories and take their positions at the table. This they agreed to do, and thus the debate commenced.

The Dean introduced the august personages (yes, it was Mr. Hakelev indeed) and then it was the Dean's honor to pose the first question.

"Why does God permit suffering?" he intoned sonorously, and then looked up with a bright expression and nodded toward the larger table. "Rabbi Herr Doktor Eckstein, if you would please begin. Each speaker, please, limit your statements to no more than five minutes."

"Suffering is punishment," Eckstein began, just as sonorously, and explained that God punished his people, causing them to suffer, because they did not keep His law. "Keep the law," Macushla wrote in her notebook, "and avoid suffering. The man who suffers is the man who sins." It took Eckstein five and three-quarter minutes to make essentially this point, which Macushla (who could have been an editor) captured precisely. She looked at the words she'd written on the page and wondered about her life. She had wanted nothing but truth and beauty and it had seemed she'd gotten nothing but ashes and tears. Perhaps Eckstein was right.

"Swami Omi," the Dean called, "if you would, could you please enlighten us as to why God permits suffering?"

The Swami nodded sagely. He held up a hand, palm out, and placed his other hand over his heart. "God permits suffering because by this alone can we atone for the sins of our past lives," he said, seriously. "I attest to this as truth itself. Every sin committed by every living creature must be balanced by retribution and kindness, and the great circle of life will continue until all have been purged of past sins, past murders, past unkindness, and brought by suffering into a cleansed, enlightened awareness of the true nature of holiness and truth. We essentially pay for our misdeeds in one life by suffering in another. God is simply that force within us all that will be unleashed to shine forth in true light after each has been cleansed of the sins of their past. Suffering is that by which we will all become gods." The palm came down, the hand came off the heart: time was up.

The Dean and many members of the audience were nodding sagely. Macushla, testing her reflexes, snapped out her hand and squashed a fly on her knee. She did not even bother to write a summary of the Swami's wisdom, which she recognized as foolishness at best, lethal deceit at worst. After her misadventure listening to that foolish sermon on her porch in her previous life, her soul's reaction upon hearing foolishness and false platitudes was slowly but surely becoming a reliable filter.

The Right Reverend stood and picked up the table microphone without waiting for any dignified personage to invite him to address the question.

"I wanna tell you all here tonight," he began, so loudly that most jumped in their seats, "that suffering comes from *lean thinking*. That's right," he said. Macushla saw his eyebrow raise, and it seemed to her that it just dawned upon the Right Reverend that a display of anger was commensurate with the thought which he had just cogently expressed, and therefore proceeded to bang the table with the flat of his hand—and too he suddenly remembered to omit his consonants. He did not wish to be confused with the overly intellectual effete, who, as was known by everyone in America, lived in cities and disdained the Word o' God, which, as everyone also knew, could only be reliably taught by those who had not yet learned the rudiments of English language grammar or pronunciation. *"Lean thinkin'*! You sufferin' from a little lack of funds? You sufferin' from the rheumatis'? You sufferin' from them unsaved hellions that live all around you, drivin' you to drink with their cursin' and dancin' and womanizin'? It's *you* that's the cause of all this," he said, pointing his finger now at the audience, "it's *you* to blame for yer sufferin'."

One woman in a gray fox fur and white hair wearing a string of pearls around her neck gasped, and her hand flew to her bosom. Men occupied themselves with their pipes. Programs became like fans in hell, going back and forth. The heat in the auditorium rose twenty degrees. "Yayuh," the Reverend continued, finger now pointed skyward, with beads of sweat standing out on his forehead. A silk handkerchief whipped out of a pocket; beads of sweat were mopped up dramatically. "It's your *own* thought life that causes you sufferin', not God! God loves you, he wants ta bless you until your *eyes* bug out, and all you do is just sit there and whine and worry about how you're hurtin, or you ain't got no money, or about that wicked woman down the street gonna run off with yer man!"

Macushla did not recognize the line of argument from anything she'd read in Scripture, and so the growing tree of her soul simply waved like wheat in a gentle wind, letting the vacuous message pass over and away.

"Think *big!*" he shouted, and leapt up in the air and came down, smacking his hand again on the table. The audience jumped, heads snapped back; women patted their bosoms like heart palpitating machines. "You want to stop sufferin' from ailments? Then you just say it—'*I'm healthy as a horse!*' and you *claim* that health! You wanna stop sufferin' from lack of that green stuff that makes the world go round while you watch them heathen rakin' it in? Then you just git down on yer knees, git up off yer wallet, put yer seed out to God's glory and his workers out there a laborin' in the vineyard, and then I'm here to tell you, brothers and sisters, you better go run git yer bucket, 'cause God's gonna *pour* down—I said pour *down*—the blessings of heaven on yer head!"

The assembled crowd of overly intellectual effetes was entertained by this performance in the way New York socialites hitting the jazz clubs in Harlem enjoy the music but never once even entertain the thought of actually letting the musicians into their circle of society. With distinguished countenances they nodded their heads as though earnestly moved; inside they were wringing the little hands of their souls in glee at the display of what was being dispensed to gullible fundamentalists in America's heartland. Not much longer now, they thought, and Christianity will be taken to be that which this laughable ass was touting—and then, just taken to be laughable. The Dean's stock went up with them all that night. They realized the magnitude of his prescience in providing them a display of the future of religion in America, and by somehow managing to tout as profoundly religious that which would eventuate in the ultimate demise of religion.

The Dean himself was trying his best not to smile, and not quite succeeding, when the lady next to him wearing a taffeta gown and glasses that looked as though they'd been made from the tail fins scrounged from a P-38 tugged at his sleeve and pointed to the little gavel that stood before him, to be rapped when time was up. The Right Reverend was taking a breath and just winding up for his next blast when Macushla (and everyone else) heard her stage whisper erupt into the momentary silence: "His time is up! Dean, bang the gavel, his time is up!"

The Right Reverend's hand, which was flying skyward, dropped suddenly. "My sincere apologies, little lady," he said, his voice suddenly deeper (and much quieter), as if his sanity had returned after stepping out for a coffee. He sat down, earnestly if somewhat absent-mindedly rubbing his hand.

The Dean gathered himself. "Thank you for that *unique* perception of faith in America today, Reverend Woolkins." The assembled professors and their wives snickered up their sleeves at the Dean's witticism. The Dean shook himself slightly, to convey a sense of a dog shaking off the water of absurdity, collected his assaulted dignity by shooting his cuffs and tucking up his lapels, and said, "Now...Mr. Hakelev...if you would please address the question of why God allows suffering?"

The worn man at the table by himself shook his head once, as though dispensing with a particularly noxious, lingering fume, and staring straight ahead (Macushla realized just then with a start that he was blind, and recalled the stick tapping up the steps to the stage), said, "Suffering makes us like God. It does not make us gods, mind you—such thinking is foolishness—but He does call us to become like Him, and only by enduring what His Son endured can we become like Him." Macushla sat up suddenly, fully attentive. In one sentence the man had put his finger on the logo of her life. The man's voice, amplified by the microphone, sounded as though it had been damaged or worn out.

"This is why He allows suffering. He loves us too much to leave us as we are, and so He permits us to suffer so that we can become more like Him. The Heart of Love Himself cannot avoid permitting His children to suffer; it would be contrary to His nature, for it is suffering alone that can bring His children to Him."

This opinion occasioned, of all things, laughter in the crowd. Eckstein interrupted—technically not permissible by the rules of the debate, but the clearly outrageous assertion demanded a stay of the rules. "Surely you don't mean to imply, Mr. Hakelev, that man can become like God?

"He says, "Be ye perfect, even as I am perfect." Here was even more from Scripture; her heart automatically warmed to the man. "Now, we cannot become gods," Hakelev went on, as though he could see the Swami's head nodding in agreement and wanted to forestall any semblance of agreement with such a philosophy, "nor should we wish to. This was the sin which felled Lucifer—Satan. He has been spouting this lie since he was thrown out of the garden." Hakelev could not see the look of utter disdain, bordering on murderous hatred, which passed like a black winged shadow over the peaceful countenance of the Swami. Macushla thought to herself that it would have made no difference. Hakelev was speaking the truth, and truth cannot be turned aside. "But we *can* become like His Son, who came to show us how man could live a life of complete obedience to God."

Here the laughter in the audience, though still muted, became more profuse. Hakelev, while blind, could see that his opinions were like pearls before swine, and Macushla watched him fold his hands slowly. "Well, that's my thought," he said, and was silent. Macushla looked down at her watch (she had to hold her arm out at a distance): only two minutes had gone by.

"Well," the Dean said, disconcerted, "well...thank you, Mr. Hakelev. Interesting perspective: now, our next question is—" he stopped as Hakelev stood up, the chair scraping across the wooden floor. Hakelev picked up the large black book, took his stick, and tapped his way unerringly back down the steps and out the side door of the auditorium while the Dean watched, confused. The woman in the P-38 glasses stared, open-mouthed, and then yanked at the Dean's sleeve, whispering again so loudly they could hear her in San Francisco: "He can't do that, Dean, we have three more questions! He can't leave yet!"

The auditorium buzzed with excitement. Here was controversy itself, descended upon their sleepy little college town like a lightning bolt. Some began to feel cheated: they'd wanted to hear this noted author rip into the Jewish question (and the Jews). Not quite the thing, some of the more erudite among them thought...no, not quite the thing at all. If this man thought he'd survive in the give-and-take, free-for-all world of dynamic exchange of opinion among men of letters with that kind of sensitivity, well then, he was gravely mistaken. No…a dilettante after all, they thought… just a dilettante. The women were distressed. Sables and fox furs were not gotten out and worn for nothing, they felt. Had the man no sense of decorum?

The Dean, not wanting to waste the evening, put the three remaining questions to the three remaining luminaries, and they went on to spout their spouts, but Macushla did not stay after Mr. Hakelev departed. She picked up her notebook and stepped out again into the night, coughing at the assault of cold air, her warm breath blowing before her, the smell of wood smoke and leaves like a tonic after the stultifying atmosphere in the auditorium. She began to wonder just exactly what she was about, working in a field in which her most cherished beliefs were considered foolishness, where those who were preferred and elevated could not even see the clear truth when it came to them in the form of a blind man.

She walked to her Bible study after stopping at the local drug store for a hamburger and some cough drops. At Maude's place, where the study was held, there were eight people—the regulars—all of whom she knew, and all knew her. Though they knew her name they called her nothing but "Dearie". She was welcomed warmly; there was a bright fire in the fireplace, and they sat around on chintz-covered sofas and chairs, some on a braided rug on the floor, each with their Bibles. A pot of tea was on the table, with cookies and some fruit. To her surprise, there on a chair in the corner sat Mr. Hakelev, a large Braille Bible open on his lap, stick next to the chair. A large, long-haired dog sat contentedly near him, close to the fire, head on his paws. He looked directly up at her without moving his head, the way dogs do. His tail thumped tiredly and he smiled (yes, dogs can smile).

"Come sit down, Dearie," said Maude, the host. "We've a guest, Mister Hakelev it is. John found him out in the street."

"Yep," said John, the school janitor. "He was just walkin' down the street with that dog, tapping away with that stick, lookin' like he didn't have a place in the world to go, carryin' that there giant Bible. I saw the snow startin' to fall and thought that a snowy street was no place to be for a blind man carryin'a Bible—a Bible study was just the place."

"Very much appreciate the thought," said Hakelev, in a rasping voice. "You were kind."

"My husband is a kind man," said Maude, looking at the old floor sweeper as though he was the King of Troy. She reached out to caress his hand gently.

"And come to find out he's a believer!" exclaimed Miss Elly, a tough old wrinkled woman with hands bent like claws, sitting in the rocking chair. "You wonder we can be surprised by anything God does anymore, don't you."

Macushla was smiling quietly, silently charmed and secure amidst the warmth which accompanied fellowship in the Spirit. Instead of replying to Miss Elly, she coughed explosively. Maude jumped. "Come you, now and sit down, Dearie. Libby, let's get some hot tea into this woman before she falls down and dies on us."

There was further clucking and rustling and Macushla found herself ensconced between two old women who made gracious room for her on the couch and buried her with a knitted coverlet.

Miss Elly ruffled one old hand across the pages of her Bible with a gesture of tender affection. "Tell me, Mr. Hakelev, what were you doing out there in the snow, if you don't mind my asking?"

"Just walking," he said slowly. His voice was rough, as though someone had scraped broken glass across his vocal chords. Over her steaming cup of tea, Macushla thought she could discern scars at his throat where his scarf had fallen away. She saw, too, that while he had appeared to have no hair, in actuality his hair was just very short, almost shaved. As he reached a hand down to ruffle the dog's head, her eyes darted to the wrist. A line of blue, like numbers inked, was where she thought it to be. So it was true, then.

"Mr. Hakelev was giving a talk at the college," she rasped. The tea was just beginning to work on her own raw throat. She held her mug before her with both hands, letting the fellowship and the tea warm her. "He's an author, you know," she went on, "and they had him in to debate with several members of the Comparative Religion faculty."

This quieted the group.

"More like the blind trying to lead the blind," he said.

Miss Elly laughed. "None so blind as those who will not see," she said sharply. "I hope you gave those white-washed tombs a belly-full of that book you got there on your lap!"

Mr. Hakelev's eyes looked in her direction. "Miss Elly, right? Well, Miss Elly, unfortunately I don't think I did so well as that."

"He did quite well," Macushla said, her own voice in her ears sounding like a frog. "I'd have thrown my stick at them after the first go-round."

"Pearls before swine," Libby said from the floor. Libby was twenty-three and worked as a maid for one of the professors. "They could not hear you anyway, Mr. Hakelev."

"What sort of name is that, now, young man," asked Maude. "Where are you from?"

"Well, Maude, it is a Hebrew name, though I am from this country."

The fellowship looked at the worn man with interest. "Tell us about yourself," said Maude quietly, and so he did.

In April of 1936, he had gone with his parents to visit their relatives in Austria. While his parents were at table with cousins in a tavern, he had wandered out to sit in the garden of the restaurant. Two men sat at a table nearby. When they heard him ask for water from the waiter in English, they let down their guard and spoke freely to one another.

"In time we will accomplish the elimination of these vermin," one said, speaking in German, looking through the wide window into the restaurant where many diners, some obviously Jewish, were enjoying their dinner.

"Not soon enough for me," said the other, crushing a cigarette.

"And you will need to quit that habit, Franz, if you know what's good for you."

"Ja, ja, it will be a trifle. They make me angry, those Yiddishers."

"Time enough," said the first man, "time enough. Our time will come. Tomorrow belongs to us, remember? Tomorrow we crush them like you crush that cigarette."

The young man from America could understand them easily; German had been spoken in his home since he was a child. He returned to his parent's table after seeing on the first man's face a look of hatred that he could not explain and would, unfortunately, see again. He knew instinctively then that war would come, and he felt an unreasoning but overpowering desire to get into the fight. He was nineteen that year.

When Germany invaded Poland in 1939, he flew to England to fight. His parents did not understand but supported him. His father knew people who knew people, and when his desire was brought to the attention of connections in the Foreign Office, it was thought that the young man, who spoke German fluently, would be an invaluable clandestine operator. Throughout the Phony War he learned how to kill with his hands, how to live off the land, how to parachute, how to run like a gazelle, how to shoot a multitude of weapons, how to use a commando knife, and about the basics of tradecraft, as it was coming to be called. When he turned twenty-four, he was a hard man, with a clear eye, a quick mind, and a desire to fight against what he perceived to be a growing pernicious offense against truth. Not two men on the Continent knew he was Jewish—or so he thought.

Just before the Battle of Britain they dropped him into conquered France with three others—an engineering expert, a demolitions expert, and a liaison to the French underground. Their mission was to gather intelligence about the German aircraft industry and after doing so, blow up as many planes as they could. They had been in France two days when their resistance contact turned them in for three bottles of champagne.

Their captors shot the engineering expert and tied a live hand grenade to the belt of the demolitions expert and pulled the pin from a distance. They were about to shoot the young man when the traitor, already mildly drunk, said, in execrable German, "You don't want to shoot this little one, Heine. He is a Jew; save him for something really special."

So the Germans tipped up their muzzles and tied his hands and shipped him off back through the lines, out of occupied France, back into Germany, and then, in mercilessly cold rail cars, watching snow fall like it would never stop, into Silesia...to a place called Auschwitz. He was twenty-five.

"I came to Him there, you know," he said to the group, referring to Christ. "I was in Auschwitz from 1941 through October of 1943, actually." Hakelev's eyes began to mist, and he had to clear his throat to continue. Something from his past was causing him pain. "An old man, Dutch I think, had been caught hiding Jews in his cellar. He spoke to me of Jesus, and...well, I had known in my youth someone who also had spoken of this man. It was the first time I'd heard of him since then, actually. This Dutch man was so full of truth and beauty that I could not deny that what he spoke of was the truth. He opened up to me the Old Testament Scriptures more so than any Rabbi I'd ever heard before; he made things so plain, so clear."

"Where is that old man, now," Libby asked, eyes wide. "Did he survive?"

"Oh, they shot him," Hakelev answered numbly. "They shot him out of hand one morning in September of 1943, just before...well, just before we left. He stumbled on the way to roll call. That was his crime, I suppose. Apparently the Russian offensive was not going so well, they were short of food, so they wanted to thin out the ranks. I lost many friends then.

"But he made Jesus leap from the Scriptures, you know, and perhaps it was the conditions, being surrounded by so much privation, so much hate, with death our constant companion, that made it easier for me to understand or see true Love and true Life. When all else is stripped away, it becomes easier to see the eternal things which are always before us, always present, patiently waiting for our consideration. It may be that seeing great light is made easier with the darkest backdrops."

The group sat listening, rapt, to a man who had witnessed unbelievable suffering.

"Is that where...is that where you went blind?" Libby asked.

His hand inadvertently went to his eyes. "Yes...yes, it was. I.G. Farben had a chemical production facility there. They were working on a formula to improve rocket fuel or something, I suppose. There was a German scientist, a chemist, who ran my section of the lab. We were just cleanup workers there, sweeping floors, cleaning the test tubes and equipment—the place had to be kept quite clean, you know. One day I dropped a test tube. The scientist became very angry. He had two guards shove my face in a bucket of fuel. Then they held me down, held my mouth open, and tried to pour some of the fuel down my throat. That didn't work too well, but there was enough to burn my throat. My voice has not been the same since. After that…well, after that, my vision began to dim. There was another prisoner there, a man who'd been a doctor. He told me that my retinas were beginning to deteriorate and there was nothing I could do."

Macushla listened, horrified. The pain of losing her children, the horror of her marriage, the abuse, the scorn, the hell, all seemed to pale in comparison to the story this man related with such overwhelming detachment. She looked over at Miss Elly, who had tears in her eyes. Maude put a tissue to hers. John blinked hard and fast, hands clasped before him.

"What happened, then?" John asked. "How did you get out?"

There was silence for a while. Mr. Hakelev's head bent down, and they could see tears begin to form at the corners of his eyes and begin to roll quietly down his face. He was no longer so detached. His hand on the arm of the chair clenched. "I killed a man," he whispered.

"Actually, I killed five guards with a knife I'd made from a spoon, and broke out with some other prisoners. My eyes were failing and I did not want to die with that hell hole being the last thing I beheld. The Germans found some prisoners and killed them in the woods, but a few escaped. I made my way up and along the coast to France, stole a small boat and rowed the channel. The last thing I remember seeing was a Messerschmitt rolling out of the clouds, trying to strafe me. I looked up, the sun was there, blinding, and then…snap…I never saw again. I never found out what happened to that Messerschmitt." He laughed sadly: "I guess he missed."

A sense of quiet descended in the room; silence as each of them contemplated the story they'd heard. Miss Elly spoke into the silence.

"…and I would place my cause before God, who does great and unsearchable things, wonders without number. He gives rain on the earth and sends water on the fields, so that He sets on high those who are lowly, and those who mourn are lifted to safety."

There was a rustling in the corner, and Miss Elly rose from the rocking chair in pain. She hobbled over to where the worn man sat by his dog and picked up one of his hands. Her hand, bent and broken by age, held his, bent and broken by hate. "Young man, we're thankful to have you here. God took you through hell for some reason. You wait and trust Him and he'll make things clear, you watch." And she went on to quote from the Book of Job: "Behold, how happy is the man whom God reproves, so do not despise the discipline of the Almighty. For He inflicts pain, and gives relief; He wounds, and His hands also heal. From six troubles He will deliver you, even in seven evil will not touch you..." She stopped, looked off over the man's head as though she saw something, perhaps in the past, perhaps in the future, and recollecting herself, looked down at him again in the chair and said, "From the pit of hell to our little home; God is truly amazing. You make sure you find out what he wants with you, young man."

Macushla heard the words as well. Her eyes misted as she called to mind that God would so care for her that he would take the time to refine her, to be with her in her pain. She bent her head and held her mug tightly. God always spoke to her in these evenings. He was so good.

Mr. Hakelev clasped Miss Elly's hand tightly. "Thank you, Miss Elly." His voice was rough, rasped. He was crying gently. "I will. I can tell you though," he said, laughing in the midst of his tears, "God did not take me out of Auschwitz to witness to Comparative Religion departments."

They all laughed, and the horror of the man's life receded before the warmth of fellowship. He told them how after the war he had made his way to Israel, and there began to write. "I have an old secretary," he said, smiling. "She makes me tea, takes my dictation, and scolds me as a poor bachelor who speaks even poorer Hebrew. But she is a Godsend, truly. She is a good woman. I am hoping she sees the truth. God knows it stares her in the face, having to write the words that God gives me to put on paper."

"Why did you change your name?" Macushla asked suddenly, coughing a bit. Her question surprised everyone, her as well. It just emerged of its own accord.

Hakelev stopped, not sure who had spoken. "Because, well, Miss..," and they could tell he didn't know her name, "because it was encouraged then, you see. The State of Israel was just beginning, and the decision had been made to make Hebrew the national language. Everyone was encouraged to Hebraicise their names. What else would we speak? It wouldn't do to be speaking Hebrew and have to throw in a 'Jake' or a 'Raymond' or a 'Pierre' now and again, would it?"

"What does yours mean?" John asked.

Hakelev folded his hands over his Bible slowly and took a breath, his voice rasping, fatigued. "Shlomo is Hebrew for Solomon," he said, "and Hakelev means 'the dog.' I had a dog once that I loved; his name was Solomon. I used to take him in my rowboat when I was a boy, with... with someone who was very dear to me." Hakelev's voice trailed slowly, reminiscing, "...someone who made me first think about what it would mean to live happily ever after. Funny, it wasn't until I fully surrendered my will to Jesus that I finally learned what that really means.

"Anyhow," he went on, now back again from some mystical place of wonder in his memory, "somehow the guards found out about the dog and from that day until I killed them, they called me 'Solomon the Dog'. They enjoyed it, I think. But each time they called me this, I would remember that little dog, and more importantly, the girl who would hold him, and the friendship—the *bond*—I had with that girl, and it was sometimes just the strength I needed. When it was time to change my name, there was nothing else that would do." He paused then, and again in that faraway voice, said quietly, "I loved that girl so much."

There was a still moment of quiet, and then a clink of glass and a small crash.

"Oh, Dearie, now, look what you've done, you've dropped your cup. Here, John, get a rag from the kitchen, would you, sweetie...there's a doll. Now, Macushla Dearie, what is it? Why are you crying, darling?"

Up on Millstone Ridge

The sky had been a threatening and portentous roiling gray mass of clouds for days before the rain began to slowly pelt down in great large drops that splattered in the dust. Chickens jumped and dodged as the rain lifted small puffs of dirt like mortar bursts. In less time that it took to notice, the shower became a downpour, and the dirt lane turned to mud, spraying up against the carriage wheels of the buggies parked in the yard. The rain washed the smell of ash from the air; an exchange of one gray assault upon the senses for another. Smoke from the rubbish pile still twisted upwards, struggling to stay hot but rapidly losing way against the onslaught of pouring rain. Half-burned logs smoked and hissed and then subsided into blackened hulks. Rivulets from the burn pile flowed down and away in small lines of frothy gray.

Colin McClure, his three children, and a gathering of friends stood under the shelter afforded by a pole barn. A large roan draft horse stood by Colin's shoulder. The horse's nose, head, and neck were under the barn's roof, while his back and hindquarters calmly endured the downpour. He was sniffing quietly, small clouds of steam clouding at an even pace before his nostrils. The smell of horse mixed with the smell of smoke in the air. Rain pattered off the barn roof and pounded an outline of the shelter into the dirt of the small pasture. Groups of people—some Amish, some Mennonite, some who just called themselves Christians, some who called themselves Christians but were not, and some who were not and honest enough not to name themselves as such—stood clumped together under umbrellas in the freezing rain. A pine box rested under the square shelter outline, resting on ropes over a deep hole. A backhoe was parked in the distance next to a flatbed trailer in the dirt lane leading to Colin's home.

"I want you to imagine going home, taking off your coats, and hanging them up in the closet," Colin began, his voice mixing with the sound of many waters. "And one day you look for the coat and realize your wife, in a fit of cleaning, has thrown it out. Would you weep? Imagine you were doing the laundry and by mistake you ruined a shirt with bleach. Or imagine you tore a hole in a pair of pants and had to put them in the trash. Would you cry and complain? My wife is not in this box you see here. My wife is with the Lord God of All Creation at the moment. Our bodies are not who we are." He touched his chest for emphasis. "Our bodies are like our clothes; they're shells, veneer…coverings that we use while we walk in a physical realm. Who we are is in here," and again, he touched his chest, "and what's in here is determined by the authority we obey, by the laws we obey. A virus can kill the body, or a car accident, or a gun, or a horse; any one of a thousand things can destroy the bodies we live in—if God so permits—but we need to worry about the One who can kill the soul. And I know that my wife's soul now rests with her Lord, because she tried hard to obey Him throughout her life. She *knew* Him, but more importantly, *He knew her.*"

Colin's voice carried over the sound of the rain to those at the back row in the crowd of swaying umbrellas and hunched shoulders.

"Sometimes we constantly badger God about Aunt Millie's pain in the knee, or Uncle Jimmy's cancer, or Mom's Alzheimer's, or Dad's kidney problems. We cry and fuss at God when he takes his own home. Who are we to complain to Him? Who are we, when we cry about death and complain to him about the loss of a loved one, to argue with the God of All Creation? What are we thinking, standing around at funerals with long faces? I'll tell you what we're thinking. We think that the ultimate goal in life is life in the flesh, life in this body, and making it last forever." He yanked at his coat as he spoke. "That's exactly what we think. And when we fuss and complain to God about poor sick Aunt Millie or Cousin Jane or the poor widow lady down the street who's laid up with the gout, do we ever once think that maybe He is afflicting these people for a reason...that maybe the One who is sovereign over all creation, the One who is doing His best for each of us every moment of the day and night, knows what He's doing? That maybe, just maybe, that person will not become who God wants them to be without that physical burden? And what do we do? We are constantly praying for God to take it away, to make them better, to heal them...as if somehow God has been laying down on the job, forgetting his obligation we think He has to keep us whole and physically healthy at all times; such foolishness.

"God heals, yes. When He walked the dirt in Israel, He healed people everywhere. It was and is His nature to be compassionate toward His sheep. But He calls us beyond an obliterating concern with just physical health. When we put our lives in His hands, we put *everything having to do with our lives* in His hands—and that means our physical bodies and our health as well. Could it be that the cancer, or the rheumatoid arthritis, or the blindness, or the failing kidneys are things God is putting in our lives to break our hold on this life, to break us to His service, and ultimately, after we break and come to Him, to bring us into *real* life, the life that truly matters? Who are we to get in God's way and presume that illness is to be avoided at all costs? Who are we to say that if we're not physically healed, we're out of God's will? We need to look to our souls more than our bodies. Do that, and when God decides to take the body, you'll know who will have your soul.

"I am going to miss my wife. My children will miss her. We will shed tears—this is a vale of tears, after all. But if you ask me if I'd change one thing about the last year, about her illness, about the decisions we made to prepare for her going, then I would say no, I wouldn't have changed one thing. I watched my wife grow closer to God this last year than in all the years she's known Him. There was a sweetness—" He paused, cleared his throat, looked down for a moment, and then up, over the heads of the crowd out to the woods on the horizon. "This illness was from the sovereign King of the Universe. Who am I to dispute His will? I know that we will see her again."

The horse blew out its nostrils and shook its head and neck, scattering water like a fine, misted cloud. Colin caressed his shoulder with a slow hand and the horse blinked, chewed a bit, and settled.

"Thank you all for coming to this little ceremony, and while typically these things have an attendant air of sadness, I want you all to know that for my wife this is the end of a year of pain and difficulty and the beginning of eternity in peace, with no more tears or heartache. She is with the One who is Faithful and True, the Alpha and Omega—the Beginning and the End of all things. Do you think she is sad? I think not; I think she is rejoicing. We should rejoice with her, and for her.

"You have all been extremely kind to come, and the food and things you've left will be cherished. We're extremely grateful. My one last request is that you leave realizing that life does not consist mainly of our physical bodies, but our spirits—*who* we obey defines us more than anything having to do with how we look or our state of health or what we do for a living, because *who we obey shapes who we become*." Colin leaned forward, intense, trying to push the words into their very souls. "The authority source in our life shapes our very souls. We all become like the gods we serve, people, did you know that? A person's god is simply the thing that is most important to them. It's fair to say that every one of us worships the thing most important to us. It could be our jobs, our husbands, our wives, our children, the concept of family, the status we have or want to have, money, power, physical pleasure—whatever it is, we all become like the things we worship. We become like the thing we consider most important in life.

"It's getting cold. Please come inside for something to eat. And remember, we are putting an empty shell, an old coat, a thing that has no life, into the ground in this box. My wife is now full of light, full of life, and full of God. If we could see her now we would all fall down on our faces in joy…some of us, perhaps, in fear. But come inside, get warm, and thank you all for your thoughtfulness and consideration in coming here this morning."

Colin nodded once and the six men lifted the ropes under the box and let it down into the hole. They began to shovel the rich topsoil of the pasture into the hole until that which had enclosed the spirit of Erin McClure was itself enclosed by the embrace of decay until that day when it will be changed in the twinkling of an eye, from dust to everlasting glory.

* * *

"I'm sorry about your mother, Grady."

"Thanks, Sam."

Samantha Jurgens sat on a bale of straw across three feet of space in the barn, particles of dust and hay filtering down as small children played in the second-floor loft. She would be fifteen this December, with shiny black hair, blue eyes that shone with intelligence, and freckles like cinnamon on silk. She wore a white turtleneck sweater under a well-worked Carhartt-brown Cordura farm jacket and jeans, with some old hiking boots. Since Grady had moved to this little northern town and taken the seat next to hers at the community's home school in fifth grade, they had been quiet friends, and had always been able to say things to each other without words. She was utterly convinced she would love him for the rest of her life.

"Will you miss her?"

"I will, Sam...I will", he replied quietly. Grady was a tall boy with his father's height and his mother's gray eyes; broad-shouldered, lean, and well-mannered. His blonde hair was cut short in the style of the day, which only made the masculine features of his face more noticeable and attractive. He leaned back on his own bale of straw and watched the smaller children running in the hay above his head. He drew in a deep breath. "But I believe what my Dad said today. My Mom and I talked a lot about it. We put nothing but a shell in the ground out there. We'll see her again."

Sam always admired Grady's trust in God. It was one of the things that attracted her about him.

"Was she frightened before she...at the last?"

"No...no, not about dying, Sam, I'm pretty sure. She knew she was going to die, and she knew she'd be with Jesus. She never doubted it, and that's what pretty much kept her through the worst of things."

The slight pause alerted Sam to another possibility. "Was she frightened of something else?" The noise of children playing washed over them both, their conversation like a small but steady rock in the middle of waves hitting shore.

Grady rubbed his face and looked at her carefully. He cleared his throat and threw a bit of straw to the ground. "Well... the day before she passed, something...something happened that we haven't exactly figured out, but it seemed...well, it seemed like she'd had some kind of dream or...or something."

Sam waited, interest heightened. Grady and his family weren't ones to swing from chandeliers; their faith wasn't based on any kind of emotional framework. If something strange had happened, it was something of substance. She wrapped her arms around her knees and Grady went on.

"She was lying in bed that last morning and Thomas and my Dad and I were there. Wren was still sleeping. Mom had called out for my Dad when he was in the kitchen and we all came. There was something different about the sound of her voice. So we went into their bedroom with my Dad and she looked at each of us and then grabbed my Dad's wrist and pulled him close. 'Keep them safe,' she said. It was like she was begging him for something. 'Don't put the children at risk.' Her eyes were wide and she was straining at my Dad's arm, and I saw she was crying. Then she looked straight at my Dad and said '*Be careful whose law you obey*.'"

"Whose law you obey? What was she talking about?"

Grady looked down at his hands for a moment and shook his head slowly. "Can't say, Sam; don't know. My Dad was confused, I can tell you that. But they were her last words. She let go of my Dad's wrist, took his hand, laid back on the pillow and let out a long breath, and then...and then...well, she..."

"She died," Sam said softly. She took his hand again gently.

He nodded, eyes welling, and replied with a gentle squeeze. "She began to really live," he whispered. "I just know it."

He put his head in his hands then, and his shoulders began to shake, and Sam's heart broke as well.

Thomas McClure, ten years old, sat silently on the floor of the kitchen, leaning back against a cabinet, watching the crowd of people flow through the house, causing him to think of how heads of wheat looked when wind moved over a field—random, different, never the same twice. He tried to identify patterns in movement, or in faces. In his mind he plotted a differential curve that related people with red in their clothes to where they were in the house, speculating about what the area under the curve would mean. Mostly he listened to their words—different accents, different tones, different motivations, different life patterns, different spirits. He saw colors that went with the sounds he heard and they mixed together in his vision like a kaleidoscope, or like the explosion in his eyes that happened when the sun had hit a stained-glass window he'd seen one day when his mother had stopped at a church to ask directions. He had learned not to yell when that happened.

He watched an ant move across the floor, dodging monstrously large shoes, hoping it would make the journey across the kitchen floor safely. He tried to predict which way the ant would turn by estimating its scope of relative divergence from the mean path of the pheromone trail. He stopped when the ant disappeared under a muddy sneaker. He looked out the window. It was still raining. He began to count the raindrops that passed through the square framed by one window pane.

Wren McClure, five years old, sat on her father's lap, nestled securely in the crook of his arm, looking out with large chocolate doe eyes, wide open, taking in everything around her. She was safe here, surrounded by the smell of her father's shirt, its rough feel on her face, the scent of horse mixed with soap and an indefinable 'man smell' that made her think of wood and dirt and trees and safety. Her father was talking to the Holtzmans. The Holtzmans had a dairy farm three miles away. The Holtzmans were Mennonites with five children. The Holtzmans loved God because, as her father had told her once, they tried to do what God said to do.

"We thought it was interesting…about the horse, I mean," said Marjorie Holtzman "under the barn roof and all." She wore a white prayer cap on her head and a pale blue dress under a black apron. Her hands were thin and strong, calloused from milking cows and working the farm with her husband. She spoke softly but directly, with clear eyes that looked out at the world without fear. Marjorie's daughter, Lilly, sat on her lap. Lilly was four. Wren and Lilly played together often. Lilly held Regina, her doll. Wren held her father's fingers.

"Bear," her father replied. "He's eighteen two. His mother died giving birth. Erin milked the dead mare, brushing away her tears, and then raised that horse by hand. The horse thinks Erin is his mother."

Byron Holtzman nodded slowly; he'd seen it before. "But how did he get so big? That isn't normal with an orphan."

"The vet came out after Bear's mother died and told Erin to give the horse as much formula as it could drink. She took him literally—we didn't know any better at the time—and the horse drank the stuff as fast as she could make it.

"When Erin got sick, she couldn't do the chores any longer, and wouldn't you know it, but that horse became almost unmanageable. He would race around the pasture and paw the ground constantly. He kicked out three sections of fence before Wren figured out what was bothering him."

"And what was it, sweetie?" Marjorie asked, looking directly at her.

"I thought that Bear just wanted to know if my Mommy was okay. So Daddy took a chair and a blanket and my Mommy sat out near the pasture where Bear could see her and he was just fine."

"That's true," her father added. "Strangest thing...the horse completely settled down. We finally ended up changing the fence so that he could graze under her window."

"I think animals know more than we think they know," said Byron. Marjorie nodded in agreement. "I could tell you stories about cows."

"I think that's why their eyes are so big," Wren peeped quietly.

"What do you mean, sweetie," Marjorie asked.

"Because they can see more than we can," Wren answered.

Her father went on with the story. "When Erin...when she passed on, we were in the bedroom. After she left—just after—I looked out on the pasture and there were all the horses, standing there in a line, heads down, looking in toward the window. They knew. When we put her remains in the box and began digging the hole with the backhoe, Bear started charging the fence, pawing the ground, and snorting. When we put the box on the ropes, the horse jumped the five-foot fence and came over to stand near the front door of the house until everyone showed up for the ceremony. Then he pushed his way in under the roof right up against me when I stood there to talk to everyone as we put her remains in the ground."

"He was standing guard," Wren said, nodding, from the shelter of her father's arm.

"Right...he was standing guard," her father confirmed solemnly, "strangest thing."

"I wonder," Marjorie said in a quiet voice to no one in particular, "I wonder who he was guarding?"

Ten days after the funeral, on a bitterly cold January morning, three large black armored Chevrolet Suburbans pulled up into the square of gravel and dirt that served as a parking lot for the community's school. Men emerged, some carrying guns, all in body armor. The school was cordoned. Local police began stringing yellow crime scene tape from the trees surrounding the property. Special Agent Beverly Farholme hesitated for a moment on the solid flagstones that lined the ground in front of the doorway. She saw words chiseled in granite on a large boulder that guarded the door—something having to do with a rock and wisdom; the word made no sense to her. She firmly turned the knob and pushed opened the door without knocking.

Susan Jurgens was bending over the desk, pointing out the different ways to conjugate a verb in Greek to Amos Moeller, eight years of age, when she looked up to see a tallish woman standing somewhat imperiously in the doorway, looking around the room.

"May I help you?" Susan asked in English. Susan was wearing her prayer cap and plainly attired; she was a Mennonite. The visitor took in her dress and cap with barely concealed disdain, and then looked around the room at the children.

"Are you…are you teaching these children?" the woman asked.

"I am," Susan answered, smiling, straightening up. She swept her arm around to take in the entire room, fifty by eighty feet, where the students all sat, eyes wide, staring directly at the tall woman wearing a large camel-hair overcoat over black slacks: "all forty-three of them."

The woman's eyes took in the children—some dressed plainly, some dressed in clothes she would consider normal—and wondered at the mix, blinking her eyes. A wood stove rested in the corner. Pieces of wood rested nearby in a box, waiting to spend the value of their existence by unleashing their stored energy, thence to be returned to the system and their Creator.

"We need to speak privately. Now."

"Certainly," Susan said with suppressed curiosity, "Amos, work these through please, ser gut?"

"Danke," the boy replied.

Susan walked to one side of the room into a small attached enclosure. The visitor followed. As she passed the window, Susan saw large black cars in front of the school building. She paused, pulled back the curtain, and saw Rowland Gaines, the town sheriff, pulling a roll of yellow tape from the trunk of his police car. She looked at the visitor, who just looked toward the little office space with her eyes and tilted her head.

Susan closed the door as the woman entered. "How can I help you," she asked again.

The woman stood with her one hand in her pocket and the other holding a briefcase, and collected herself. "Ms. McClure has died, has she not?"

"She's passed, yes" Susan replied. "Did you know her? I'm sorry, but her funeral was—"

"No, I didn't know her. My condolences; it's just that she was registered and approved by this State as a teacher, and…well…"

"And you are wondering if I am?" Susan prompted. The woman looked nervous, ill-at-ease, but disturbed somehow…no, not disturbed…resentful. Susan could see one fist clenched in the coat pocket. There were thin lines of tension near the jaw, her eyes darted everywhere, and when she did look at Susan directly, there was a glimmer of hostility.

"I was wondering exactly that," she replied. "Actually no, I wasn't wondering. I know you're not. I was wondering if you knew that what you're doing here is illegal."

"And why must I have certification from the State to teach our children?" Susan asked.

"Because they are the State's children, and the State says it is illegal to teach without being certified," the woman snapped. Susan's expression conveyed the impact of a particularly noxious faux pas, and Agent Farholme noticed.

"I'm sorry, I didn't mean to be brusque, but the State has a responsibility to ensure that its children are educated to proper standards."

"I'm not sure I agree, Miss...?"

The tall woman pulled out a badge and opened the flap.

"Special Agent Farholme...I'm with the FBI."

Susan's eyebrows went up. "The Federal Bureau of Investigation is wondering about our little school, Ms. Farholme?"

"Special Agent Farholme...and yes, we are. Too many children are abused in these situations, and some have been transported across state lines by parents to avoid state law."

It was at this point that Susan first began to be concerned.

"'Abused' is an extremely strong word, Ms...Special Agent Farholme. And to be used in such a way, with absolutely no grounds whatsoever, is reprehensible."

"We have information that such a concern is...warranted," Farholme replied vaguely, looking down at the table and then at the walls of the small office. Her eyes could not avoid the constant references to Scripture pasted on the wall, which disturbed her for some unknown reason. And there was no noise coming from the unattended children in the other room; she thought the absence of noise strange.

"And what information is that?" Susan asked, now tensing against this intrusion, wondering at the same time what God was doing.

"Information...to which you are not privy," replied the woman, still not looking at her. "And you must realize...certainly you've read the papers, followed the news. Cults like…well, groups like yours are breeding grounds for all sorts of perversion and…and in these cases children are basically brainwashed to do what their parents tell them to."

"Children are expected to obey their parents," Susan replied evenly. "Would you have things otherwise?" She was beginning to disapprove of the woman standing before her and Susan had taught enough children to recognize when she was being lied to.

"Children should be free to chart their own course in life," Special Agent Farholme argued. "You have no right to dictate to these children what they should wear, what they should learn, or what they should believe."

Susan clasped her hands together for a moment and sent a quick prayer to her Father: *God, tell me what to say*, she begged. She took a deep breath and stared back at the FBI agent, who was becoming more confident as the rote words which encapsulated the State's mantra were trotted out between them, dominating the little space with their dark threats of overpowering sovereignty, as surely as death comes to all men aiming to kill the soul of every little child sitting out there at a desk.

"And the State does?" she asked, shaking herself, now intensely angry.

"The State does what?"

"Are you telling me that the State, not a child's parents, has the right to dictate what these children wear, what they learn, and what they believe?"

"When parents demonstrate an inability to protect the freedom of children to choose their own path in life, then yes, the State does have that right."

"Don't you mean instead, Miss Farholme, that when parents demonstrate that their opinions on deportment, education, and faith differ from those of the government, the State has the power to compel the parents to adopt the government's dictates?"

Agent Farholme's mouth tightened and thinned. She pulled a paper from her case. "This…is…a…warrant," she said in clipped tones, chopping the words like a butcher chops meat, throwing a piece of folded paper on the table between them. "I'm not here to argue with you. I'm here to execute this warrant. The children will be taken into the State's custody until such time as the State can place them into more suitable care."

Susan blinked. The unthinkable had just been tossed baldly in her face—the dark sword of an ungodly power unsheathed, its stench almost overpowering her soul. "You cannot do this," she gasped weakly.

Farholme leaned forward slight and said with evident relish, "The State, Ms. Jurgens, can do whatever it deems necessary. Now…you can help me do this and we can avoid upsetting the children or you can oppose me and cause an enormous amount of trouble—for you and for the children."

Susan leaned against the wall, stunned. "You…you can't get all those children in three cars," she stammered, not knowing what else to say.

"We've called for a bus," the woman replied tersely. "You will tell them that they have to get on the bus when it comes, and that they should do so quietly. We don't want to upset them any more than we have to."

Susan's mind flashed to that portion of Scripture in which Paul wrote about the 'sword of the State', that man's government did not bear power in vain, but rather, as the text described, it exercised power so that righteousness and justice could flourish—God's righteousness, not man's—and evil men would not overpower the good. But here she was, one Mennonite woman, forty-eight that January, confronting the specter of the world's largest, richest, and most powerful government, its representative manifested in the flesh, now come to her little school house and demand that she feed the community's children into the maw of a system that was poisonously opposed to God's righteousness.

"I will not," she said, standing straighter, annunciating her words precisely. "I will *not* tell them to get on the bus when it comes. I will *not* tell them to cooperate so as to save you the embarrassment that will surely result from doing something you know is wrong. And you, Miss Special Agent, should be ashamed of yourself."

Special Agent Farholme picked up the warrant from the table. She smiled bitterly. "Fine," she said, "just fine. Do it your way. Be martyrs. Make trouble. Get on your high horse and put your nose in the air and march off to the sounds of Amazing Grace or whatever; it doesn't matter a bit." She turned around, yanked the door open, and marched toward the entrance, heels pounding echoes against the hardwood floor. She slammed the door as she left the building. The children's eyes were now wider than ever.

Susan took a deep breath, recalling that all those who desired to live a godly life in Christ Jesus would be persecuted. She and many others in their community had spent so much time talking about the possibility that they would see the day—in their lifetimes—when such persecution would come. When its foul breath struck in reality, however—well, it was different than reading or talking about it. Now here it was, the great red dragon of a godless State in all its stench and power and cunning, bubbling up on their doorstep, jaws gaping to devour their children, wrapped in a warrant.

* * *

It was snowing on the day when the hearing was held, adding to the blanket which had accumulated everywhere but in the main streets of the county seat. The sky still had the look of slate, with no sun to be seen. People were beginning to wonder; they hadn't actually had a sunny day in weeks. Winter relentlessly squeezed the roads, the soil, the water, and the people. This winter was the coldest on record; the previous year had broken the previous record, and so forth, for the last five seasons. No one argued about global warming anymore. There were less than 25,000 people in a county where five years ago 70,000 lived. More than a third of the county's population was on welfare. More than a fourth were addicted to prescription pain killers distributed by a bankrupt state treasury. Unemployment was skyrocketing as businesses fled the State due to increased taxes to compensate for the reduced number of people and the entitlement mentality so prevalent among those that remained. An inconvenient truth about democracy was that it was only sustainable until the people realized they could vote themselves money from the public funds—after that, it became bread and circuses. This truth was borne out in the county for all to see, for few to understand.

Sheriff Gaines stood at the front of the courtroom. He was a tall man, a former Green Beret—some said he'd been in the last war in Venezuela; others thought that he'd had something to do with covert operations in one of the central Asian countries—no one knew for sure. What everyone did know was that he was the antithesis of the 'donut-eating small-town buffoon', as most local sheriffs were painted. He was trim, muscular, and possessed an air of business-like lethality.

"All rise." The voice took the crowd by surprise, and they automatically stood, not thinking about the symbolism of the act itself—standing in honor of the representative of an authority source that through the assumption of such enormous power had become antithetical to their way of life. Some things we just do without thinking. Colin McClure, however, did not rise. Sheriff Gaines looked at him grimly. The Sheriff had spent his entire life acquiescing to established authority. Not one to ever question the nature of that authority, he was bitterly suspicious of anyone who would.

The judge was a graceful woman in a soft gray business suit, blondish-gray hair, with reading glasses on a little chain around a frilled white high-necked blouse. She entered the courtroom and sat like a queen upon a chair on a raised platform facing the assembly. The meeting room in the courthouse was filled with most of the children's parents. The State's attorney was there, a short fat woman in an excessively short tight skirt, a leopard-spotted top, and a white blazer. At her feet were two suitcases of files. Special Agent Farholme sat next to her. The court-appointed defense attorney, Mr. Monroe, a young man of twenty-five or so, just out of law school and wearing a pin-striped suit and a pince-nez, was by himself at an opposite table.

"You may be seated." Those that had stood to honor the appearance of the judge and the authority she represented sat down again. Sheriff Gaines looked hard at Colin. Colin remained seated, hat in hand, head bowed, shoulders broad but burdened under his chore coat, still decorated with bits of hay, stained with manure and mud, completely unaware of the enemy he'd just made.

"Are we ready to start?" the judge asked, looking directly at the State's attorney.

"We are, your Honor," she replied.

Mr. Monroe, the defense attorney, hesitatingly broke in. "Excuse me, your Honor, but—"

"Then we'll begin. Mr. Monroe, catch up if you're able. The State's case, please, Ms. Robinson."

"Certainly, your Honor. Basically, the rights of a rather large group of children are being abrogated by their parents, apparently due to the parents' specific or particular religious beliefs. The State alleges that this violates the freedom of each child, and will therefore plead to remove the children from parents' collective custody and place each child in a more suitable environment conducive to choice."

"Thank you Ms. Robinson. Mr. Monroe...your response?"

"Thank you, your Honor. Well, er, we're not quite prepared at this time to provide a complete response to the court, your Honor, but...well...if I may, let me say that there appears to be little question about the rights of parents in the case where children are involved. And while I understand the religious aspect of it..."

The judge looked over her glasses at the young attorney and sighed.

"Forcefully stated, Mr. Monroe...as always. Please be seated."

"Why, yes, certainly, your Honor." Mr. Monroe sat down obediently.

"The issue seems clear to me on precedence," the judge opined, surprising Mr. Monroe, causing Ms. Robinson to smile. "And I'm not sure this needs to be a lengthy matter; what else do I have on the docket?"

The court clerk opened a book and consulted the page. "You've three other cases this morning, your Honor, and four this afternoon."

"Then let's go on the record." She gave a nod to the stenographer, who took up her position at the little typing machine, and then to Ms. Robinson.

"Yes, your Honor: citing the U.S. vs. Warriscovitch, the U.S. vs. Lingle, and Canada vs. Bore et. al., it is apparent that the State has the right and the duty to remove children from homes where excessive religious doctrine, assessed to be harmful to the interests of either the children or the State, is being taught."

At this, Colin darted a glance at Mr. Monroe, who sat silently. Ms. Robinson continued.

"We can make a clear case that the doctrines of the community in which these children were being schooled are directly in opposition to good order and discipline in a society. The parents are collectively restricting if not eliminating each child's right and freedom to choose their own way in life. Finally, the State alleges that some of the children may have suffered severe and, in some cases, irreversible intellectual, emotional, or psychological damage from this type of…instruction."

Another glance at Mr. Monroe, who remained glued to his chair, was fruitless. Colin put his hat down on the bench and stood. "That's not true," he said.

The reaction among the court and its attendants was as if writing had magically appeared on a wall before their eyes. Several people reacted at once.

Sheriff Gaines vaulted from his chair as if it had been suddenly electrified. The judge looked out over her reading glasses, shocked that someone had broken protocol and spoken in her courtroom without her permission. Many spectators yanked their heads in Colin's direction, shocked that a layman would interrupt the sacred courtroom rites.

She rapped her gavel once or twice to get attention focused back in her direction. "What is your name, sir?" she asked, head tilted up slightly, like a snake before it strikes.

"Colin McClure."

"You address the court as 'your Honor', sir. This is the custom in a civilized country; you are familiar with such customs, are you not?"

"I'm familiar with such customs, but nothing I've seen or heard relating to this matter indicates to me that we're in a civilized country any longer."

"You may be held in contempt, you realize, Mr. McClure."

"I would return the courtesy, ma'am."

At this Sheriff Gaines took three steps toward Colin, fist clenching, another hand reaching for the truncheon on his belt, but the judge held up a staying hand. "I see...well...perhaps you may yet, Mr. McClure...perhaps you may. But we've other matters to attend to now; the matter, particularly, of your children. I presume you have children in this issue?"

"I do."

"Well then, if you'll permit us to continue, we can perhaps get to the truth of the matter and move on? Thank you. Ms. Robinson, again—"

Colin spoke up persistently. "Excuse me, but your case has no relation to any truth that we here recognize, Mrs. Jacobs." At the use of her proper name, the judge's eyes widened. This was now personal.

"Mr. McClure, if you would like to be held in jail for the next thirty days, by all means refer to me again by my name." She leaned forward in her chair and with a vituperative look, continued, "Otherwise you *will* adhere to the conventions of this court, of this State, and of this country, do you understand me sir?"

"You have, beyond all right, beyond all reason, in pure tyranny, taken my children—you've taken the children of most of the people in this room—and you talk to me of convention and respect?" Several of those nearby Colin began to tug at his sleeves, pulling him down and out of the line of fire. Others made gestures, imploring him to be seated. The judge noticed everything.

"Your compatriots do not seem to be similarly inclined, Mr. McClure. Isn't there something in your book about respect to those whom respect is due?"

Some of the crowd began to nod their heads, agreeing with the person who appeared to have the power to return their children. Whispers floated up to him like flies in summer:

"Come, Colin, sit, don't make trouble."

"Colin, we are to be peaceable, we are not to be argumentative."

"Come, man, this is unseemly, she *is* a judge, after all."

A number of the Amish looked down at their feet, embarrassed that one with whom they were even loosely associated was causing such acute disruption in a place dedicated to law and order.

Colin put both of his hands on the back of the bench before him and leaned a little forward, looking at the judge directly. "Ma'am, when Jesus confronted the Pharisees, they used the same argument."

Suddenly the courtroom erupted like a disturbed anthill. The stenographer stopped pounding her little machine. The bailiff's hand went to his holster. Sheriff Gaines pulled handcuffs from his utility belt.

"*Mister* McClure!" the judge snapped in a strained hiss; veins stood out in her neck, grace and comportment vanishing in a flash. She injected a punch and sting to the rhythm of her words. She did this whenever she was upset. "You *will* refrain from the use of inappropriate language in this courtroom. I suppose you...you *people* are not aware of the fact that the United States Government finds the use of that...that *name*...to be disruptive to our society and extremely offensive to any number of groups of honest, hard-working, sincere people who this government is pledged to protect and support. Do you *understand* me, sir? You *will* be silent in this courtroom until I direct you to speak." She was pointing her gavel at him, almost up out of her seat completely. "Do you *understand* me, sir? If you do not, then I will have you physically removed from this courtroom and you can find out what will happen to your children by reading the papers...if you can read, that is. Now...*sit down*, or *be removed*."

Colin sat, heartsick, angry, aching for cords to make a whip.

The proceedings occurred without any further disruption. Ms. Robinson delivered extensively detailed testimony. Mr. Monroe stuttered through a half-hearted rendition of his own theory on parental rights being essential to a free society, all while the judge refrained, barely, from smiling. The remaining officers of the court did not, nor did Ms. Robinson. The judge found, to no one's surprise, that there was every indication that the children's rights had been violated and that the State therefore had every right to secure those rights by removing them from their harmful environment. They would be placed temporarily in more suitable custody until such time as a final determination of the disposition of parental rights would be made. That hearing would occur three months from the current hearing date. The judge, again composed, in control, and with a self-satisfied look on her face, smacked the gavel. Court adjourned.

"We're off the record, now, Cynthia."

"Yes your Honor," the stenographer replied, setting her hands in her lap.

"Good. *You* sir," she said, pointing her gavel at Colin, "are fortunate to be going home and not to jail. I have never been so insulted in a courtroom in my entire career. Your behavior has been abominable. Those with whom you associate should be *ashamed* of you and of themselves for considering any further association with you. I have always held the...the plain people in the highest regard. Your conduct here today has brought *extreme* dishonor and shame to them and to their community. Now you will *leave* my courtroom, sir—at once."

* * *

One evening a week later, after a bleak dinner of cold soup, Colin put on his snowshoes and trudged through the still-falling snow to the community's meeting hall, nestled in a small valley a mile from his farm. Others were making their way in the gloaming as well, carrying candles or lanterns to light their way. Colin stopped at the top of a rise. From where he stood, breath steaming in the early evening like clouds of steam from an engine, it seemed as though there were just a few trickling bits of light making their way into a central core of warmth and sanctuary—and what lights remained were being choked by the encroaching darkness. He moved off down the hill in the grip of a loneliness unlike any he'd ever experienced. The absence of his children was like a knife wound, and his wife's last words ate at him like acid.

The plain rectangular meeting hall began to fill. The building had been built by the community with local logs for walls, local lumber for the tresses, and tin from their roofing business covering the roof. There were short, plain wooden benches arrayed in a circular pattern around the room, different from the typical arrangement where each bench would face forward. The community was different in many things such as this. There was no steeple on the roof. There was no pulpit, lifting one man higher than the rest. There were no choir robes, no segregated "ministries" where families were fragmented into men, women, and youth when they came to worship. The children, of whatever age, sat peacefully and obediently through the entire service, in the arms of their parents, in their laps, or by their side.

While not the first crisis the community faced, this theft of their children was the most intense. The meeting came to order when the local Amish bishop appeared in a sledge. The community was comprised of ten Amish families, eight Mennonite families, and five families who were called to a life in Christ separate from the world, yet not called to enter into the specific disciplines of either the Amish or Mennonite orders. In truth, none were strictly as their denominations had once been. This particular group of Amish was quietly but determinedly evangelistic, reaching out to anyone who expressed a desire to live a separate life of peace in Christ, encouraging them to consider the costs, counseling them as to the discipline and joys involved. The Mennonites were less concerned with plain living than with avoiding the pride that might arise due to their "plainness". They focused on bridging the rapidly-closing gap between those living plainly and those Christians not called to that life style. The Christians too were beginning to find themselves with less of a desire for things of the world and more of a desire to live separately, to put away those things that hindered them from a focus on the life of the Spirit. As they each cooperated with the Spirit of God to become more like Jesus, they found themselves growing more like each other, or rather, more like Jesus, and in this did they find a unity and a loving single-mindedness. Their differences no longer had more power than that power exerted by the Love that bound them.

The Amish Bishop opened the meeting with a prayer, expressing hope that God would provide peace, and guidance, and wisdom, and direction, and keep their children safe from the predations of the enemy. A Mennonite woman spoke out after a short period of silence, begging God in a quiet litany of gasping sobs, tears flowing, for her children and those of the others to be returned safely. This aching, heartfelt appeal broached the reserves, and soon, quietly, in order, but with passionate intensity, parents—husbands sometimes, sometimes wives—would speak out to beg God for their children's safety. As each prayer wound on, the listeners began to hear in each an emerging theme—that while each supplicant begged God for the safety of the children, with increasing frequency, they began to ask at the end, and then sometimes at the beginning, that God's will would be paramount—that what *He* wanted would occur, rather than what they wanted—regardless of the consequences. As this theme began to emerge and weave repeatedly in and through the prayers, a peace descended on the gathering. It was something they recognized as God's hand, and something for which they were intensely grateful.

The prayers ended. There were still some sobbing, and God was for a time busy gathering tears for His bottle.

"We are here tonight," said the Bishop, in German-accented English, "to discuss what we must do—if there is anything we must do—about our children. We have prayed; we know that God has heard us. Yet we know too that there are times when He requires us to act, and there is wisdom in the community that may not be found in a single home. And so, let us talk about what faces us, and what should be done." He sat down again, a wise old man with a plain, untrimmed gray beard in a black suit and a white shirt buttoned at the neck.

A tiny woman in a sheepskin vest over a black turtleneck sweater stood up. "Is there someone who knows what the State is planning? I mean, what can they do? What did *we* do? I still haven't understood why they've taken... why they've done this thing."

Tony Jackson stood, in jeans and a farm coat. He was a hog farmer who joined the community a short ten months ago.

"I think I can say, Jean. You're familiar with what happened out in Texas...well, it must have been quite a while ago...you know, with that group of polygamists who were living all together in some kind of community? Well, apparently a crank caller alleged that there was some abuse going on—and there probably was, what with sixty-year old men marrying fifteen-year old girls. So they came in and took around forty kids. Some were in their mid-twenties, so they weren't really kids, but the whole point is that this thing in Texas was the first time the Government made the case outright that the State, not the parents, should be the final arbiter of the welfare of children. I mean, if anyone's been through a divorce you know the State jumps in the middle of that kind of dispute right away, and suddenly both parents find their authority over what happens to the children washed away. But this case in Texas kind of broke the dam, so to speak, and when there wasn't much complaint from folks about it, they began to think that no one was watching. I mean, how could you complain about keeping kids safe from a bunch of old guys marrying ten or twenty young girls? They *were* Mormons, after all, living out in the middle of nowhere. So no one complained, and the Government got bolder. They went into Florida and took three kids away from their parents because sometime in their past they'd been orthodox Jews. When no one complained about that, they took fifteen kids from a private Christian school in Massachusetts three years ago. They've been doing this off and on for the last few years. They're taking Jewish kids all the time now, people, and it's not getting much press because...well, I'm not sure why. It's pretty much common knowledge, and there are a few of us who were wondering when they'd get around to coming after the home-schooled Christian kids in the more remote communities. Lancaster is being hit like this, too, Bishop," Tony said, with a look toward the old man, who nodded in agreement, his mouth compressed with disapproval. Tony sat down again, brushing his hands on his thighs.

The tiny woman who first asked the question spoke up again. "But... but Tony, what do they do to the children? What happens to them?"

Tony looked down at his hands. It was plain that he didn't want to answer the question. A lady named Michelle stood. Michelle Jacobsen was a Messianic Jewess and a single mother of three who ran the community's bakery. She was a lean woman with dark red hair and brilliant green eyes.

"Unfortunately, Jean, I can tell you what happens to them. You can believe me or you can think I'm crazy, but I'll tell you. The State sees these kids as the last obstacle to complete and total control. Oh, I'm not one of those folks that think there's a conspiracy behind every rock, but I can read history and I can read my Bible, and I know that when governments have power, they work hard to keep it—it's just their nature. When people in Government put away God's authority, the only source of authority left is their own. This is why they think it's okay to take half our incomes with taxes. They think the land is theirs, not ours, which is why they tax our property. And they think since the Government is the final authority source, they can direct parents how to raise children…especially parents who might have the gall to actually teach their children that there is a different authority source in the world—God. The Government will go after those people, and those children, with a vengeance. I think this is why they're doing what they're doing, Jean."

Erik Swenson stood; Erik was a cattle farmer who provided most of the community's beef. He wore blue coveralls and an old yellow farm coat. "Unfortunately Michele is right: the greatest threat to the power emerging today is a free-thinking population nested in a strong family—that's always been the greatest threat to totalitarian regimes everywhere, which is why they strangle free speech, cut off radio broadcasts, and most of all try to break up the integrity of the family unit. Hitler did it, taking kids out of the home at incredibly young ages. This is always the way, but now, you see, there is a more insidious evil—it isn't just some kind of national government, with some crackpot dictator trying to retain hold on a little nation and its revenue and the power that comes with it. Now it is an overpowering source of global authority that seeks to be worshiped by everyone on the planet— and you know about what and whom we're speaking. Governments and religions are lining up with this philosophy of working together to create some kind of heaven on earth. The last obstacles to this effort are those who worship the true God—the God of Abraham, Isaac, and Jacob—who believe that man *can't* make heaven on earth—that the only thing man can make will be hell. While we older folks are a threat they can deal with, remember, they're also very economically driven. They don't like to waste money or resources. If they can poison the children, that will be one less generation of Christians and Jews that they'll have to deal with."

"So are you saying, Erik, that the children are in danger?" the Bishop asked.

"I'm saying, sir, that they will take these children and re-educate them. They will do whatever they need to do to change how our children view the world, how they think about God, and how they think about their obligations to His people. They will actively attempt to poison their souls." He took a breath. "Yes, Bishop, I think the children are in danger—but not physical danger; they are in danger of having their eyes blinded to the truth. Their souls are in danger."

This last assertion caused a commotion among the families. Everyone began talking at the same time. There were cries and a few louder sobs.

Roman Velasquez, an older Mennonite man in a checked lumberjack shirt and quilted vest stood up and asked for quiet. The hands he waved to gain their attention were scarred and battered, like seasoned oak paddles. "Please, please, my brothers and sisters, please, remember who we are and who we serve. Please, I beg you to remember, is not God sovereign? Is the Ancient of Days unaware of what is happening to His lambs? Does He give us rocks when we ask for bread? Snakes if we ask for fish? The question is not, 'What is the State doing?'...the question instead is, 'What is God doing?'"

With this wisdom came encouragement; the murmurings abated somewhat. Sheep are so easily disturbed and yet so easily put right when reminded that the Shepherd is close by.

"So let us turn to this question, Roman," the Bishop said forthrightly. "We cannot know what to do unless we are first to some degree aware of what God is attempting. What is He trying to do? And let me refine this," the Bishop continued, holding up a weathered hand, "by saying that we are not focusing on, or unaware of, what He is doing in these days. Let us concern ourselves simply with trying to understand what God is doing in our lives and in the life of our community."

A tall woman rose in the middle of the packed group of seats. "It seems to me that God is wondering what we're going to do to get our children back. Is there any doubt that He doesn't want them in the hands of a culture that would bend every ounce of its strength to poison their souls?"

"So you are saying that this event has been orchestrated by God to test us, to see if we will act to defend ourselves and our children…that the onus for action here lays upon us?" the Bishop asked.

"I'm saying that someone needs to do something."

"I hear what you say," Velasquez replied, in the lilting accent of a native Spanish speaker speaking English, "and the course you suggest has many advantages." Everyone knew that this was the plain people's way of indicating that there was about to be a disagreement. "But if God is sovereign, then could we not say…could we not say that this has been planned by Him, that He knew it would happen, and that such a thing is His will? And is not all authority on earth permitted by Him? And if we believe these things, are we not opposing Him in opposing a properly formulated Government? Are we not to obey the rulers appointed over us? This is the law, and it is so stated in Scripture. We have lived before in places where the law does not agree with our faith. Many of those whom we revere had their faith tested by fire and trial and came out the greater for it. What if they had turned away from the test by opposing the makers of such laws? Would such opposition not be considered opposing God Himself, and what He wants to make in each of us?"

This line of argument gave the group pause. Most were confirmed pacifists, opposed to any form of adversarial confrontation with formally-constituted authority, and this call back to their first principles struck hard when their children were at stake. The room quieted dramatically as the gravity of the conflict began to sink into the very depths of their souls.

An older farmer stood, another Mennonite, with a hat in one hand and his gloves in the other. "And to add to your point, Roman, is it not also true that no one takes away a person's free will—no one, not even God Himself, can override a person's will to choose to serve Him. If we believe this, then doesn't it mean that our children will still have a clear and free choice about the path they take in their lives, regardless of where and with whom they live?"

There were now a number of blinking eyes and confused looks among the group. They'd heard these arguments before. It was hard to hear them used to defend a course of action that would result in their children being raised by someone else.

Colin rose to speak. "Roman, what you say has merit, and yet there is a principle I see throughout Scripture," Colin said slowly, "and I see it most clearly in the life of Jesus. He directly disobeyed the formally-constituted religious authorities of His day—and remember, in the life of every Jew, those formally-constituted religious authorities had as much power over their lives as did the Romans. We remember what He told his disciples: 'Render to Caesar what is Caesar's, and to God what is God's.' When Peter came and asked Him about paying taxes, He made the point that those who own something should not be taxed for it—but so as not to give offense, He provided means whereby the current governing authority was placated— miraculously, pulling His tax bill and Peter's out of the mouth of a fish. When we consider *all* of Scripture—how obedience to God is the single most important element throughout His Word—what can these things mean but simply that we are to obey the Lord God of All Creation before anything or anyone else? When we can obey governments and remain within that overarching requirement, then good, we obey the Government. If God needs to give us the means to do so miraculously, He will. Yet I believe that it was obvious in the crafting of the Lord's reply, and by what we know of Him, that He thought obedience to God more important than obedience to man."

As he spoke and the logic of his argument rolled out, Colin's natural intensity and passion began to flow. "But consider—God has made note of the fact that there are spiritual forces in high places; powers and principalities arrayed hierarchically, as is most of worldly government. Shall we obey authority simply because it possesses authority? Could we assert that those who hid Jews during World War II—and in so doing opposed the natural constituted authority in Nazi Germany—were sinning? When *any* authority source, be it temporal or spiritual, begins to claim for itself sovereignty over a man's soul by requiring a man to directly oppose or disobey what is clearly directed by God, then I submit that that authority source loses what force it possesses to compel human behavior. Why? Because the universe is ordered by God and by God's laws, and no force, no power, no authority can contradict or overturn those laws. No human authority source or spiritual power or principality or man-made law or government can lay claim to an obedience that supersedes the weight of God's authority in creation without causing extreme disruption—in nature, and in people's lives and souls.

"We know what God has directed us to do regarding our children: we are to raise them up in the nourishment and admonition of the Lord. Is this not so? Is this not a clear mandate for parents from Scripture? We are to care for them as He cares for us. We are to protect them and shelter them from all manner of harm. And elsewhere we are instructed to *oppose* evil; we are to stand and resist the devil." Colin was impassioned now, using his hands to make his point.

"Imagine this, Roman," Colin said, turning directly to the Mennonite man who'd raised the question, looking intently at him. "Imagine a stick floating downstream. Does the stick cause turbulence? No…does the stick disturb the water? No…why? Because the stick is going in the same direction as the current; the water surrounds and supports the stick. But imagine instead now a stick in this same river, *not* moving with the current, stuck somehow in the mud or caught on the river bank. Then you see turbulence, and bubbling, swirling water, a disturbance of the natural peace in the river all around this stubborn stick. And why is this? Because the stick does not flow with the current; it opposes it. This is what will result whenever any government or law or authority source or human being is in opposition to the will of God. And I am concerned that any of us might be found uniting in purpose with any government or agency that would push against the current of God's will.

"Losing our children means losing our future *and* our ties to the past. While each one of us professes a strong belief in an eternal future, we are also aware that life eternal is not something our children inherit. At such early ages, children can be diabolically influenced away from the path of righteousness. Christ himself warned of dire consequences for those who would cause little ones to stumble, demonstrating clearly that children are vulnerable, and also making it clear that children *can* stumble. Did not Christ speak of a farmer who so cared for one sheep that he left the ninety-nine to look for the one lost? If we cannot oppose evil when our children are at stake, then I fear for our sanity and our souls, for we will become a people who will not oppose evil at all."

Colin sat down. After a few moments a heavy black crow of regret flapped down and perched on his shoulder. He tended to express his views with too much intensity and forcefulness, and it was a source of never-ending distress to him. The plain people, having so much longer lived in cultures where community was more important than the individual, had a much better way of gently expressing their opinions. He remonstrated with himself, pulled his hands into the sleeves of his work coat, stretched the coat across his shoulders as tightly as possible, and hunched down lower in his chair.

Roman stood to respond. "Colin, you feel deeply about these things and it is obvious you have thought about them. Yes, we are told to fight evil. We are also told that our fight is not against flesh and blood, but against powers and principalities in the realm of the spirit. I do not think that you are, but...but I must ask. Are you advocating that we exert some degree of violence to reclaim our children?"

Here then was the horrible word displayed before them all; the one inviolate theological proscription possessed by many in the community. The Prince of Peace was not a God of violence. Violent men and violence itself was thoroughly and roundly denounced throughout the book which served as the authority source for many of those listening to the discussion. This authority source had dictated the course of each of their lives; it had driven them, in obedience, to endure loveless marriages, to put away careers, to end close associations that were unfruitful or not edifying to their lives in Christ. Any recommendation or line of discussion that advocated a departure from the precepts or behaviors described in that book—which all there that evening believed to be a magic book, full of living truth, and displaying the Living Truth—would not be countenanced.

"Tell me, Colin...and I ask you this before everyone here because I would that everyone consider the same question: are we guilty of idolatry?

By this I mean, are we in danger of considering our children more important than obedience to God?"

Colin considered Roman's assertion quietly as every eye in the room turned to him, waiting expectantly. A hush descended—light itself seemed to pause, softening, dimming, dancing more slowly around the two men as they wrestled not so much with each other as with the depths of what their faith required of them.

"Roman...may God keep me from ever putting my children before my Father in heaven. I know it's a very real danger, and I think everyone here desperately hopes to avoid such a pitfall. But your question presupposes a condition that acting on behalf of our children to oppose the formally-constituted authority of the State would be in disobedience to God. This... this I am not convinced about.

"Would acting in disobedience to the law to protect those whom God has given into our charge be wrong—acting against the law created by a government, may I say, that is now actively and directly opposed to the law and rule of Christ in the world? Do we fulfill the law of righteousness by submitting to the rules established by Satan?"

"We must not take to ourselves the role of God," Roman replied emphatically, "acting as a supreme protector, above human law. If we disregard the rule of law, Colin, our society degenerates, and we have no ground upon which to stand before God. He has directed that we obey the laws of the rulers appointed over us. And remember, He gave us this injunction when He knew that Satan was the ruler of this world, the Prince of the world's systems, with power over the kingdoms of the earth. Paul wrote this at a time when the Romans ruled most of the known world, and Roman law makes today's laws seem moderate in the extreme."

Colin's eyes flashed. "Surely you do not think that God intended that we acquiesce to the laws and value systems of Satan's kingdom? Does He not constantly call us to come out from them, to be separate, to be sanctified?"

Roman paused to let the intensity of Colin's question diminish somewhat; it was a technique used by those schooled in the gentle art of communal conversation. "Well, Colin," he said quietly, drawing out the 'well' so as to soften his reply and avoid any impression of argumentative conduct. "I believe He intended that we obey the established authorities in the midst of whatever evil government man imposes."

"To what degree, though, Roman...that is the question." In his own ears he sounded like a hammer against an anvil, in contrast to Roman's gentle, persuasive ripostes. But Colin had not lived in a community most of his life. He had been reared in the modern world where independence shaped every fiber of his being. It was something he deeply regretted, but he continued nonetheless. "What if the authorities who make this law are violently opposed to God? What if established authority required us to fight in a war—what if it *commanded* us to be violent in a way that was clearly against God's will?"

There was a pause: Roman thought for a moment. "I see your point," he said, contemplating. "This kind of thing—a request or direction from government that we exert violence against our fellow man in violation of our beliefs—has happened before, and we have opposed it."

"Then you would agree that there are times when the law of the land can be directly opposed to the law of God, and each man must choose which law he will obey?"

Roman nodded his head ever so slowly. "To God what is God's, to Caesar what is Caesar's...yes, I see. Put thus...yes, Colin, I would agree that there are times—truly, they try men's souls—when we must choose who we will obey, God or Caesar."

Colin replied slowly, haltingly, as though he was attempting to convince himself with his own words. "We are in a situation...where we feel equally passionate about...divergent courses of action." He lifted one hand, palm outward, in a poignant, old-world, European gesture that at once was appeal, imprecation, and amelioration. "So what is violence? Can I ask this? We say we are opposed to violence...and we believe this is the way God would have us be. But what is violence? Is it an act or is it instead a state of the soul? When a man takes a hammer and strikes a nail with the requisite force to drive it, do we say he is a violent man? Do we say that he is using violence against the nail? Of course not; he is using a tool suited for a purpose in its proper fashion. When a man harbors thoughts of beating or killing his fellow man because of his own sin nature, because of something he might gain at that man's loss, but does not actually carry out his imaginings, do we say that this is a violent man? We do, yes, and we would be correct. And lastly, let me ask this: when the Son of God returns with a sharp two-edged sword and lays waste to His enemies so completely that there is blood up to the horse's bridles, that His own robes are stained with blood that He himself sheds, would we say that He was a violent man? No...may it never be. How then can such a thing be rectified? How can we say that any physical violence is wrong when the Son of Man—that same man who made a whip of cords and physically whipped people out of the temple and with His own hands exerted force to overturn the tables of the money changers—perpetrates such acts? Is violence the same as the exertion of physical force? Is violence equivalent to taking a life? No...I do not believe this is the case. What then is the difference? Again, look to the Son of God. What was in His heart when He cleansed the temple? What will be in His heart when He returns to claim the earth as His own?" Colin paused here to look around the room. He put his hands down on the back of the wooden bench before him and leaned forward, trying to look into the depths of each soul in the room.

"The difference between an act of violence and righteous exertion of force is *not* measured in the degree of that force, friends. It is measured by the degree to which the action is in accordance with the will of God— the degree to which that action is performed in obedience to God's will. *Obedience*—obedience is the key. Any action that is not in accordance with His will is violence, whether it involves physical force or not, for violence is in its essence spiritual, and such violence against His will, as we know, usually results in a violation of our obligations to our fellow man and eventually harms creation itself. Any action that *is* in accordance with God's will, regardless of whether or not that action requires force, is not violence but obedience. The enemy will bruise Christ's heel; Christ will bruise his head. In this one phrase we see the difference. Satan has no thought of obedience to God, and the action described in the phrase is violent. Christ, acting in obedience to God, will bruise the enemy's head, crushing his entire kingdom, and this is obedience, not violence.

"The meaning of this word *violence* has been abused, and in so doing we have missed the essential element of obedience. Obedience to His will rises above every other obligation. Jesus saw this clearly. Jesus was not a violent man. He was a man who fully obeyed His Father in heaven—He was an *obedient* man."

"And here is a hard thing, but I must say it. I believe that there are times when *failure* to act, times when one might fail to exert physical force to prevent violence, is itself violence. Do you understand me? I believe that *failing* to accomplish anything which is in our power to do to prevent true violence is itself sin, and right now a violent State is committing violence against our children's ability to obey God. Would Jesus *ever* fail to oppose sin and evil? Of course not—again, remember what He did in the temple— because sin and evil are not in accordance with the will of God, and it is God's will that such things be opposed.

"Paul adjures us to live peaceably with all men. By this I believe he means that we are not to wander about stirring up arguments or conflicts so as to manufacture situations where we in our fallible human nature may feel obligated to exert physical force or engage in contentious discourse to address what evil we think we've found." Colin held up his right hand, all the fingers gathered together, his thumb pushing hard up against the crook in his forefinger. "But when the enemies of God step in the straight path before us and threaten our relationship with Him, or worse, threaten the lives and souls of those too weak to defend themselves, then it would be an act of violence to *refrain* from action—even if that action required physical force. And this...this to me would be sin...and this I cannot do."

There was a hush in the hall. The sound of the snowflakes hitting the windows resounded softly throughout. There was no more talk, no more discussion. As if by an unspoken agreement, everyone realized that they needed to go home and think about what had been said. Like wind rippling across grain in a field, eventually their eyes sought the Bishop with a silent imprecation. Sensitive to the Spirit in the group, he stood and bowed his head. Everyone else did so as well.

He spoke in broken English with a hushed tone. "God…God, speak to us about the things we have heard here tonight. You can make your will clear to us…you can provide direction and wisdom. Talk to our hearts, convict us, and restrain the deceitful hand of the enemy that he may not blind us to the truth you wish us to see. God almighty, we love you. Help us obey you."

They walked out of the hall into the night, into the valley, holding their candles under still-falling snow. There was no calling out, no laughing, no cartwheeling through the drifts, no snowballs…their children had been taken from them.

* * *

Jenny Cordstrom was thirty-five that January. She'd grown up in the little northern town all her life, went to grammar school there, finished high school as an honors student, was a cheer leader, and played on the high school volleyball team. She had married Bill, her high school sweetheart, and they had two children, a boy and a girl. Bill worked at the feed store. She had a great job as the administrator for the county running the state's juvenile detention facility. It actually paid better than Bill's job in the winter months. She went three times a week to the local gym so she could keep her figure; she was still fitting into the clothes she wore in high school, and she was proud of that—so was Bill.

Jenny was a little disturbed this morning. The State had seen fit last week to pull in the kids from that cult out on the farm road in the northern part of the county and it meant just no end of work for her. She had to file every one of their names, along with their ages and any distinguishing characteristics, in the State's database, and that meant so much work that she was pretty sure that she'd miss the Wednesday evening Bible study at the church with Bill and the kids. Apparently the federal people were interested in this situation, and that meant she couldn't just check out at five and leave what wasn't done until tomorrow. She'd tried suggesting that first thing when Mr. Lance dumped the edict on her by email from the Capital earlier, but he squashed that idea right away.

"These things need to be in the database by close of business today," he'd written. "We'll be moving the children down to the State's home near the Capital soon, and the information needs to be collected." So Jenny resigned herself to a long night of work.

Jenny had a mother's heart, and she paused to think about how these kids must feel, away from their parents, but when she thought about that, she called to mind the stories in the paper, about how the adults at that cult place were in the habit of beating the children regularly, starving them, making them work in the fields from sunup to sundown. The story even hinted that maybe there was even some kind of sexual abuse happening. That kind of thing made Jenny stone-cold angry; parent or no parent, when people let those things happen, they gave up any right to have children.

There was little light and lots of snow. It was just plain weird, the dimness outside, and it was already ten in the morning. She hoped Bill would drive safely to the study. Shirley Jackson had lost control of her car just the other day and run off the road into a ditch and it took a bulldozer to pull the car out. Lucky she wasn't killed or left to sit in the car and freeze all night...God's mercy is all it was.

There was a low rumbling and a grinding of gears, and she looked through the front glass door to see a bus pull up in the front parking lot. A tall man got out of the bus and came to the door, stomped the snow off his shoes, and pushed it open. He wore a blue parka with a large hood over his head, which he tossed back as he entered.

"Morning, ma'am."

"Yes, hello...kind of cold out there, isn't it?" Her tone was formal; she was, after all, the administrator, but Jenny also liked to make sure the working class had no excuse to think her patronizing. She did disdain men who weren't capable of doing anything more important than driving a bus, however.

"It is that, ma'am, true."

Jenny watched him pull off his gloves and take off his hat. He wore blue workman's pants, a plaid shirt under the same blue workman's jacket—he looked like a bus driver. The jacket had his name—Ralph—stitched in a little white circle on his chest. He had a policeman's belt, that thick black type with patterns in the leather with all sorts of pouches for phones and cuffs and ammunition and what-not. He was thinner than she imagined bus drivers to be.

"So," Jenny asked, "how can I help you?"

"Well, Ma'am, I'm here to pick up them kids...you know, them kids they took from up north? I gotta transport 'em down to the Capital, down to the juvenile detention facility."

He was a state worker; that explained the belt. Jenny was surprised, but immediately her mind flashed to the possibility that this might be an answer to prayer, because it meant that if those children were gone, she could make the Bible study with Bill and the kids tonight. And while this was unexpected, she never underestimated the power of God to do miracles.

"I guess Mr. Lance wants the children down there pretty quickly," she said, allowing a tone of offended surprise to edge her words.

"Yes ma'am, I guess so," he replied, suitably humbled. He spoke slowly, as if his speech was slightly impaired. Figures, Jenny thought; I just hope he can drive a bus safely.

He tossed a thumb back over his shoulder: "The weather's gonna be nasty and it'll make the drive down there pretty rough. If you get 'em loaded, I'll git the heater turned up in the bus."

Jenny stood with alacrity from behind her desk. She'd put him in his place, and now best not to give this man any excuse to drive away and leave her here with a workload from hell. "I'll do just that. They'll be out in a jiffy."

That evening at Bible study Jenny listened to Sally Gervase talk about how her neighbor's elderly mother was having a time with her drunken husband—the antics of that man were just too much—and how that family needed *prayer*. Bill was in the other room with the men, talking about how important it was to make sure they were good fathers to their children. The children were in a third room, being entertained by a DVD featuring talking vegetables. So Jenny didn't see the email from Mr. Lance that came in at seven thirty, wondering where the data was on the children from that cult group. Like a good Christian, Jenny had disabled her Blackberry. There were some things that were just more important than work.

The bus pulled up in front of the community hall and disgorged forty-three children into its warmth. There they waited until parents, notified by messengers traveling in haste on foot, came to collect them. As the parents appeared out of the dimness under falling snow, they gathered their children to their hearts with a mixed sense of joy and trepidation, with a threatening question unspoken: what would happen now that Colin had blatantly violated the law of the land?

Colin, still wearing the blue parka, cleared his throat once and knocked on a table top and the crowd silenced gently.

"I know that you are all wondering what to do now. I am sorry if I've put you in a difficult position, but taking them all was the only way for me to rescue my own. If you wish, you can simply wait here until the police come, and tell them the truth—that you had nothing to do with my actions and that you will not object to returning your children to the custody of the State. As for me and my children..." he looked at Grady, standing tall, holding Wren, with Thomas by his side, "we are going to disappear for a while. My advice would be that you all do likewise, but that is something between each of you and God."

Three weeks later Jenny Cordstrom was sitting in her Bible study talking with Sally Gervase about one of their mutual friends who had recently found herself pregnant out of wedlock when her Blackberry buzzed. "Sorry," she said apologetically, and reached down to cycle the wheel and read the message.

"Honestly," she exclaimed, "that man..."

"Who is it?" Sally asked.

"Mr. Lance...*again*...I mean, really, the man just doesn't understand that there are some things more important than work, you know?"

"What does he want?"

"Oh, he wants to make sure I get the files on the three kids we brought in, those Jew kids, uploaded into the State's database before tomorrow close of business. I told him I'd do it, but ever since...ever since that maniac stole those cult kids out from under our noses, he can't let things rest."

"Whatever happened to those kids, anyway?" Sally asked, picking up another piece of cake.

Jenny leaned forward and whispered conspiratorially. "Well, no one will say, but I *heard* that most of the kids disappeared. I mean, some of the parents did the right thing and surrendered their kids back to the State, but most of them just disappeared into the woods. I *do* know what happened to that maniac who stole them, though—that bus driver guy. Sheriff Gaines shot him—shot him dead with a long gun from about eight hundred yards. Bill said it was a wicked long shot, and Bill says he doesn't know anyone else who could have done it. The sheriff must have seen them while they were walking on the ridgeline up there. He took the shot from his car sitting on Route 1; I mean really, can you imagine just pulling over and shooting someone from your *car*? Tommy—I mean, Sheriff Gaines—said he was just lucky. I guess that guy and his kids were trying to make it into the northern territories."

"Nobody survives the northern territories for long," Sally mumbled, shuddering, mouth full of food.

"You are absolutely right, girl," Jenny said, "and that crazy man is better off dead. God will not let those freaks have their way with innocent children and stand by and do nothing. He's a *righteous* God...a *holy* God." Jenny's words went up an octave whenever she proclaimed upon God's attributes. "And He *loves* the children, let me tell you. And Sheriff Gaines did what was right and proper, if you ask me."

"And he's kind of cute, too," Sally said, giggling, spilling crumbs.

"Well, I've got Bill and the kids, you know," Jenny replied conspiratorially, winking, "but you go, girl."

In a vast wilderness, in a distant cabin hidden under great drifts of snow and a supernatural covering which prevented those diligent servants of the State from peering too far into its depths, dozens of children and their parents sat around a blazing wood stove. Grady McClure sat with a Bible on his lap, reading to the group. Some were dressed in modern clothes; some wore plain clothes. Samantha sat, eyes wide, listening to words that now meant more to her than life itself. Wren sat on Grady's lap, comforted because somehow Grady smelled like her father. Thomas sat on the floor against the wall, looking out through the window, counting the snowflakes, wondering, struck dumb by the blazing complexity and stunning magnificence of the God of All Creation, and wondering when they all would see God's face. A large roan draft horse stood tethered just outside the cabin door, nose up, smelling the wind…standing guard.

WHEN REVELATION KISSED REASON

This is the story of how Avram Belinsky, loving husband, wise and courageous father, famous doctor, and brilliant researcher, lost an argument with his gardener, and in so doing gained the wisdom of the ages.

Doctor Avram Belinsky was an orthodox Polish Jew from an orthodox Jewish family (you pronounce the name with the accent on the second syllable—Av-*rahm*—and it helps if you tilt your head slightly to one side to emphasize the fact that you are sure that this is where the accent falls). His father was a doctor in New York City, his grandfather was a doctor in New York City, and so Avram became a doctor in New York City. They were each dedicated to transforming the world for the improvement of humankind. With such a heritage, Avram decided to specialize in the treatment of autistic children.

To understand this story it is important to know how much Avram loved his wife, Miriam. Avram was fourteen when he met Miriam. He had gone with his parents to a camp in the Adirondacks. Walking by himself near the river one day, he saw a canoe suddenly overturn in the rough water. Quicker than a leopard he leapt into the frigid, tumultuous river, pulled a camper out of the foaming water, and laid her down on the bank. She was a thin, bedraggled girl, tall for her age, with long dark hair plastered over her forehead and a lifejacket two sizes too large. She coughed once, apologetically, on her knees. He went back to get the others—Avram was a good swimmer, and courageous—and eventually there were three young girls, sitting up, coughing, wet hair dripping into little pools in the sand, safe on the bank. He went back into the river and righted the canoe and pulled it up on the grass. He was about to ask if they were feeling well enough to get back in the canoe when the first girl he rescued stood and looked at him.

Now, it is a certainty of astronomical proportions that young girls are completely unaware of the impact their direct gaze has on young men. This young girl—Miriam was her name—had eyes as dark as space and bright as stars, and when she saw Avram standing there on the bank, she was pleased, because she could tell right away that he was a young orthodox Jewish boy (the tallit katan under his shirt, now dripping, and the payess, weren't things one normally saw in knights errant who rescue damsels in distress), and it would make it easier for her parents to accept the man she would marry if he was orthodox, like her parents...and like her. Of course Miriam had decided on the spot that she would marry this boy—eventually, in time, when the planets moved appropriately, when the springs of their lives rushed together. This may sound strange, or needlessly romantic, or simply foolish...to those who have never once fallen in love at first sight.

It is said by some wise men that a person's soul is made for one specific mate, one other soul to which the interlocking elements of our own hearts fit—not perfectly, because we are human, and there is no such thing as human perfection. In their meshing, imperfections are filed away, mutual strengths are strengthened, joy is heightened, sorrow is buffered, hearts are joined, and the two become more than what either could become alone, while at the same time each diminishes into the other. This, say the wise men, is symbol; it is one way a magnificently and amazingly complex God speaks to His creatures. And if the two are especially fortunate, they mesh with a Third, in which the two, having learned to put to death their own wills in deference to the other, put to death their own wills in favor of the One, and lose themselves completely and utterly in the Totality of the Universe. So there are some—courageous, far-sighted, boundlessly optimistic, walking around every day with more hope in one pocket than a martyr carries to the stake—who know themselves and can see into the very depths of another's soul. They can see those interlocking elements and how they will turn and mesh and blend through the years, and they are pulled by the most irresistible desire for unity—a consuming, utter, abandoning, crazy-wild uniting—with another person, one particular person. And if they are particularly astute, they will recognize that this screaming desire, this passion for unity, that fills every thread of their being is intended to be a mere tap on the shoulder from God, who wants us to know what His desire for unity with each of us is like. Yet for those sad souls who do not believe in love at first sight...there are other paths by which God can make Himself known.

So there Avram stood, struck by the intelligence that poured out from Miriam's eyes like the jet stream from a liquid cutting beam, dividing truth from falsehood, separating light from dark, emitting joy, banishing loneliness. Knowing himself, he saw into Miriam's soul and perceived those elements that would mesh with his own, and he too fell in love. In looking at her there on the sand, standing with grace that a recent dunking only enhanced, Avram felt completed, brave, incredibly joyful (as though he'd found the answer to life's second-greatest question), and focused. These things true women can do for honest men by simply looking at them with love.

And so it was. When Avram was twenty-six and Miriam twenty-four, they married. Avram had finished medical school and was beginning his residency. Miriam taught at the local University because she had completed her doctorate in record time and the faculty could no more resist her when she went to interview than a stick of butter can resist a hot knife. They lived with Avram's parents because there was room and the parents were getting old and they loved each other—why move away? Avram and Miriam never felt the need to establish a life separate from the lives of their parents and their families. Together, with each other and in the bosom of their (incredibly large) extended family, their life was tall in the way sequoias reach to heaven, rich with wisdom in the way chocolate is rich with mystery, and as exciting and swirling and full of joy as a davening supplicant is enraptured by the very presence of God.

Avram and Miriam had no children, and true, this was a sadness. They did, however, have dozens of children into whom they poured their life, who broke their hearts, and for whom they ached no less than they would have had those children been from their own bodies. At the time an autistic child was thought to be a unique anomaly in the creation of the universe, but Avram had a very different opinion, based upon a theory of his which was in turn based upon his relationship with God during that stage of his life.

Avram's life would be marked by a single great epiphany, but a number of lesser insights would creep up on him and surprise his intellect in such a way as to go before that single great epiphany, combining together like voices in the wilderness of his intellect, crying out about the coming of a great and wonderful revelation. The swelling, gathering power of this breaking wisdom would come upon him and eventually strike him down in his argument with the gardener in much the same way Job was struck down and lifted up before his God.

A first lesser insight occurred one day as he watched a davening Jew— his cousin, it happened—at temple. Avram froze, watching his cousin move back and forth in prayer, oblivious to the world around him. When he arrived home, he spoke urgently to Miriam.

"Did you see Meyer," he whispered, intently, in the grip of an understanding like none he'd ever experienced. "Do you remember him, what he did, what he was doing?"

"He was praying, was he not?" she asked. She wondered what she was missing. She trusted Avram implicitly and there was never any disparagement or acidic, degrading, or denigrating communication between them.

"Do you remember what he looked like while he did so, though," said Avram, touching her gently on the arm with affection, remembering Meyer's davening as if he was still before him, eyes bolt open, connections to truth flashing one after the other like sparkplugs in an engine. His hand reached for hers, gripping it tightly with the electric excitement that occurs in men, seeking wisdom as silver, when they find it.

Avram took his wife by the hand from the kitchen into the bedroom. They sat down together on the bed. Birds sang beyond the window.

"Miriam...you know that autistic children display what seems to be purposeless movement, like flapping their hands, rolling their heads, or rocking their bodies."

"I know this, Avram...yes?"

"And you know that they exhibit compulsive behavior which is apparently aligned in some way to a set of rules which only they know. They align toys or cans or objects in a certain way." When Avram was focused on his work, he spoke like a medical manual, or an encyclopedia.

"Yes...these things are symptomatic."

"And you know that there is an almost slavish devotion to *sameness*—a terrified resistance to change—in their routine, their habits, and their surroundings. There is ritualistic behavior that stems from this devotion to sameness, Miriam, where daily activities are performed the same way, at the same time, each day. They restrict their behavior to activities which to us seem severely limited in focus, and...and there are some who intentionally hurt themselves...they will bite themselves, or cut themselves, or..."

"Avram, yes, yes...what does it mean?"

Avram sat back against the headboard and looked up at the ceiling, eyes suddenly suffused in grief, in shame, in sorrow. Sun filtered through the lace curtains and speckled a pattern across his black silk jacket, a pattern that Miriam would remember ever afterwards and associate with this truth. "These children are showing us what we look like to God."

From this truth, from this lesser epiphany, Avram Belinsky would go on to become the most successful practitioner in his field, and yet, with all his wisdom, all his insight, even with this first tenuous grasp of the numinous, he would still lose the great argument of his life—blessings upon such a good fortune—with his gardener.

After sharing his insight with Miriam, they went to find Avram's father.

"Abba," he said, using the Hebrew word for 'Daddy'; they mixed Hebrew and English in the home, with Yiddish occasionally, and some Polish. "Abba, we need to talk." Avram laid out his line of reasoning to the old man, sitting at his desk reading in the Book of Job, as it happened, when Avram and Miriam came into his study.

"Abba, I think that we have been treating these children in the wrong way."

The older man, once one of the city's most renowned specialists in internal medicine, placed his spectacles down gently on the table. "Why is this, son?" the old man asked patiently, running his hand over the open book, smoothing the page tenderly.

"Consider this," Avram replied, who, in his excitement, dropped to the floor at his father's feet. Miriam took a chair and folded her hands in her lap. "We know the external symptoms of autism, do we not? Purposeless movement, compulsive behavior driven by an unknown set of rules, the bitter tyranny of slavish adherence to sameness and the resistance to change such adherence brings, and that some will even do violence to themselves… we know these things, Abba, but what else do such things remind you of?" The wise old man and the wise young woman stared at Avram as he sat on the floor, waiting.

"Us!" Avram cried excitedly, spreading his arms in a gesture to that embraced the entire human race. "Us! Look at us! What is it that causes the God of All Creation such heartbreak and sadness? Instead of engaging in the activities He sets before us, do we not wander in purposeless movement upon the face of the earth, engaging in compulsive behaviors that cause pain, disillusionment, tragedy, and destruction because of rules—rules we devise because they make us appear higher or brighter or more holy than others—rules that we establish ourselves, rules that make no sense to others? Do we not repeat these same mistakes over and over again, generation after generation, like slaves to a pattern we can't escape, a pattern of behavior that we embrace, a pattern we are loathe to change? And Abba…Abba, look around, do we not do violence to ourselves, does not man harm man, do we not kill and maim and slaughter mindlessly?"

"All the things you say are true, Avram," his father replied slowly; such lines of reasoning could be dangerous. "But what does this have to do with how you treat autistic children?"

"Abba, if autism is in truth a microcosm, a concentrated symbolic manifestation in one human being of mankind's condition without God, then there is hope for them, because there is hope for mankind."

The old man paused for a moment and passed a caressing hand over the pages of Job. "Avram, what will you do, read them Torah?"

"Are you saying," Miriam began hesitantly from the corner, "that God is judging these children for mankind's purposeless behavior? That they are being judged for mankind's behavior?"

"No," Avram said, smiling at his wife with respect, "It does not make sense that God would afflict children in this way for the parents' sins. It is not His way. But if these children—for some reason which I don't know yet—are symbols of man's rebellion against God, then...then there must be a way to bring these children out from their prison, from their circumscribed life. God would not—*does not*—abandon us, blessed be His name. He would not abandon these children, especially if they are being used by Him as a symbol of mankind's condition in His eyes. If there is a way man can come to live in accordance with God's rules, to come to know Him and His intentions for us, then there must be a way..." and Avram stopped, looked as if he were going to say more, but did not. He soon lost himself in speculation.

"A way for what, Avram?" his father asked.

Avram thought for a moment, and then spoke slowly, as though he were working out the solution as the words came to him, which he was, as they did. "There must be a way in which we ourselves are brought out from the prison that is a life without Him."

* * *

From this first understanding came Avram's conviction that while autism might have physiological causes, it was in reality an analogy physically manifested in the lives and behavior of autistic children that represented mankind's spiritual condition apart from God—and which therefore in keeping with Avram's theology (or perhaps more accurately, his desperate hope) would have a cure. Avram believed that God did not create man to leave him flapping around upon the earth, ignorant of His purposes and will. Avram needed but to identify the means within the spiritual realm whereby man draws close to God, then translate those means to the physiological side of the analogy. Yet Avram found himself at a loss at this point. As his father had noted, one could not simply read them Torah. Avram would have to discover how men drew close to God and then learn how to translate or model that spiritual methodology so that it would benefit his patients.

Such thinking ran greatly counter to the established wisdom in the field but, Avram reasoned, not many established practitioners believed that there was a God in heaven, supreme over all life, all men, all events. To consider that God was sovereign over all things, even the daily affairs of life and health and science and the hearts of men, was to them the height of folly. Avram, on the other hand, did believe such things, and sought to see in everything around him the hand of God. He still wasn't clear exactly how he needed to treat these children, but he did believe that a rational starting point would be an environment wherein they might more easily discern God's hand, which is why he suddenly was taken with the desire to move his practice to a place where those things which the children might attribute to God would be most easily seen.

So they moved out of the city, bought a farm in upstate New York, built a thoroughly-equipped, professional, but non-obtrusive clinic on the property, and put up a number of cottages for Miriam's parents, the Uncles (of whom more later), and the parents of the patients. At this new clinic they were surrounded by the things God made instead of the din and cacophony and twisted metal and concrete and chaos and dichotomies that spewed from the constructs which emanated from the minds and hands of men in things called cities. It was then, just after Avram's first small epiphany and just after they moved to the farm, that the gardener appeared.

The gardener was not what they expected a gardener to be, nor was he hired, in the clear sense of the term. One day he simply appeared at the farm and began working. He was not a young man. He looked in his sixties, to be kind, and was probably older, although he would move with great deliberation and, it appeared, possessed wondrous flexibility. One day Avram was sitting by the window in the kitchen with Miriam. He looked out over their pastures into the woods and saw an old man digging with a spade. The man had a white shirt, rolled at the sleeves, an open brown vest, and khaki trousers. He seemed remarkably fit for an old man. He looked Jewish—there was the long, untrimmed beard, the payess, and... yes, Avram could just make out a tallit gadol and a kippah. Avram could see beads of sweat in the man's face and dark loops of perspiration on the man's back. Avram could not remember hiring a gardener. Perhaps, he thought, it was one of the Uncles who had decided to work in the garden.

The next day, again at breakfast, Avram looked out to see a line of tiny but robust maple saplings, like boys practicing to be soldiers, lined along the white board fence where, yesterday, not one had stood. This was a prodigious feat of arboreal legerdemain, and Avram spoke to Miriam and asked her to remind him to find the Uncle that did such a wonderful job with the saplings along the fence and thank him with blessings.

It went on this way for forty days, Avram seeing a new arboreal or horticultural event each day but never getting around to actually finding and speaking with the hard-working mysterious gardener until the fortieth day, when, as he walked around one of the cottages to find an Uncle to discuss with him the finer points of how to make a good kosher stew with only onions, garlic, and carrots, he almost tripped over the man. He was kneeling in the dirt, vigorously working the soil with his hands.

"Uncle," Avram exclaimed, "my deepest apologies." And—finally—Avram looked closely at the man and realized in an instant that this man was neither his Uncle, nor was he in any way related to the teaming mass of humanity under his roof.

"You're not an Uncle," Avram said, drawing his head back slightly as if he was nearsighted, which he wasn't.

"I am not an Uncle of yours," the man corrected, looking up, sitting back on his heels. Avram's knees hurt just watching him do this. "Nu, is this something that you worry about?"

"Well, no, certainly not...but...are you related to one of the children?"

The old man shook his head. "Not like you think...no, I am not, Avram."

"Then...forgive me, but what are you doing here?"

The old man rested his hands on his thighs and looked down with sadness at the little plot of ground he was working. He then gestured toward the dirt as though someone or something had disappointed him, as if to say, 'isn't it obvious?' "I am the gardener," he said, "and I am trying to understand why this particular stretch of soil will not speak to me as the soil does in many other places where I work. And so I am reasoning with it."

Avram's eyebrows went up like a glider catching an updraft.

"You think this is funny?" the old man asked, without looking at Avram.

Avram pursed his lips, shrugged his shoulders, turned both his palms outward, tilted his head to one side, and said, "Did I say it was funny?" in English. In Yiddish, such body language was nothing short of a burst of riotous laughter.

The old man raised an open hand, waving it by his ear back and forth in short, choppy motions. "Nu...so tell me, Doctor Belinsky, if God, who knows us from dirt, can reason with man who came from dirt, why can't I reason with this dirt here?"

As light will sometimes fracture and display a brilliant, shimmering pattern when reflected through the strangest things, so was Avram suddenly struck with another of his lesser epiphanies. He dropped down onto the garden bench like a bag of grain and blew out his breath, suddenly in his mind fully engaged in wrestling with the continuing attempt to find a solution to the other side of the analogy.

"Uncle," he asked, forgetting that the gardener was no Uncle, "do you believe God reasons with man?"

"Of course He reasons with man," the gardener replied, blinking up at Avram from the dirt. "Why shouldn't He? He made us so that He could walk with us, talk with us, and work with us. He talked with Moses, didn't He, like a man talks with his friend? What kind of friend orders you about all the time?"

"The Christians believe that man cannot argue with God."

"I think you are wrong, Avram, about Christian theology. I know from Christian theology. Christians—real ones, not the ones you see spouting foolishness, deceiving old women, raking in millions of dollars—believe that God desires very much to reason with man. But first you say *reason*, then you use the word *argue*. Which do you mean?"

"What's the difference?" Avram asked. "And what do you know from Christian theology?" Avram looked pointedly at the man's tzitzit—fringed tassels that spoke of a meticulous devotion to the Law of Moses.

The old man stood up and brushed dust and dead weeds from his pants. His hands were black with ingrained dirt, heavily lined, rough, and strong. "Reasoning with someone," he said softly, with a voice that sounded like deep, rich, dark loam, "is like coming upon a man who has fallen to the side of a road, perhaps beaten by thieves, and taking him up gently and putting your arm under him to support him so that you and he can walk together to the right place. Arguing is to come upon that man and hit him with a shovel so that he gets up and goes to the same place on his own."

"Abraham argued with God, did he not, over those in Sodom?"

"Abraham *reasoned* with God—and Abraham knew to whom he was speaking, make no mistake. Abraham wanted the best decision, because he wanted the Judge of All the Earth, may His name be praised, to do right so that the Blessed Name would suffer no reproach."

Avram looked doubtful. "Abraham wanted to make sure God didn't destroy his nephew. Abraham had his own agenda."

The old man shook his head slowly and looked at Avram with deep, sad eyes. "No, no...no, Avram, if Abraham had been concerned only with what he himself wanted, he would have asked God to spare Lot directly."

Avram leaned forward on the bench, in the grip of intense disputation. "Ah, but what if Lot had become an unrighteous man and Abraham, not wanting to ask directly—like you say, he knew who he was talking to—what if Abraham wanted to leave it open for God to perhaps give Lot some mercy if Lot hadn't exactly been a mensch in that cesspool of a city?"

The old man looked directly into Avram's eyes for a long moment. Avram felt unsettled. The old man shook his head admonishingly. "What is with you, always dancing around the little black points?" The gardener looked disappointed with him. "Do you have a child, Avram...a son, perhaps?"

Avram looked away, caught by the shift in the conversation, sudden pain in his eyes. "We have no children," he said reedily, voice shaking. How such a void can open a wound in a man from even the greatest distance.

The old man looked around at the farm, with the cottages and the hills and fences and woods and buildings and children here and there. "Nu... what are all these children I see running around?" Before Avram could answer, the gardener said, "No matter...so one day, you'll have a son. So think, Avram Belinsky, on that day, when you hold your son in your hands and lift him up with inexpressible joy, presenting him to God so that He will bless this new life...do you think you could one day hold up a knife to slay that son of yours, that son that you desperately hoped for, prayed for, longed for, ached for?" The gardener was holding one hand, palm up, in front of Avram's face and the other clenched in a fist, as though holding a knife, raised, ready to strike down into the imaginary baby in his palm. Avram was looking up at him in horror, the sun reflecting through the man's uplifted hand, and he could almost see the knife. As the old man spoke Avram felt the overwhelming grief and heartbreak that Abraham must have experienced. Piercing agony flashed into the water of his soul like a hunting bird arrows down from heaven deep into a cold blue lake.

The old man went on sternly. "This man Abraham, who would do such a thing for the Almighty King of Creation; this man who would not withhold his only son from God, who was convinced that since God had promised him descendants like the stars in the sky, God would, after he plunged in the knife, resurrect his son and provide those descendants… such a man, you think, was after his own agenda, his own meager wishes?" Wind whipped around the small courtyard in which they sat. Above the valley clouds raced into dark rolling knots like wrestling sea serpents. Avram suddenly became cold. The gardener seemed to become taller, with a suffusing light from within his peasant clothes, and the open hand holding the imaginary baby morphed into a closed fist with one finger shaking like an admonishing rabbi, the other open, held over his heart. Avram was overcome with remorse.

"Abraham was a good man who reasoned that God would raise his son from the dead to keep his promise, Av*ram*…to provide the promised line of descendants. This is reasoning based in trust, not argument."

Avram began to weep. The poignant description of what Abraham must have endured to obey God was bitterly real to Avram. He knew what it was to desperately hope for a child. What a breathtaking loss losing Yitzhak would have been, and yet Abraham would have gone through with it, killing his longed-for child with his own hand…there was no doubt in Avram's mind. He was struck by the enormity of Abraham's obedience and devotion. Avram put his head in his hands in a swirling, confused tangle of grief and anguish and worship. His tears fell to the ground. He did not see the old man's rough hand hover just barely above his head.

The old man whispered in a voice that Avram could not hear, yet angels could not ignore: "'For the mountains may be removed and the hills may shake, but my lovingkindness will not be removed from you, and my covenant of peace will not be shaken." When Avram looked up, many minutes later, the sun was falling below the tree line and the gardener was gone.

That night, Miriam conceived a child, a boy. At the bris, she who had carried to the mohel babies of other women laughed with joy as she watched her own carried by others, and they named him Yitzhak.

* * *

Just after Yitzhak was born, Avram had another conversation with the gardener. After the first talk with Miriam and his father, he had not discussed with anyone his thought, his first epiphany, that autism was in fact a symbolic manifestation in man's most precious resource of man's rebellion against God. But one day he was walking along the path that led up to one of the Uncle's cottages and came across the gardener building a stone wall to border the path. The gardener was lifting what appeared to Avram to be an extremely heavy stone. "Here, Uncle, let me help you," Avram replied, rushing to get his hands under the rock.

"No need, no need, Avram," the gardener said, setting the stone in place in its prepared bed of mortar. "They are not so heavy." The gardener sat down on the pile of stones for a rest, and Avram stood quietly while he wiped perspiration from his forehead with an old red handkerchief. "And how is Yitzhak this morning?"

"Yitzhak is wonderful, praise the God of All Creation."

"Miriam is happy, nu?"

"Miriam is deeply grateful," Avram replied.

The gardener nodded slowly, smiling. "Gratefulness is good," he said. "And what about you, Avram; have you come to an answer yet about whether man can argue or reason with God?"

There next to the gardener, sitting on stones next to a stone wall which would in all probability remain for the next century or so, Avram was struck suddenly with an overwhelming sense of permanence, of weight, of the truly substantial gravity of life, and it made him want very much to talk to the gardener about that which most commanded his thoughts. A light breeze swirled through the trees, easing the burden of the heat, and with it seemed to come an almost ethereal calm, a banishing of artifice or cynicism and the very deep, internal anxiety from which such things typically ooze. Avram felt as though Truth Himself stood close by.

"Uncle, I want to tell you...I want to tell you about what we do here, and I want to ask your opinion of something." That Avram would address the gardener as an Uncle spoke of a subtle shift in his spirit.

The gardener waited on the pile of stones, looking around, turning his face to the breeze, closed his eyes, and nodded.

Avram took this as a sign to continue. "We treat autistic children here, Uncle. The symptoms they exhibit, the characteristics of autism, I think, are...I think they may be symbols. Most people think that there is some physiological cause, some type of error in the wiring of the brain, and that may be. Yet I think that the symptomology of autism also closely resembles the characteristics of how man rebels against God. It may be that in some cases autism is another way God is attempting to...to *reason* with us, to get our attention in some way." Avram stopped, in that small wooded space with the breeze coursing through the trees and sweeping up the hill, and with a strange pleasant tinge of surprise recognized that there was no concern whatsoever about the validity of his thought or whether the gardener would think him a fool. There was simply peace, truth, acceptance, and a deep desire to share his mind and commune with another human being.

The gardener wiped his forehead again with a red sweep of cloth. "I think this is very possible," he said slowly. "For those with eyes to see, Avram, these children may be used by God to show mankind what their rebellion looks like, and to show them how their rebellion keeps them from functioning in the way He intended."

"But Uncle, I am still wrestling with why...*why* would God do such things to children?"

The gardener stuffed the red square back into his pocket, looked up at the clouds for long seconds, and then rubbed his calloused hands together. "Avram, if you wanted to put up a sign that said something very important, let's say a warning sign, and you desperately wanted people to see it because it was terribly important, because you loved them and didn't want anything bad to happen to them, where would you put it?"

Avram thought for just a moment. "You put the sign where people would most easily notice it."

"And where do people most often look in their lives?" the gardener asked. "Where do they look for their future, for their hopes, for their dreams…to where do the hearts of people most easily turn, when they have hearts at all?"

Avram nodded then, slowly: "To their children."

"Precisely…at least those people who have not yet become monsters… so if you were God, wouldn't it make sense to put such warning signs in the children of the world so that we might all see exactly what we look like to God, so that we might fall on our faces and realize how foolish we are, how far we are from truly communicating not only with God but with each other?"

Avram realized the truth of this without a moment's hesitation. "But… but there must be some recourse, some cure," he wondered out loud, "because God does not abandon us completely. There is hope of a life with Him. Moses talked to Him face-to-face. He spoke with the prophets directly. He gave the Law that we might live."

The gardener looked down at the stones in the wall that he'd built and put one rough hand out to swipe an unruly speck of mortar from the pointing. "The Law, Avram, is not the way man can be put right with God. The Law is beautiful precisely because of the characteristic it has of showing us that we cannot be put right by adhering to it."

Had Avram not been within that time and space wherein Truth suffused every fiber of wood, water, stone, tree, and flesh, he would have vociferously defended what he could only perceive as an assault upon a central rock of the Jewish faith. As it was, he attempted to understand. "We are made righteous before God by the Law," Avram said ponderously, with significant portent, "there is nothing else by which man stands or falls but by obedience to the Law."

"And tell me, Avram," the gardener replied, leaning forward slightly, pointing at his chest with the hand that held his red handkerchief, "can you keep the Law… the *whole* Law, in each and every stipulation, in all its aspects, perfectly?"

Avram sat down on the wall and thought about this…about the six hundred and thirty-some rules and restrictions levied upon orthodox Jews— and every other human being on the planet. He thought about the reams of commentary and rules and interpretations of the Law and interpretations of the interpretations and the little black points around which Jews had been arguing for centuries—as if the act of arguing itself garnered to the debater some sort of mantle of holiness—and he had no answer.

At the farm in the Adirondacks where Avram treated autistic children, which Avram called the Adirondack Autism Institute, but which was known by hopeful (Jewish) parents and all of Avram's relatives fortunate enough to reside therein, as 'the Bosom of Avram', the Uncles were a dominating and imposing presence. Ten of them—enough for a minyan, any would be quick to point out—resided within the Bosom of Avram, each in their own cottage, each with their own burgeoning family. Five were brothers of Miriam's father; four were brothers of her mother; one was the brother of Avram's father.

They dressed alike, each in the garb of the traditional Hasidic Jew. They seemed like plump wingless crows or great thin cadaverous bearded statues come to life, constantly moving about the grounds, in their way and according to their nature friendly, curious (which translated into English from the Yiddish means *nosy*), rapaciously intelligent, incisively argumentative, aloof one moment, engaged furiously as if the world depended upon their opinions the next; inhumanly vigorous, deathly still; mystical and mysterious; an ethereal, harmonious embodiment of mankind; the epitome of what it meant to be human. They were imperious, impetuous, contending with the King of the Cosmos, may His name be praised, and, by their line of argument, prevailing. They were, in a word, Jews. Among those possessing a modicum of cynical, secular urban humor, the Uncles were known as 'Avram's Bane'.

But truly it was not so. Avram delighted in the presence of so many of his relatives, and the Uncles were alternately a fountain of wisdom, a walking display of the strengths of Judaism, a strong bulwark of tradition useful in standing against ever more powerful incursions of modern culture as it sought to erode the pillars of their faith, and the bedrock of their own community of orthodox Jews there in the mountains of upstate New York.

It did not hurt that one was a specialist in internal medicine, another a superb orthopedic surgeon, and another one of the world's leading pediatric physicians. They circulated around the grounds like blood circulates in the body, and no visitor would leave the Bosom of Avram without remembering the Uncles. Few would leave without encountering three of four directly, conspicuously, and, sometimes, argumentatively. But the Uncles were always gentle with the parents of the children; they knew that the human soul can bear only so much.

And so one can understand why, encountering the gardener, Avram was not confused or taken aback or surprised by the conversation. Such conversations occurred constantly in communities where God is the central theme. When God is at the center of a man, a life, a community, or a people, there is no limit to the depth or richness or complexity or elegance or beauty or truth that accompanies that man, that life, that community, or that people.

Avram would discuss his medical and spiritual ideas with the Uncles and their reactions were to be expected. They were not dismissive; rather, the collective opinion was that these insights were small breadcrumbs God was dropping so that Avram could discover something God wished for him to learn, and they each, in their own way, encouraged him to continue the search.

"Reading them Torah is not a bad idea," said one, "your father is very smart to suggest this. How else will they know God's law?"

"Bring them to temple," said another.

"Teach them to daven," said a third, davening.

"Teach them the history of the Jews," said another, "for in such history is the lesson that there is always hope, and that God does not forget His children. The God of All Creation will not let His children perish," this Uncle proclaimed intensely, "I care not how things appear. God makes an agreement, He keeps it." The Uncle walked off imperiously, waving a newspaper in disgust, wherein was found an article speculating upon the inevitable destruction of Israel from a nuclear weapon, a biologically-engineered plague, or some other devastatingly thorough means of genocidal murder.

"You must teach them the *Shisha Sedarim*—the Talmud," said another Uncle. "These laws order the Universe; in them will their own minds find order from confusion."

In such fashion did each of the Uncles speculate upon the method by which autistic children might be made to know about God and, in so doing, break out from their prison. Avram considered each of their suggestions with great seriousness. Yet, though he tried almost every one of the Uncle's suggestions (defying the questioning glances of his assistants), none succeeded, and still he remained utterly at a loss as to how he might break through the impenetrable barrier erected between those in this life and those imprisoned by autism.

The gardener, on the other hand, was of a slightly different opinion. As Avram would contemplate the various suggestions from each Uncle, he would come across the gardener working in the dirt, or pruning a tree, or building a stone wall. Avram would greet the man, who would smile and talk quietly with him about the latest solution posed by the Uncles. A relationship was building over the years that Avram found hard to define, but, as it progressed, seemed to revolve around the differences between Christian and Jewish theology. There was never any small talk; it was as if they were both supremely aware that essential elements of the Universe were of such importance—and time so short—that to be diverted in the discussion of anything other than eternal profundities would have been a sin against creation.

One day Avram came across the gardener as he was building a stone wall around a vegetable garden. "Your boy," the gardener asked, looking up, "he is well?"

"The Creator, may His name be praised, is keeping the boy well, thank you," Avram replied.

"Nu...so...what is the most recent big solution to the problem I see in all these children around here," the gardener asked, waving his hands in the air at nothing in particular.

Avram stood still, hands in the pockets of his long black coat, looking out over the farm. They were standing on a hill, a point from which they could look down on most of the land. "You have heard most of them, nu?"

"I have," the gardener replied in Hebrew. Their conversations moved back and forth in the languages spoken most often at the farm—Hebrew, Polish, English—like a river courses down a mountain, seeking the path which offers the best opportunity to run deeply and silently when it needed to pause and repose, or rapidly over rocks when it needed to sing, or over a great steep precipice when it needed to display its power, or, when they desired to fully express irony or cynicism or the iron of soul that reposed within the Jews, they spoke Yiddish. That the gardener, so well-versed in the history of the Jews—even to the degree that he spoke so many of their languages—would continue to advocate a different theology was a large grain of sand in the oyster of Avram's life.

"It seems to me," Avram continued, speculating, "that each of the solutions has one thing in common. Each presupposes that the patient needs to know about God to be cured, and each solution offers a way to do this."

"I agree that this is what they all have in common," said the gardener. "And what do you think?" The smell of honeysuckle was redolent, and the smell of trees—strong, woody, attached to the earth, ancient—surrounded them like the frame of a picture. The gardener's chisel worked as if it lived, knowing the very soul of the stone itself, seeking out and chipping away at unseen imperfections.

"We have talked about this," Avram said, "and the problem it seems is that each solution presupposes that you can talk to these children, that you can communicate with them directly—and we know that this is impossible. Our means of communication is utterly incomprehensible to them. It is as if we were trying to talk to ants, or birds. I think that the condition itself presents to the patient a barrier to the cure. In some way, physiologically, the patient is hindered from communicating normally with the world around them. I think this is a parallel to man's spiritual condition. It is like the person who doesn't know anything about God; not knowing about the Author of truth and beauty, they are similarly handicapped, unable to accurately perceive the world around them, and unable to communicate clearly to those who do know about Him. Of course the logical solution would be to help these children know about God. I only worry about the disparity between offering a spiritual solution to an obviously physical malady."

"There are those who say that the spiritual world drives the physical world," the gardener replied.

"True, true," said Avram, nodding slowly, "but it is a big leap to consider."

"So you think the cure will be found if you could find a way to help these children know more about God."

"I am considering it, yes," said Avram.

"Won't work," said the gardener, flatly. His chisel struck the stone sharply, and a large chip flew away.

Avram was taken aback by the gardener's cursory dismissal. "And why not?" he asked with some asperity. "The solutions the Uncles put forth have kept our people and our traditions alive for untold generations. If we are looking for spiritual solutions, I would look no further than that which Jewish tradition has offered down through the centuries. Our traditions have served to keep us a coherent People. No one else knows as much about what God requires of man than does the Jew."

The gardener looked up at him slowly. "Avram, what do you know about working with stone?"

Avram blinked once and shook his head. "Nothing," he replied.

"But you could learn, right? You could get a book, read about the different kinds of stone, read how the greatest stonemasons of the world created their masterpieces, nu? You could read about the basics of the trade, how and with whom to apprentice, and what tools to use, and what projects to undertake to become a good stonemason. You and your people could read about working with stone and write about it for centuries, becoming experts in the descriptions of various techniques and interpreting each other's interpretations down through time?"

"We would know quite a bit…"

"You still wouldn't be a stonemason, Avram, until you took a piece of stone in your hands and worked it. There is a great difference—a vast distance, a distance across which no man can leap—between knowing *about* something intellectually, and *knowing* something experientially, in the heart. God is apprehended with the *heart*, Avram, not with the mind. It is the difference between the Tree of Life and the Tree of the Knowledge of Good and Evil. And it is just this gulf which stands between a true believer and men who choose to establish their own traditions, their own set of books or bodies of knowledge about who and what they think God is or wants. For I will tell you, Avram," and here the gardener looked fiercely intense, "it is just this intense passion to know about God which has kept your people from truly knowing Him; you have fallen in love with your own words, your own ideas, and your own thoughts about who He is, and have ignored Him Himself. Your traditions have become to you that which you worship; your traditions have become to you God, and God's heart breaks because of it.

"Tell me, Avram," the gardener continued, "do you know *about* your wife, or do you *know* her? Do you know about her as a woman who has been described to you in a letter? Is your knowledge that of one who has read a letter she's written...or do you have experiential knowledge of her through constant, daily interaction, through a vibrant, ongoing, intensive, passionate relationship?"

Avram found the implications of the gardener's argument intensely offensive. "You would have a relationship with God degenerate into nothing but simple emotion or the vagary of experience?"

"Foolishness!" the gardener replied, lifting the hammer in the air effortlessly. "Emotion has no place in this discussion other than a natural and laudable byproduct of such a relationship. We are not talking about the unstable waves that roil a man's life; we are talking about the difference between knowing *about* something, and knowing it. And why disparage experience? Did not the patriarchs all have an experience with the living God? Abraham spoke with Him, Yitzhak knew Him, Yaakov wrestled with Him. Did not He speak to the prophets? Did not He speak to Moses face to face, like a man speaks with his friend? I will tell you, Avram," the gardener said, his chisel pausing for a moment, "that you *cannot* know God unless you experience Him—unless He comes into the very fabric of your life and in so doing changes it irrevocably.

"Getting these children to know *about* God will do them no good," he said firmly, rough hands still caressing the stone. He pointed his chisel directly at Avram. "You must find out how a man comes to know God *experientially*—how a man can *experience* God. You must find the way whereby man can talk with God face-to-face, to relate to Him, and thence to obey Him, directly. Step from the law to the spirit of the law, Avram. Teach them to *know* the Lawgiver. They will have the law in their hearts, then—not in their heads. You will not reach these children until you can discover how man comes to know God, for it will only be in that parallel that will you find your solution."

* * *

Young Yitzhak was the cherished prince of the community. As he grew, none could fail to note his precociousness. One day when he was twelve he fell to arguing with the Uncles after a minyan.

"Uncles," he said respectfully, when the Uncles argued with him about the preeminence of the documented traditions and writings in the Talmud, "why such a focus on the written law? Is not the law intended to point to the Lawgiver? I can read about a rose all day, but does it compare to a minute spent smelling one? Should not our focus be the Giver of the law and what He wishes of us? And is He not capable of speaking to us directly? Is not that which is written—beautiful and truthful as it is—intended simply to lead us to discover He Who is Beauty and Truth itself, Who would, logically, be all the more beautiful and truthful?" You may think this was a strange way for a twelve-year old boy to talk, but you must remember with whom he lived, and Who and what it was they spoke about constantly.

All who heard him marveled at his wisdom. Since each saw in the young boy their own genes sprouting forth to transform the world for the betterment of humankind, each therefore smiled upon him with satisfaction and devotion. "But you should watch him," one Uncle or another would say to Avram off to the side, in whispered tones, wagging fingers or heads or beards. "He has strange ideas." When Avram heard of Yitzhak's comment about the Lawgiver, he began to suspect the gardener was having an influence on his son's development.

As far as Avram and Miriam were concerned, Yitzhak was the chief joy in their life. He was an only child; Miriam could not bear another. He was meticulously obedient and delighted to work with his father in the practice, helping in any way. He would file or type or carry or fetch, and he was especially gentle with the autistic children themselves. As he worked closely with his father, he came to understand in the depths of his soul the mysteries and the tragedies of this condition which isolated children from the flow of normal human discourse. Miriam came upon him one day when he was five, on his knees helping a young autistic girl to perceive words in a children's book, tears coursing silently down upon his cheeks as he slowly turned the pages.

Over the years Avram had been working in concert with the Uncle who specialized in internal medicine to discover the physiological dynamics of autism, speculating along one line of inquiry that perhaps the disorder was due to some chemical malfeasance in the brain. No one knew what physical imperfection or fault caused autism, nor how it might be cured, and while Avram still intently pursued the line of research down which his lesser epiphanies were leading, he did not give up on exploring the potential of physiological causes. It was along this line of chemical research that Avram had what he referred to as a 'sideways breakthrough'—not something directly curing autism, but something which, however unlikely, might help. He and one of the Uncles found a way to chemically induce autism in laboratory animals.

"But Avram," the Uncle said, "this is of no use; you cannot restore the subject to normalcy. This formula could be one of a thousand that causes the condition. That you can cause the disorder does not mean that you can cure it."

"One step at a time, Uncle," Avram replied, undaunted.

As the years progressed, they worked together to refine the formula that would bring about replicable symptoms of autism in laboratory subjects; they found that the formula would only work on the young—on young rats, young monkeys, young guinea pigs—possessing a blood type that was rare in each species. As the subject aged, the formula would no longer produce the symptoms. None of the subjects were able to be restored to normalcy in all the years of their research and experimentation.

"No one must know about this," Avram said to the Uncle.

"Who would want to know?" was the reply, which translated from the Yiddish, was "I wouldn't tell a soul about anything as crazy as this."

One day when Yitzhak was thirteen, an eleven-year old girl was brought to the Institute. Her parents, obviously not well-to-do, were from Minnesota and had driven straight through to the farm in New York. They arrived unannounced, with no reservation, no prior consultation, and simply walked into the lobby of the residential treatment facility and asked for Doctor Belinsky.

"A cousin told us about this place," the father said. "He said that you could help our daughter." He was a plain man with a lean jaw, unshaven, haggard, dressed in a short-sleeve flannel shirt and jeans. He held the car keys tightly clenched in his fist. The other hand, finger poking on the counter, emphasized his urgency. The mother—short, wiry, and high-strung—wore a print blouse and slacks, and stood smoking, nervous, and agitated.

Naomi, the temporary receptionist, was a daughter of one of the Uncles. She was brilliant (taking a few days off prior to commencing an internship in neurology) and therefore did not ask the insultingly foolish question about whether they had an appointment. She had memorized her appointment book twelve seconds after looking at it that morning and these people weren't in it. Fortunately her intelligence was married with and surpassed by remarkable compassion, and as quickly as an osprey dives for a fish, she grasped the situation.

"Of course; if you would be so kind as to wait for only a moment, please, Mister...?"

"Rivkomen," the man replied, "my wife, Sarah...our daughter, Rebecca." Naomi looked over the counter to see a thin, tallish, dark-eyed girl with straggly hair, a dirt-streaked, unkempt face, scratches on her arms and legs, and a torn pale-green dress, tatters of which hung down and dragged upon the floor. She was tapping her foot, staring at one of the pictures on the wall (which Avram had placed there for the specific purpose of helping autistic children focus during what would to them be a threatening or confusing activity). She began to twirl around slowly in widening circles. Her mother yanked her hand roughly. She moaned at first, with a high, keening cry that culminated in a great wail that continued even as her mother held her hand firmly.

"We're very sorry," the mother apologized.

"We see it all the time," Naomi said, with a gentle wave of her hand, heart breaking. "Don't apologize. And you can let her twirl if you wish." She punched up the number for Doctor Belinsky and spoke into the headphone in rapid Polish. The mother maintained her clamp upon the child, who continued to wail plaintively.

"He'll be right out," she said, in English. The father, up to this point a tight ball of tension and energy, collapsed slowly against the smooth marble wall and slid down like pudding until the floor, fortunately, arrested his decline. He hadn't drawn a breath since he left Minnesota. The mother tightened her grip.

It was the keening cry of a prisoner in agony that brought Yitzhak in from the field. He heard the cry and recognized it as the sound of a soul in pain. He saw many such children at the farm. It was his father's business, after all, to treat children trapped in a prison of unconventional perceptions. But there was something peculiar about this cry, as if there was a thread of hope, but only a thread, and a great deal of fear. The fear was normal; the abnormal surroundings of the farm, so outside an autistic child's normal routine, would be frightening. The hope, however, was not. In a thirteen-year old knight's heart, he heard a voice: "Come rescue me, please, someone...anyone!"

When Yitzhak walked into the lobby he saw Rebecca collapsed toward the floor, still keening, held up only by her mother's iron grip around a wrist. "Straighten up," the mother hissed, yanking. The girl kept crying out in a long, high, steady peal of agony.

"Here, ma'am, I'll take her," Yitzhak said.

"He works here," Naomi said to the surprised mother, who reluctantly released her grip.

Yitzhak steadied the girl as she descended to the floor, crumpling like a broken swan. Her keening quieted to some degree. Yitzhak observed her closely. She was not making eye contact—this was normal. There was a thin line of liquid from the corner of her mouth. He wiped it with his sleeve, gently. He arranged her limbs so that she could sit comfortably. Her keening stopped.

The mother started as though someone had pinched her. "What did you do, young man?" she asked with no small degree of wonder and a hint of threatened malice. "She doesn't stop for hours once she starts. What did you give her?"

"I told you, Sarah" the father said from the floor, as though the marble itself had spoken, "they say this place works miracles."

"I just set her down, ma'am," Yitzhak replied, answering the mother's question. "I didn't give her anything. She'll be okay. Doctor Belinsky will be here very shortly." Yitzhak looked back at Rebecca. "What's her name?" he asked. He tenderly brushed a stray lock of dark, stringy hair from her face. The girl did not respond.

"Who are *you*?" the mother replied.

"This is Yitzhak Belinsky," Naomi replied, "Doctor Belinsky's son."

The mother made a gesture, tilting her head to one side, which communicated grudging approval laced with a tinge of 'let's wait and see'.

The father, still against the wall, tears coursing silently down across a stubbled expanse like streams flowing down a mountain, said in barely a whisper, "She is Rebecca...she is my daughter."

* * *

As Yitzhak matured he assumed more responsibility in ministering to the patients. Avram was proud of his son. Yitzhak had a way with autistic children; he could get them to do things, to make progress, in ways no one else could. There are some people in life who communicate on different levels—they are said to be good with animals, or good with children—and it was in just this way that Yitzhak could make tenuous connections with a few of the patients.

Yitzhak spent much time with Rebecca at the request of his father. The young girl was severely afflicted; she could not speak, and would frequently attempt to harm herself by striking her head against a wall or hitting herself with various objects. Yitzhak had a pronounced effect on Rebecca. She seemed to know he was in the room, and there were times when Yitzhak could soothe her. Whenever he would speak to her, she would look away. The mother, noting this one day, said bitterly, "She does this all the time. When I talk to her, she looks away, as if she doesn't want to hear what I have to say. How can you reach someone like that, who completely ignores you?"

Yitzhak looked up from the floor of Rebecca's room where he had been quietly talking with Rebecca. "Mrs. Rivkomen, some autistic children perceive the world differently. It may be that they can either hear, or see, but they cannot do both at the same time. Rebecca might look at you and see so much more—entire spectrums of light and color that are in some way related to her emotions or your emotions or the temperature of the room or your spirit or her spirit. It may be that she sees and takes in so much with her eyes that she is mentally incapable of processing speech with her ears while looking at you. To hear what you are saying, she needs to stare away into the distance, to stare at something that will not present such a flood of visual sensory input. She's trying to hear what you have to say."

Mrs. Rivkomen compressed her lips in frustration. She could not gainsay the theory, since she was obviously a lay person, but the unfulfilled heart of a mother who had for so long sought a daughter's companionship—willingly withheld, from all appearances—argued otherwise. Yitzhak seemed to know this.

"She truly does want to communicate with you," he said gently.

"What do you know?" the woman spat. She turned on her heel and stalked out of the room. Rebecca began to keen.

"Softly, softly," Yitzhak said, "softly…she can't help it, Rebecca. They are like this in the beginning. They come to understand, though, they really do. And you will talk to her one day…you will."

Rebecca curled into a fetal position, wrapping her arms around herself tightly, and began to cry, moaning, dribbling saliva, rocking herself against the wall. Yitzhak held her as she rocked, and she quieted.

Avram was impatient with the progress of most of his patients, but more so with his own inability to come to grips with the solution posed by the gardener. The need to find an answer that paired with his conviction that autism was a manifestation of a spiritual inability of man to communicate with his God pressed upon him increasingly, like a man carrying a hundred-pound pack for miles and miles—the pack only got heavier, bearing down upon him, until he felt he could not take another step. This burden pressed down upon Avram until he found it difficult to eat, or sleep, or think of anything else. He felt that the cure to autism was inextricably bound up in this parallel, and that if he could find the physiological parallel to the tenets and doctrines and teachings of Judaism—teachings that led men to know about the God of All Creation—he would achieve his life's goal of transforming his little part of the world to benefit humanity. It was this burden, this oppressive, crushing weight of expectation and constant casting about for an answer that brought him to the doorstep of the great argument of his life—with the gardener.

The gardener was in the stables one day, loading manure in a wheelbarrow to fertilize the roses he had planted near the reception building. Avram was walking by, having an intense conversation with the parents of a young autistic boy of twelve. The boy was making no progress at all, and the parents were considering removing him from the Institute and submitting him to electric shock therapy. Avram was stridently arguing against this, and in their discussion they wound their way to the stables. The talk ended with the parents noncommittal, and an attendant escorted the young boy back to his room while Avram remained in the stables, discouraged.

"You are discouraged," the gardener said from behind a wall, knee-deep in manure, shoveling it into a wheelbarrow.

"I am not discouraged," Avram replied as if to no one in particular, looking around, and then, seeing the gardener, continued: "I am simply frustrated. These people have no patience. They cannot, they *will* not see that their child only needs a key to unlock his ability to communicate with the rest of the world. He does not need to be strapped to a table and shocked to within an inch of his life. They'll kill him; they'll destroy everything that is human in him."

"You must enable him to experience God, Avram," the gardener said quietly, the shovel scraping and squelching through the manure on the concrete floor.

"And just how would you propose such a thing?" Avram said, both arms suddenly shooting straight up in the air over his head, fists clenched, arms pumping. "If I could pull God down from the heavens I would. I would pull Him down and grab Him by the lapels and demand that He speak to these children, to wake them up, to rescue them from their prison!"

In the silence of the stable, the old gardener said, gently, "He did such a thing once, Avram." He leaned on his shovel, staring directly at Avram, "in a place very much like this." The gardener raised his arm and swept it to encompass the muck and wood and straw and filth of the stable.

"He did *no such thing*," Avram replied hotly, stamping his foot in affirmation, resenting the gardener's insinuation. He moved toward the gardener, looking at him with blazing passion fueled by the dense, pitch-soaked logs that were centuries of tradition. "He will, one day, send the Messiah, but *He has not yet come*." Avram held up a finger and said, "'*Shema Yisrael Adonai eloheinu Adonai ehad*'. Hear, O Israel, the Lord is our God, the Lord is one.' He does not make three of one. He does not split Himself."

"Avram…"

"How long have you worked here, Uncle?" Avram said to the gardener. "Are you completely unaware that it is impossible for us to agree? Judaism is a monotheistic religion—we believe there is *one* God, not three."

"Avram…"

"I will not tolerate discussion of this pagan perversion of Judaism. I will not have it!" Avram was close to shouting. "I know what you think, what you believe. I do not know why you have worked here, for so long, among us Jews, but we have tolerated you as you argue and wrestle and— yes, okay, *reason*—with the Uncles, but we cannot have any proselytizing, mister gardener. And you will *not* speak to Yitzhak about such things, do you understand? You will be dismissed. I will not have it!"

"Avram…"

"What, by God! What?"

"Avram, you are standing in the manure."

Avram looked down. He was standing in a thick, wet, clumpish, muddy pile of fermenting manure up to his calves. Such a thing had never happened before. In all his years at the Institute, Avram had never even so much as lifted a stone on his property. That he would be standing in a pile of manure was shocking to his sense of cleanliness and order. And then he looked at the gardener.

"You are standing in the manure as well," he said, still shaking.

"Avram, we are both standing in the manure. I am standing here because it is where I belong. You are standing here because you have lost your way; you have ordered your steps incorrectly. But we are both here in the manure, Avram. What does that tell you?"

Deflated, the great doctor lowered his arms and sagged, his intensity disappearing with his dignity. "I don't know, Uncle…what should that tell me?"

"It should tell you, my friend, that we are in the same pile of manure in this life—you, a Jew, and me, an old Christian. Do you not see? The degree to which either of us moves closer to truth—for there is truly only one Truth, Avram—is the degree to which we move closer to each other. The degree to which we move away from that Truth, in our pride or selfishness or our elevation of tradition or lust or power, is the degree to which we move away from each other. This formula, this algorithm, this intertwined relationship between the Jew and the Christian does not apply to all the religions of the world; this is not some 'all roads lead to the top of the mountain' foolishness. Christianity springs from Judaism. Judaism is to Christianity what the roots are to the branches and the leaves and the fruit of the tree, and no true Christian can or should ever lift a finger against a Jew. The central figure in Christianity was a Jew, for God's sake sent to the lost house of Israel. Christianity is to Judaism as the olive is to the tree—it is the fruit, the oil, the sweet essence from the tree which alone is able to bless men. This dynamic doesn't work with other faiths in the world, Avram, because God chose to reveal Himself through the Jews. Why do you think the Jews have had such a hard time of it all these centuries? Man's nature is to hate anything that implies or makes evident to him that God has a sovereign right to rule over mankind, and the very presence of a Jew is the same as God standing there in the manure pile of their lives next to them, poking His finger at them, saying, 'I am the Lord God of All Creation, I made all things, I made you from the dust of the earth, and I am sovereign over my creation, therefore I am worthy to be worshipped *and obeyed* by that which I made.' Men hate this, Avram; they hate it. So that they can ultimately rule upon the earth, they will not stop until they eliminate every Jew from the face of the earth, and in these times to come, they will try to eliminate every true Christian from the earth as well."

Avram looked at the gardener with new eyes, wondering, still a little suspicious. "So…maybe God should choose another people for a while," Avram replied, with the age-old joke from the pogroms. "But we part company over this carpenter from Nazareth, Uncle. God does not split Himself; He is one, not three."

The gardener shook his head in a typical gesture used by a Yiddisher to express disagreement in a collegial fashion. "Avram, let me ask you a question. Do you see those olive trees there?" The gardener pointed to a grove of olive trees that he had planted ten years ago. People said he was incredibly foolish, for olives don't grow in New York, but against all local wisdom they were flourishing. "They will take almost forty years to bear fruit," the gardener said, "and when they do, they will have olives on them, will they not?"

"They will, Uncle."

"And what will you call the fruit from those trees, Avram?"

Avram leaned against the wood of the stall, forgetting the detritus about his feet. "They will be olives…what else can they be."

"You are right, Avram, they'll be olives, just like the trees."

"No," said Avram, seeing where the gardener was going with his argument. "They will *not* be just like the tree. You might call them the fruit from the tree, but not the tree itself."

"But Avram, doesn't the olive have a pit inside it, a seed, which, if you plant it, becomes an olive tree?"

Avram had no answer to this.

"The olive is the tree manifested so that we might benefit from it," the gardener said, "so that we can understand what the tree has to communicate to the world, manifested in a way that gives us joy and nourishment and sustenance. And Avram," he continued, "olives are wonderful to eat, this is true, but to obtain the greatest gift from the tree, you realize that the olives must be crushed to yield their oil? The olive must be pressed until every drop of its life comes out of it, and in this process do we obtain the oil that cools us, that is poured out to flavor our food, to ease our life, to put fat on the bones and smiles on faces above the plates of life. In just such a way did the God of Abraham, Isaac, and Jacob crush His Son so that we might benefit from the oil which flowed thence forth. So tell me, Avram…who are you to tell the Creator of the Universe, blessed be His name, what He can do with His own tree?"

Avram looked at the gardener leaning against the shovel. He was an old man, true, but in the years since he'd come to work it did not seem as if he'd aged a day. Avram considered his own situation. Flies congregated around his shoes, which he would dispose of as soon as he returned to the house. The gardener's argument festered within him like the smell of manure rising up around him, causing an objectionable reaction, but somehow, in this automatic recoiling from the traditional Christian theology, Avram could not help but sense a grain of truth—an earthy truth, admittedly—in the gardener's argument. But earthy truths are no match against centuries of calcified tradition.

"I need to get cleaned up, Uncle," Avram said dismissively.

"You do, Avram," the gardener said heavily, fraught with portent.

"But," Avram said, "with respect, neither you nor anyone I have met in my life has yet explained to me why God would need to send a Son, if indeed He would have a Son, to walk among us. It makes no sense to me."

"It may, perhaps, in time," he said, and after a pause, said "and about Yitzhak?"

Avram waved a hand gently in the air. "I am sorry I spoke to you in such a way, Uncle," he replied. "Of course you can speak to the boy. He has a good head on his shoulders."

"The Uncles disapprove, however, do they not?"

"The Uncles are not stupid. They have known you were different from the day you appeared here, but they have yet to make a sufficient case, though God knows they complain enough. They have told me constantly that you should be dismissed. They think you are going to make the boy goyim. I don't know why they come to *me*, since I don't remember hiring you in the first place." Avram turned and walked gingerly back toward the house.

"The Uncles have always disapproved of me," the gardener said, curiously, "but I love them nonetheless." Avram did not hear this as he squelched off toward the house to recover from the shock of being immersed in that which fueled the growth of so many green things. The gardener wondered if the manure would have the same affect upon the green sapling that had been planted in Avram's spirit.

* * *

One day in the summer of Yitzhak's fifteenth year, Avram, Miriam, and Yitzhak were eating a light lunch of tomatoes, cucumbers, lettuce, pita bread, herring, potatoes, and olives on the patio. There was ice water in a carafe, and lemons, and melons in a glass dish. Light poured down from the sun like a great golden river, washing the farm and the ground and the children with its warmth. It was cool in the Adirondacks, however, unlike the heat that would bake the city, and the family Belinsky was enjoying a pleasant afternoon lunch. The Institute kept them all very busy, and they did not get to see each other often in the middle of the day.

Avram would remember later how quiet things were. He could hear bees flying, dancing directions, searching for pollen. He could hear the wind rustle across the tops of the wheat in the fields. He could hear a hummingbird make its rounds in the garden. The interweaving instruments of nature's orchestra—the heat, the light, the air, the smells, the sounds— all brought to his mind the memory of that day when he rescued Miriam in the river. He looked at her, there at lunch that day across the table from him, and it seemed as if she had not changed a bit; she had simply aged in beauty the way a good wine ages—its outward appearance doesn't change, but the depth and quality of its character enhances over time. It had been so with his wife. He was overwashed with gratefulness. He reached out and grasped her hand, and in that touch she absorbed all that he had been thinking and feeling and her love for him pushed further upwards.

Avram looked then at his son. Yitzhak was fast becoming a man. His shoulders were broadening—no doubt from the work he was doing in the fields with the gardener, Avram thought. He was growing tall; taller, now, than Avram himself, actually. The first wisps of a beard were appearing on his face. He was no longer a boy. The thought brought both pleasure and pain to Avram. He swelled with pride to think of his son as a man, stepping confidently into a life of his own, carrying forth the traditions of his fathers...yet the father in him longed to once more hold a little boy in his lap, to comfort him in his perplexities, and to hear the little boy again reach out to him with tiny arms, calling 'Abba, Abba.'

Just then Yitzhak looked up at him and smiled. It was if the sun had come down to the table and beamed at Avram from across a bowl of olives. Avram's heart was pierced with a love for his boy so sharply that he could not draw breath, and his eyes began to mist from the pure sweetness of it.

"What is it, Abba?" Yitzhak asked.

"Are you okay, Avram?" Miriam asked. She reached out a hand and touched him gently, lovingly, on the forearm.

"Fine, fine...I'm okay," Avram said, wiping the back of his hand across his eyes. "It is just that it is such a beautiful day, and I am such a lucky man." He looked into the eyes of his wife, lifted her hand, and kissed it.

"And you are a good son," he said to Yitzhak.

"You are a good father," the young man replied, standing.

"Where are you going?" Avram asked, not wanting the boy to leave.

"There is wood to be brought in, Abba" he said. "I've cut up several trees, and if we are going to get in twenty cords this year, I've got to start now."

Husband and wife watched with grateful eyes as the boy made his way across the property and disappeared into the tree line.

"He is becoming a man," Miriam said, with an ache that Avram understood all too well.

"It is what boys do," he replied, "and we are luckier than most. That God would give us such a boy, who works with his father, honors his mother, loves the Uncles, and is happy to simply be here in the bosom of the family...we are blessed."

"He will want to start a family one day," she said.

Avram nodded. "One day, true," he replied, "he will find a girl and begin a family. But Miriam, he is only fifteen! We do not need to build a *chuppah* tomorrow, nu?"

Miriam looked off in the direction her son had gone, as though she could still see him. In the voice of a prophetess, she said, "He is not fifteen, Avram...you know this as well as I do. There has always been something... different about Yitzhak, something older—you can see it in his eyes." She paused to take a breath. "And he has already picked out his bride."

Avram was startled by this revelation. He turned most of his upper body to face his wife. To his knowledge Yitzhak had not been off the property for any period of time. "Has he met one of the siblings?" he asked, referring to one of the sisters of the patients, girls who occasionally came with other members of the family to visit their autistic siblings.

"Avram," Miriam said quietly, her eyes looking down at her hands in her lap, "he is in love with Rebecca."

Avram was shocked for only a moment, until he realized the truth of his wife's pronouncement. He had watched Yitzhak over the years work with the girl, extending to her tenderness and consideration and grace. Truthfully, though, there was little progress. She was a disappointment. She remained tightly encased in her own world, unable to break out, unable to communicate. Yitzhak had made some progress in that she no longer tended to physically injure herself, but beyond that, she still could not care for herself. Her father would occasionally come to visit; the mother they had not seen for years.

"He wants to talk to you about her," Miriam said softly.

"What is there to say?" Avram asked with passion, lifting up both of his hands in questioning supplication, as if he were being accosted at God's bar over something for which he was innocent. "What can he be thinking? What kind of a relationship does he think he can have with such a woman? He will be looking after the girl until the day she dies, which could be many, many years from now. Is this the life he wishes for himself?" Avram reached out a hand for reassurance and in fear, taking his wife's hand in his own, and leaned toward her. "He could never do this, Miriam—he could never take his wife's hand and look into her eyes and tell her how much he loves her, and see in her eyes how much she loves him...if she did."

Miriam's eyes brimmed and she squeezed Avram's hand. "I know this," she replied. "I cannot explain it. Perhaps the time he has spent caring for her has created some idea, some dream, that he can rescue her. God knows he is romantic enough for ten boys. Where he gets these ideas, I don't know." She smiled at her husband through forming tears.

"This is impossible," Avram said, as if the pronouncement would seal fate. "There is no way he could have a life with her. I won't permit it."

Miriam looked off into the woods, wondering how much Avram could or could not permit. "You cannot take him away from Rebecca's treatment program, Avram...it would be cruel. She responds only to him, you know."

Avram, caught between his love for his son and his duty as a physician, struggled.

"He is a good boy," Miriam said. "He will see the right way. Let him find it." She patted her husband's arm.

"You're right," Avram replied after a moment. "He will come to his senses."

Yitzhak stopped by Rebecca's room on the way to the forest to look in on her, as was his habit. He pushed open the door and saw her sitting on her bed, curled up, fingers twirling the edge of the bedspread, the edges of her clothing torn in thin strips. Her hair was bedraggled, stringy, and unkempt. She was drooling. He moved slowly toward the chair next to the bed and sat down, folding his hands and composing himself. Rebecca began to moan, which Yitzhak had over the years learned meant that she was taking notice of his presence and was trying to audibly filter the cacophony of input so that she could process anything he might want to say or do. Yitzhak opened a book and began to read quietly. Rebecca stopped moaning; she had adjusted her filter and was ready to process Yitzhak's communication.

Yitzhak read to her in a voice barely above a whisper: "My beloved responded and said to me, 'Arise, my darling, my beautiful one, and come along. For behold, the winter is past, the rain is over and gone. The flowers have already appeared in the land, and the voice of the turtledove has been heard in our land. The fig tree has ripened its figs, and the vines in blossom have given forth their fragrance. Arise, my darling, my beautiful one, and come along!'"

Rebecca's hands fluttered and she seemed to try and bury her face in her hands. Yitzhak stopped reading and placed one hand upon the arm of his chair, closest to where Rebecca sat upon the bed against the wall. Face turned away from him, pressed into the padded surface, with one hand she pounded and pounded...and the other stretched slowly across her body to rest on Yitzhak's hand as lightly as a hummingbird touches a flower.

* * *

At sixteen, Yitzhak was a head taller than his father and much broader of shoulder, but he still followed him everywhere, working at his request with various patients, always making an improvement in their lives. Avram's relationship with his son was such that he openly discussed Rebecca with him.

"Tell me about her," he asked, not long after the conversation he'd had with Miriam in which he'd discovered that there might be something between his son and a severely-disabled autistic girl.

Dashing Avram's hopes that he had come to his senses, Yitzhak instead confirmed the opposite. Yitzhak was not shy; very direct, he would not dissemble, and said, "I was made for her, Abba. It is the only way I can explain it. I feel as if it is the other half of my soul, languishing there behind those green eyes of hers, trapped with her in that prison."

Even while the father's heart was breaking he exulted in the nobility and courage of his son's soul. But he could not let the question go unasked. "Yitzhak, what kind of a life would you have with her?"

"Father, I do not know what kind of life I would have with her, to say honestly. But I can tell you that without her I would have no life at all. Oh, things would be fine here, I would continue to work with you and mother and the Uncles, helping, doing things as you need me to, but my heart, Abba, my heart is locked up with this girl…with Rebecca."

Had it been any other sixteen-year old boy, Avram would have dismissed this as mere uninformed, youthful ignorance. Yet he knew that his son was neither uninformed about love nor ignorant. Yitzhak had seen, and they had talked endlessly about, true love, relationships, and what a man must be and do in a relationship so that two souls can blend into one. And more than talk, Yitzhak had seen such a thing modeled before him in the lives of his father and mother. He had spoken with the gardener about these things as well, and despite their differences about the carpenter from Nazareth, there was a great similarity in how the old man with dirt constantly on his hands viewed the role and responsibility of a husband in a marriage. And there was one other thing that Avram heard in his son's voice—a tone, actually, that he had not heard in many years, since another young man stood on a sandy spit of land, watching a wet, bedraggled girl stand and look at him, when both recognized in that moment that their souls were knit. Such instantaneous impressions were death to most young people, raised as they were in the shallow soil of the prevalent culture, but Avram knew that Yitzhak was anything but shallow, and he saw with the pain of recognition that same awareness in Yitzhak that had surfaced in his own heart about Miriam.

Avram loved his son. Avram loved the children who were brought to him as well, but he loved Yitzhak in the way that only a parent can love the child that springs from their body. Perhaps it was this love, and the fact that Avram trusted his son completely, and knew his son well—because, after all, he was his father—that Avram took the steps he did.

* * *

One evening in the last days of the winter of Yitzhak's eighteenth year, when Avram felt he could no longer delay, when he felt he could no longer bear to watch his son's suffering as Yitzhak grew increasingly attached to the incapacitated young girl, as he watched her become a woman, yet a woman descending into a dark abyss before his eyes, as he came to believe that there was but one hope remaining, he asked Yitzhak to speak with him in his study.

It was dark, with stars splashed across the sky like spectators in a great, hushed celestial auditorium, waiting for a show they had seen once long ago to be replayed. Yitzhak came in from the field. From the look on his face, Avram could see that he had been in prayer, agonizing again, beseeching the God of Heaven and Earth for the soul of his beloved. Tears had frozen on his face in the cold wind; his cheeks were red and chapped. His hands were raw and impervious to cold. Yitzhak wore only a short-sleeve shirt as the snow began to fall in the dark. He shook the snow from his feet against the stone steps leading to his father's study and looked at him grimly. Avram could tell immediately that Yitzhak knew they would be discussing Rebecca, and the determination he saw in Yitzhak's face spoke volumes to him about the course of action he would take this night.

They gathered around Avram's large cherry desk. Miriam was there, sitting next to her husband, face red from crying but trusting him nonetheless: she was trembling like a bird. There was a fire in the grate; candles were lit against the wall, and Yitzhak sat down facing his parents.

"Yitzhak, we must talk...about Rebecca."

The young man nodded. "I thought as much, Abba. I still feel the same; more so, if anything, since we last spoke of her." There was steel in his son's voice, not rebellion, but Avram had expected it.

"I know, my son, I know. But I have a question for you. Do you... do you think it would be possible for you to reach Rebecca as things now stand, if you were to continue on the way things are?"

Yitzhak thought for a moment. "You would know better than I, Abba. I haven't seen much progress, frankly, in the years that she's been here. I cannot explain how or why I feel the way I do; I only know that my soul is knit with hers, and I would do anything to free her from her prison."

Avram nodded slowly; this was what he thought Yitzhak would say. Avram felt he could not go on. His voice was choking from emotion, his heart breaking, but he had to continue.

"Yitzhak, there is something...something your mother and I must present to you—an option, shall we say—that you must disclose to no one."

"What is it, Abba?"

"We think...we think there is a way that you might reach Rebecca."

For Yitzhak the words exploded in the night air like sparkling light around a door suddenly opened in a dark recess of black sky; for his parents, they were like words that threatened to choke out what light existed in their world. Avram thought of his first conversation with the gardener eighteen years ago and shuddered.

"You have seen how, for some reason, one autistic child can sometimes more effectively communicate with another. Yitzhak, I...I and one of the Uncles have developed...a formula...that can make a person autistic. It only works when taken by someone not beyond a certain age, who also possesses the rarest of blood types—Bombay blood, of the sub-type h-h."

Yitzhak's entire body pulsed forward; his hands gripped the edges of his chair, and tears sprang to his eyes, for Yitzhak knew the implications of these conditions as well as he knew his own blood type—Bombay blood. "Father, if you can...if you can truly do this..."

"Wait, wait, Yitzhak, please, let me finish," Avram said, struggling to speak coherently through his emotion. His son's reaction—the courage, the sacrificial spirit, the nobility—was breaking his heart. Avram held up a hand, palm out. "I think...I think we can put you into that world, Yitzhak...the world of the autistic person. But as I said, we can only do this with the young. If we wait, say, until you are in your mid-twenties, your thirties, it will not work. Typically a man waits until then to choose the woman he...he marries...at least, this is the current wisdom." Miriam put an arm on his to steady him, and her touch recalled to him how old he was when he first knew that he would marry his wife, and it helped him to continue.

"So...because of your love for this girl, and because of our love and the trust we repose in you, and because you are the only person we know within a thousand miles that has the necessary blood type, and because of how you feel for this girl, we must put this great, terrible, daring choice before you now, and not ten years from now, my beloved boy, my precious son. I can put you in that world, but Yitzhak...you must know that I have no idea how to bring you forth from it."

The prospect of losing fellowship with his parents struck Yitzhak then like ice water. More intense even than his love for Rebecca was his love for his mother and father. "Would I know...would I know who you were again if...if you did this, Abba?"

Avram bent his head in his hands and wiped the tears forming there in his eyes. His voice was not above a whisper. "I...I cannot say for certain, Yitzhak. I do not know how such a thing might work, either way, going or coming. It might not affect you at all, or it might put you in a completely vegetative state—we do not know."

There was silence for but a moment. "You will find a way, Abba," the boy replied. The degree of trust Yitzhak had for his father brought tears to his mother's eyes. She could only see a young boy of five, crying for another small child who could not speak or understand. "I will find her, if you can only put me into her world. I will find a way to reach her, I *know* it. This is what I was born to do. Only...only do not forsake me, Abba. Bring me home to you."

Avram had no idea what gave Yitzhak such confidence. Perhaps it was only hope, speaking upon the shoulders of love, which affirmed in his son's heart Avram's ability to bring about that which he had been unable to do for most of his professional life. Yitzhak saw his father's hesitation.

"Abba, you *must* do this. Tell me what I need to do; I will do anything to reach them—and I *will* reach them, Abba, do you understand? If I can reach Rebecca on the wings of my love for her, what will the power of your love for all these children not fail to accomplish through me? Let me go, Abba...let me do this thing." The young man, tall, broad-shouldered, courageous of heart, knew exactly what his father was offering. Avram thought that perhaps love for Rebecca blinded him to the possibilities of failure—love for Rebecca, and trust in his father.

So it was that they consulted the Uncle. There was a quick session in the laboratory and a vial was produced, which Yitzhak would drink that very evening. Avram said it would begin its work very quickly. "Expect to see changes in twenty-four hours, my son. If you can, share with us what is happening. It would be..." here Avram choked on his words again, struggling, "it would be valuable information to help others."

In his bedroom, his mother and father kissed him and Avram laid his hands on the boy's head and recited a blessing in Hebrew. The Uncle handed him the vial, and Yitzhak, trembling, beads of sweat on his forehead, looked directly into his father's eyes and said, "I will see you again, Abba, and I will know you." The ghost of the gardener's point about knowing God wisped like a tendril of smoke through Avram's consciousness. The boy looked once into the cup and saw Rebecca reflected in the blood-red liquid. "Thank you," he said, looking up, and drank the cup.

Throughout the next days, Avram was by his son's side constantly. The formula had begun to work at once. The morning of the first day, Yitzhak marveled aloud to his father.

"Abba…Abba, everything is light; fractured, piercing, splaying around me. Wait, no, do not move…please, stay still. Move your hand, there…like that. My God, watch the light! Abba, see the light from your fingers! What is happening? What is happening? I can see that you are nervous and upset. Light is shooting from you like an explosion! Is this what they see? O God, how can they live in such confusion?"

By the second day, when Avram would say something, Yitzhak would visibly recoil. "Oh, Abba, it is so loud, it is like the sound of…of many waters, all around me, rushing past…make it slow down, please, Abba, make it slow down."

On the third day Yitzhak's eyes were wide open and he was beginning to rock. "I cannot feel my body, Abba. Where am I? Where are my arms, my legs? I can only feel them when I rock, Abba." Avram's tears spilled like the water his son was describing, like great rivers. What had he done?

That afternoon, Yitzhak whispered to his father. "Abba…Abba, there are so many things here…let me count them…let me count." Yitzhak's eyes glazed, staring off into the ceiling, rocking, curled in the corner of his bed against the wall.

An hour later, suddenly, with no warning or transition, Yitzhak sat bolt upright and waved at something in the air. "Abba, Abba," he yelled, "do not forsake me!" Yitzhak said nothing more. After long minutes, then hours without further speech or movement from his son, Avram put his face in his hands and cried.

On the seventh day, after they perceived that Yitzhak had stabilized into what was unmistakably a severe autistic state, they brought Rebecca into the room.

Nothing happened.

Nothing happened for two days. For two days they sat, each in their own world. Rebecca would alternately rock or moan or dribble, or make nonsensical motions with her hands or arms, flapping, shouting, or crying. Yitzhak would sit there, quietly, making no sound, making no motion, but simply staring at the girl across the room.

On the third day the gardener, who had by means unknown to Avram or Miriam or the Uncles discerned the experiment, came to the back door of the home and knocked once. Miriam answered. "Oh, Uncle, yes, what can we do for you?" She cleared her throat once, softly. "Is there something you need?" Her face was blotchy and strained. She had lost her only son and her heart was breaking.

"Miriam, my dear, yes, please...take me to see Yitzhak."

Miriam's eyes widened. "I'm...I'm sorry, but I can't do that, Uncle, he is...he isn't..." She looked around, one hand raised slightly in desperation, turning halfway back toward the rooms within the house in a gesture that spoke of tender agony, the most excruciating helplessness.

"I know where he is, and what he is about, dearest woman. Take me to see him."

Avram spoke from within. "Who is it, Miriam?"

"It is...it is the gardener."

There was a silence in the house, as there would be, thought the gardener, for about half an hour in heaven after a trumpet sounded. He could hear Avram making his labored way to the door.

Avram came and stood before the gardener. One might have thought Avram would meet the man with bombast, with fury, with a tirade at injustice, a complaint against the bar of Heaven...but no. The act of sacrificing his only son had changed Avram in ways that not even his wife had yet to perceive—but the gardener did.

"My friend, come, let us talk," he said gently. Avram opened the door to the study and, broken as he was, the door to his heart, and the two men were, for a time, one.

After they had spoken for a while, the gardener asked Avram to take him to see Yitzhak. "I want to pray for him."

At first Avram was ready to argue, but the heart to argue had been taken from him, and so he just waved his hand weakly. "Do what you wish,

Uncle. Let us see what the carpenter from Nazareth can do, if he can do anything."

"Anything indeed," said the gardener under his breath. They walked down the hallway toward the treatment room, the gardener wearing dirty khaki coveralls over a faded red cotton shirt, Avram in black pants and a rumpled white shirt over his tallit. The older man wiped his hands on a rag and stuck the rag in his back pocket and Avram opened the door.

Yitzhak sat quietly in a corner of the room; Rebecca, in a corner opposite. Yitzhak was waving an arm toward the light that flowed in through a window. Rebecca was slowly and rhythmically pounding her head softly against the padded wall. An attendant sat unobtrusively behind a wall partition, hands folded solemnly. The gardener advanced into the center of the room and looked at the two young people. To Avram and Miriam standing behind him, it seemed as if the gardener was simply standing in the center of the room like a weathered statue, imbibing the inevitable.

But to the two young patients in the room, things appeared very differently. The light, once fractured and lacerating, became coherent, soothing, and restorative. The colors were stilled, their cacophony diminished and then disappeared, and the light began instead to soothe and caress. There was order and peace in the room, and the very motes of dust caught floating in the beam of light from the window aligned before Yitzhak's eyes. He turned in amazement to see the reason for the miracle, and saw the gardener standing in the middle of the room. Yitzhak was confused at first, because the gardener did not seem to be an old man. Rebecca, her head turning, attention arrested by the blinding, soothing wash of light that sparkled from the middle of the room, also saw.

"Now children," Avram heard the gardener say, "you should speak with each other." And he turned and walked out, followed by a distraught Miriam and Avram, broken shells.

"They will be fine," the gardener said to Miriam, patting her arm, and touching Avram's shoulder gently. "Let them be for a while, Abraham; you will see." He left them at the door to the treatment room, holding each other, stunned, distraught afresh that the old man—he was just a *gardener*, for God's sake—would step so far from the realm of his own limited expertise, so far beyond the realm of what was possible, and hold out false hope to wound their hearts afresh.

Yet it was as the gardener had foreseen. That very afternoon, Rebecca, for the first time since she had come to the Institute, began to focus on her surroundings. Yitzhak traced his hand through the air, and then moved his body rhythmically. Rebecca seemed to understand the movement. She moved closer. Yitzhak would count slowly, out loud, in a rhythm that Avram could not discern, but which, apparently, was attracting Rebecca's attention.

Three days after the gardener had entered the room, in the morning just as the light was coming in from the east, Rebecca seemed to recognize Yitzhak and crawled across the floor to his side. Yitzhak saw her as she approached and, with indescribable joy, Avram watched the light of recognition appear on his son's face, and then a look of pure, fierce, conquering love. Yitzhak put his arm around the girl and she put her head on his chest.

"Yitzhak," Rebecca said in a thin, weak voice, "you came." The young man folded Rebecca in his arms and they both leaned against the wall, crying together from relief, drained, resting to gather strength for the rest of their lives. Avram collapsed to his knees from gratitude and joy, and Miriam wept at his side.

"Abba," Yitzhak said, reaching out a hand to his father. "He brought me back." Avram took it, and with joy indescribable was struck with his one final great epiphany—that he had been given the priceless gift of *experiencing* how God felt, and understanding to just the smallest degree what it took for an all-powerful God to send His only Son—out of love for a future bride, out of love for a woman to whom his soul was knit. He saw in Yitzhak that he was of himself, yet different. Yitzhak was Avram made manifest in different form, and the parallel was so clear, so plain, so simply declared whenever a father and mother brought forth a child, that he marveled that he had not seen it before. And Yitzhak, by his willingness to sacrifice everything, carried out the very deepest desires of his own heart and the deepest desire of his father's heart as well. In essence, Yitzhak had become Avram in a form best able to reach Rebecca. Avram knew now— knew with a certainty that could not be dislodged and which he would carry to his very grave—that the gardener had been right and he had been wrong, for he knew now how God felt. He knew now why God had to make Abraham feel the pain and fear and utter desolation the loss of an only son would cause—because God wanted Abraham to know how *He* would feel, sacrificing His only Son as well. And it was in this activity of experiencing the things that God experiences that Avram came finally to know God experientially. He bowed his head in pure wonder and worship at the amazing love He must have had to sacrifice such a precious Son, and as he bowed his head, surrendered in his heart his contention with the gardener.

In the days to come, Yitzhak's ability to heal autistic children, restoring them to wholeness, would seem to be almost miraculous. He did not restore every child, for while he reached every one, some would reject his miraculous attempts to communicate, and for them, Yitzhak realized, there was no hope of breaking free from their prison. They would continue to flap, or moan, or count, or pound themselves against their surroundings until such time as their physical bodies relinquished their hold on life and their spirits pounded their way down into eternal damnation. But those who responded to Yitzhak were brought forth out of their darkness and with tears of joy he led forth the captives into a world of light and clarity and understanding and truth.

And Rebecca, whole of mind and body, brought forth a son, Yaacov, upon Avram's knees. And there was great joy in heaven.

"Come now and let us reason together," says the Lord, "though your sins are as scarlet, they will be as white as snow. Though they are red like crimson, they will be like wool."

Note to Horatio

This town has a beautiful river. I moved here two years ago after losing most of my earthly possessions, even more of my money, and all of my heart because of one blatant act of disobedience twenty-five years ago. When I am sitting by myself in the quiet of the evening and think about it seriously, I realize the river is what drew me here, and my fascination for it convinced me to lay out the remaining chunk of savings I'd accumulated throughout a decidedly ill-advised life. I remember this river for a lot of reasons but mainly because there were times when I'd walk onto the bridge and look down into the infinite, swirling dance of constantly-moving perfection, and the water and the foam coursing over and through the rocks would call to mind that in the midst of constant and chaotic movement there was a singular direction and flow, and that within its seemingly gentle appearance was inherent power and the potential for dangerous transformation. I would stare at it endlessly—moving water has a fascination for me that I cannot explain. I only know that as I watch it, I see infinity, and the hand of the Infinite, in marvelous liquid complexity. I once stood on a beach and watched waves crash against the sand and had one of my first conversations with God in which there was the give-and-take of dialogue that one normally has in a conversation with a friend, face-to-face. I would pose an assertion or ask a question, and the reply would be there in my mind, unbidden, not something that came from my own mind. It was undoubtedly an interposition of external thoughts and ideas. The written word is one thing: keen, precious, a standard beyond measure, immutable. The Living Word is He who is described in the writing. I have always thought that the written word was like a love letter from a suitor to his beloved, and the Living Word the suitor himself. I believe now that the written word was intended to introduce us to the Living Word, the Logos. I believe the men who wrote the New Testament would not have confused what was written with the One they wrote about.

I bought a hundred acres up on what passes for a mountain in these parts, with a farm house that looks down on that river. I was forty-seven that year, with a depressing but persistent spare tire, graying hair, five years to go on my alimony payments and a list of three fairly well-received novels to my credit. I hadn't written anything worth reading, anything that could be said to artistically represent truth or beauty, in twenty months. Writing is like music; you need to have the heart for it. Your heart needs to be free to rise up and sing as the passion and beauty and sweetness and the bitterness of heartbreak becomes real to you—like the taste of grapefruit juice when you are desperately thirst—before you can push it out of your soul wrapped in words. But when your heart has been ripped away as if someone has roared by in a freight train and reached down and lifted your suitcase as you waited at the station…well then, there isn't much you can do.

So I took a job writing proposals for an old friend. He works for a defense contracting firm trying to break into new markets. Fortunately the firm doesn't have anyone on staff who can write cogently enough to guarantee at least a reasonable chance of success, and in this lack do I find my current job security. God looks after writers by populating businesses with engineers. Once they become prosperous, engineers stand up at rubber-chicken dinners and make jokes about "those who can, do, and those who can't, write". Nonetheless, engineers cannot do what I do, fortunately, which is to sell—convincingly—on paper, and so they let me write from home. I work quickly, do my own graphics, and do not charge them an arm and a leg. Internet connectivity has just come to the county. You can call Jeanie at the Internet place and she'll get you signed up in about a week or two. If you want DSL, they may have to run a line out from the nearest junction box, though, which means they'll need to get Artis out, and he's pretty busy these days. Little did my company know just how thin a thread sustained their proposal efforts. A short, fat telecommunications specialist named Artis, who does not yet shave and devours yo-yos and chews gum at the same time, who drives to each site in a horribly rusted pickup truck laden with enough tools to fix Guatemala, wields an electronic sword of Damocles over the necks of eighteen PhD's.

Home was now a farmhouse in the northern woods in Maine, with Snap—Snap the Border Collie, who also happens to be the smartest dog in creation. Home was where the great lesson of obedience would be repeatedly burned into my soul with the Refiner's fire as I nestled into a threadbare recliner near the wood stove on winter nights and pulled from the Gospel of John the rich descriptions of Christ's unfailing, unflinching persistence in doing His Father's will; from MacDonald, who wrote with such tender compassion and deep wisdom about God's love and the imperative necessity of obedience in the Believer's life. I would read these truths and others and recall my past—my disobedience and the pain it caused others—and, like piranha swarming, like a roaring, crushing bear, like a black and poisonous lizard on my back, these memories, my past sins, would rise and mock me and I would crumble into great wracking sobs of remorse and repentance, gasping to Him, wondering where my children were, wondering if they were safe, wondering if… wondering if I would survive this.

* * *

The first day after I bought the farm I was walking up the hill (I won't call it a mountain) along the back edge of the property when Snap alerted. He crouched down in that posture Border Collies assume when they're ready to work, like missiles about to be launched should you but press the button. There was a rustling in the woods ahead. I'd heard all the neighbors and the real estate agent joke about being careful—it was moose rutting season—but seriously, who thinks they'll encounter a moose in the woods? One sees moose on post-cards, not in the wild, in the flesh.

It wasn't a moose. It was man, wearing an old Vietnam-era faded green field jacket plastered with patches, jeans that could have used patches, good hunting boots, an orange cap from Bob and Ted's Gun Shop, and carrying a very old but nicely-cared-for .410-gage shotgun…on my property.

"Well, hey, fella, how you doin'?" he says, in that flat Maine accent with those long, drawn-out syllables, the last of which are usually like eyebrows on Groucho Marx; they go up so high you just can't believe it at first, and they're up all the time, but then you get used to them.

"Hello sir," I reply. "Any luck out here?" I didn't want to mention the fact that he was on my land. He was, after all, a strange-looking bearded man with a gun; I was a much-less fit man, beardless, with a small pen.

"Oh," he says, making the word sound like a food processor into which someone has just dumped a handful of gravel, "there ain't nuthin' out here. I'm just takin' a little walk." He pauses and looks me up and down, then looks at the dog.

"That there's a smart dog," he says immediately, after sizing up Snap for maybe twelve milliseconds. Some people can just look at a dog's face and know the dog, and others just see teeth; life in a nutshell. Snap wags his tail. Dogs are smarter than we think.

"He does okay," I reply.

"You the fella just bought th' old Marlboro place?"

"If you mean that old run-down farm right…well, right here, yes sir, that would be me."

"Killie Swanson," he says, and sticks out a hand, as though I'm the first of a thousand constituents with ten more counties to hit before the vote, but I'm the most important. The .410 is cradled in his other arm. I shake his hand and glance over his patches. Some are off-the-wall patches you could buy at a gun show, but there are others that one doesn't normally see for sale; patches you have to earn, by risking your lifeblood. I see a combat infantryman's badge with a wreath—you don't get those at gun shows. There was a strange patch I'd never seen, but only heard about, with some sort of Latin inscription underneath a picture of a rat carrying a flashlight and a pistol. I have an inordinate amount of respect for men who have risked their lives, enduring the prospect of death or injury by bullet, rocket, mortar, or shell so that we might have a civil society uninterrupted by those who would deny us such blessings. There in the woods, translating the Latin, I realized what Killie Swanson had done in the war.

I took his hand and shook it. "Jeremiah...Jeremiah Giordano."

"Well, nice to meet you, Jemmy." I was taken aback by the man's use of the diminutive; the only other person who called me that was my mother, before she passed away. I had no idea how this old man latched onto it right away.

There was something open and honest about him, standing there in the woods, the scent of hardwood and pine filtering down through the blue Maine air in a light breeze, the dog standing there smiling up at him. If Snap likes somebody, that says a lot to me. He's got a sort of built-in bad-man detector—I've seen it in horses, too—that I'd trust over an entire brigade of psychoanalysts. Swanson just stood there, smiling, sizing me up, as though he thought this encounter the keenest thing in the world. Strange...as I got to know him, he would seem the most natural, the most relaxed, and the most, well, the most *where he belonged* when he was in the woods. There was something that came over him—or, rather, something that departed, that shook off his back like scales—when he stepped into the woods with a gun. He seemed most at peace then. I'd visit him in his trailer or ride around with him occasionally in his ancient, battered old Toyota pick-up truck, and he'd still be the same gentle soul, but there would always be something nagging at him, something pulling or grabbing for his attention, something under the surface constantly—as if he'd been sitting on a sharp rock for just a little too long—that disappeared when he was in the woods.

"Well, come on, young fella,"—yes, he actually calls me *young fella*, and yes, real people still use such phrases—"let's git on down the hill." He starts walking back down the way I've come; I start walking with him. There is something irresistible about the man's friendliness. It hits you like a wave; it smashes into you from one direction and then pulls your legs in the other—regardless, you can't stand still.

"So how much ya pay for the place?" This question from any other human being on the planet would have been downright invasive. In my previous life, I would have bridled (at least inwardly, while striving to maintain the proper external Christian demeanor) and demurred. But there was something about the man—it is *so* hard to describe. He just looked at you with eyes that were happy and sad at the same time. He so plainly expected an answer, so plainly didn't have any thought of offending, and so plainly thought that the question was the most natural thing in the world, that, well, he just asked. And I just answered.

"Pretty much an even one-sixty," I said…the very truth.

He smacked his free hand up against his orange hat. "Ojeez," he says, laughing, or groaning, I couldn't discern which. "They seen you a-comin'." Now, this is not something one who has just been through the most crushing divorce in the history of civilization needs to hear. It is not something calculated to boost one's confidence, nor is it something that one typically hears from complete strangers one meets in the woods carrying weapons, and it most certainly is not something one hears from those who are set on making friends. Yet I listened to him and smiled and it was fine. His warm and friendly heart burned through any crust social conventions might have layered onto my reception equipment.

While I'm walking down the hill with Killie I do not wonder why I feel so comfortable. This is strange, because I'm typically shy, wickedly intense about my privacy, and in forty-seven years have garnered maybe two, possibly three people I'd call close friends. Yet if this man asks me to tell him the story of my life while we walk, after knowing him for all of about four minutes, I don't think I'd hesitate telling him my deepest fears or my worst failings. Maybe this is a symptom of going through a divorce that shakes a person to their core, convincing them that they are worthless and starving them for any sign of human compassion that doesn't smack of condemnation. I think this is strange for maybe two seconds, but then I look down and see Snap trotting by his side, tongue lolling, head up, trying to get Killie's attention. He reaches down and pats Snap's head, and the dog gambols, enraptured, like the first dog being petted by the first man.

Snap never does this. Snap is as shy as I am. But I don't wonder about these things, which is also a wonder in itself.

There is sort of a strange golden, backlit, streaming diffusion of light that filters around or sparkles over everything—the man, the dog, the gravel in the road, the sun pouring down through the tops of the trees standing there like armed guards at a convention of world leaders. Peace—*that* is what this unreal sense of reality is. The recognition of an amazing sense of relaxed contentment and security comes upon me, as surprising as if an alien from New York City—who I would recognize from magazines— suddenly appeared next to us in the woods.

This sensation is strange to me because I can't remember when I've felt this before. I try and recall when in my past life there was this sense of utter and complete abandonment, a feeling that you could lay back into the arms of God and he would take care of the world, and there wasn't a thing called stress or anxiety or pressure or pain. I think the last time I could remember this feeling was when I was twelve, and my parents bought me my first war game (it was the one with little cardboard counters with pictures of ships printed on them, and you would steam them around on your table or living room floor, under the table legs, and blast each other into floating wreckage with their monstrously accurate naval guns). I think one of the best days in my life was that day when I realized that I would have an entire holiday free to simply lose myself in that era of great sea battles, to utterly disappear into an alternate awareness in which I could do great deeds, endure risk and the splash of shells and the smell of cordite and salt water and the blast of explosive powder, all to possibly save a great empire, to crush those who were truly evil. I never played against anyone or with anyone; the experience for me wasn't about competition but, as I now realize, the opportunity to simply step out of a stressful and difficult childhood and into another time. I didn't want to clutter such an opportunity with competition. Besides the occasional few hours granted over the years immersed in truly great novels, I think those days were the happiest I'd known; sad, when you think about it.

Or maybe it was the day my daughter was born—such a peace I remember that day; such a glow, a spreading, diffusing sense of illumination in a new and wondering realization of the beauty of life, as if God, in manifesting this little miracle, let some of the magic out of the bag during the process and it spilled into my soul—my daughter, who grew eventually to become a stranger to me, someone who hated the One I came to love; my precious daughter, who became dark, dressed in black, who wandered in strange places at night in college, whose artwork reflected such talent, but contained such disturbed, frightful, angry, bitter, heartbroken images. Strange, that the birth of a human creature—whose nature, like all humans, is flawed—would bring such an advent of peace and yet afterward eventuate in a crushing weight of guilt and sadness. Yet even so, walking there in the woods with this man, feeling that same sense of golden peace like light layering down gently in one's soul, I cannot say that I wouldn't embark upon fathering that daughter again, even in the face of all the subsequent pain. O God, would that I could, knowing what I know now…would that I could…and with this thought, another came: perhaps this is how God feels about us.

"So what do you do fer a livin', young feller," he asks.

"I'm a writer," I reply, coming out of a very dark hole in the canyons of my memory. "At the moment, I'm between books, so I'm working to help out some business partners."

"I figured as much. You look like you write a lot."

I can't decipher exactly what it is in my appearance that would cause anyone to conclude that I write. I don't usually sport unsightly ink stains on my fingers. I have no quill pens or nibs protruding from my pockets; no scraggly, unshaven countenance; no raggedy, thread-bare black frock coat down to mid-thigh.

"Do you have land up here?" I ask, hoping to steer the conversation away from anything that will get too personal too quickly.

"My Granddaddy's place, right up there," he says, pointing back up the hill, thick with new-growth pine and hardwood saplings. "Got a small camp; I like to git away now and again, come up and just sit and listen to the trees and watch the animals go by."

"You get anything today?" I ask, noting his reference to animals, wondering about his shotgun.

"Naauuuggghhhh," he says, worrying the word like a terrier would shake a particularly recalcitrant rat, making that food processor sound again. "Ain't really up here to hunt...got plenty to eat. Just up fer a walk."

I nod, deciding not to mention the potential navigational error that guided him onto my property instead of his. Somehow, up here in the midst of such an amazing display of majestic, divinely-created beauty, a miserly concern over some line in the dirt was inappropriate at best.

"God made a good day today," I say, thinking of the trees, the river I loved, the smells, the stones in the earth that spoke to me of God's strength and permanence, and the strange peace that seemed to embrace the encounter.

"O, no doubt, no doubt, Jemmy. You a big church-goer, are ya?" Killie never did fuss about with conversational subtleties.

"Killie...there was a time in my life when I would have said yes, and felt proud about it. Now, I go to church to hear God talk to me," I replied. "All the other foolishness is, to me, just that—foolishness. And lately, there is so much of that that I'm not sure I want to spend the time going to church any longer. But I don't link obedience to God with going to church, if that's what you're asking."

He nodded while I spoke. I could see him thinking about what I'd said. The road we were taking spilled like a river of crushed rock out of the overhanging trees into a clearing. The trees gave way to a meadow that ran down the hill and opened up to a dramatic view of the entire valley. We could see for fifty miles—rolling hills like waves covered in thick green foam, cut by lines of roads or rivers, dotted with homes filled with people whom God loved. There was a lake in the distance, resting like water in the palm of God's hand. He waved the muzzle of his shotgun in the air slowly, transcribing a circle that took in the entire scene. "There's plenty of God to see up here," he said.

I just nodded. I'm not a confrontational person, and while I knew all the arguments and doctrines and Scriptures that would have shot holes in his 'woodsman's theology', I didn't have the heart, nor did I feel led to embark upon that line of discussion. I didn't know him well enough to understand as deeply as I needed to the words that were simply the tip of his spiritual iceberg. And I'm not sure Snap would have approved if I'd have fussed about it.

I was sitting in my kitchen two days later when the gravel in the driveway announced a visitor. I didn't get many visitors. In my state, I wasn't sure I wanted any. I put down the book I was reading, picked up the cereal bowl, set it in the sink, wiped my hands, and opened the door to the mud room.

An older man and a lady I took to be his wife stood there next to a relatively functional farm sedan. Cars up here are graded on the degree to which they look capable of surviving the winter without falling apart from rust or sliding off the road into a ditch.

"Hello," said the nice lady, extending a yellow covered dish with little white flowers around the border. She had a towel under the dish; it was hot.

"Hi," I said. "Thanks for coming by." They'd come to visit, and there was no reciprocal wonderment on my part why. It was what people did here.

"No trouble," said the man. He was stocky, with blue work pants and an old but clean flannel shirt under a Carhartt jacket. One glance at his hands told me that he didn't write for a living; here was a farmer and no mistake.

"Come on in," I said, opening the door wider, and after putting their coats in the mudroom and setting the hot dish (hamburger casserole) on the oven, we sat down at the small wooden kitchen table. In this part of the world—come to think of it, in most parts of the world where people earn their bread with their hands—people visit in kitchens.

"Welcome to the neighborhood," they said, in the same long, drawn-out accent that Killie had. "I'm Tommy Larson, and this here's Katy. We thought you might do with a good hot meal. Katy makes a pretty mean stew mash."

"Jeremiah Giordano, and thank you very much," I said. "It'll save me from cooking tonight." There is a strange but prevalent assumption among Americans that single men do not cook, as if cooking is some type of genetic characteristic possessed only by the female of the species. I like my cooking; actually, I like my cooking better than most restaurants I've been to. But cooking for others is one way to extend kindness tangibly. 'Here,' a gift of food seems to say, 'let me present you with something that took some of my money'—which translates to value—'and some of my time'—which translates to something of more value—'and, using my creativity and industry, fashion you something that will satisfy your body and perhaps feed your soul.' Against such things there is no law.

"So you bought the old Marlboro place," the woman said. She must have been in her late fifties or early sixties, with soft brown hair just slightly beginning the inevitable dash through gray to blue.

"I did that, Katy. And I'll tell you why. Look out the window there," and I pointed toward the kitchen window that looked unabashedly down upon the town's river, not a half-mile below. "I could stare at that river for a month and still not digest all the complexity it has to offer."

They stared at me as if I'd just spoken in Greek. I could tell that this sortie into the poetic was not something they were used to. I caught myself up. "It's just that I liked the view."

"Well, sure, we can understand that. Old Susie Marlboro loved to sit out there on the porch and just listen to that water. Strangest thing was old Susie." Katy looked off for a moment, probably remembering an old woman who my writer's brain conjured as sitting in a rocking chair with a shawl, peeling potatoes or carrots, dropping them with a plinking sound like slow rain into an old tin pan, rocking back and forth, listening to the river like other people listen to their doctor.

"You all settled in?" she asked.

"I am, thank you. I've figured out where the hardware store is, and where I can buy eggs and milk, and I've got a line on someone who'll drop about six or seven cords of wood by for the winter."

"You got a wood stove, then?" Tommy asked. "Marlboro heated the house with oil."

"Of course he's got a wood stove," Katy answered. "Oil was a hundred dollars a barrel then; it's three hundred a barrel now and no end in sight. He's a smart young man, of course he put in a wood stove."

She turned to me. "Now we want you to know, Mr. ...Mr. Jordani (the folks up here in Maine aren't too facile with names that end in vowels), that you're invited to come by church on Sunday. We'd sure like to have you. It's a nice little group, been there for almost two hundred years, and it's a warm community. I think you'll like it." She wasn't smarmy or saccharine or embarrassed or sinuous. She was truly hoping that I'd come to their church because, most probably, she thought it would do me—actually, that it would do anyone—some good.

There is a strange thing about America, something I've seen on the political maps that show the states colored in hard, clearly-lined, strident, argumentative red and blue. It seems that wherever there is a profusion of wealth, wherever people have moved to and work predominately in the cities or dense urban environments and involve themselves with the things which primarily revolve around what *man* does, or what *man* has produced, or where great sums of money are made, people tend to move away from a dependence on an individual, personal God and begin instead to believe that man himself—or their own special higher power, "Man" in the collective—can fashion his own Utopia. It must be that the skyscrapers, the freeways, the computer-controlled sewers and power stations and construction projects and malls exert some strange fascination, some weird urban spell that convinces those in their proximity that such things are, in fact, Utopian, and that man himself, if only given complete reign, could make things even better. So the blue states are those where the people vote for the politicians who seek greater and more intrusive control by the State over people's lives, because it is only through centralized control that man can bring about his Utopia. Yet where people tend to hold on to their own land, where men and women scrabble for their food from a hard and rocky soil, where men weep in quiet desperation when the rains fail and women scrape their knuckles in cold, frigid air, trying to wash clothes before the baby wakes—it is in these places that people are not fooled by this false hope that man can make his own Utopia. They know human nature better because they are more familiar with it. There is nothing worth watching on the television out this far anyway, and so people instead spend time getting to know each other. With a more refined awareness and an unflinching assessment of human nature, a man-crafted Utopia seems to them to progress from being silly to sadistic, and then finally to something unflinchingly satanic. Unfortunately, there is no party or political recourse to which these people can any longer appeal. If there is a more blatant sign of emerging tyranny, I haven't seen it.

It was with these noble thoughts in my mind that I launched myself to church that next Sunday, hoping to find the salt of the earth retaining their strong flavor. There was a steeple on top of the building (someone explain to me why churches have steeples—I search and search and cannot find any such architectural oddity referenced, either in the Old or New Testaments). There was the very typical pulpit, up to which the Pastor mounts to stand and look down upon the faithful, all of whom are looking at him (not at each other). There are the traditional side rooms in the traditional annex where mothers drop babies and little children like a P-47 drops bombs; zooming in, dropping the ubiquitous diaper bag, toy bag, food bag, and change-of-clothes bag, and then zooming out to look for their friends, chattering like machine guns. The men congregate in little knots, soldiers looking for a foxhole into which they might leap in their suits and ties, dressed in 'holy array', as the Word says. Yet they talk of crops and tractors and games and businesses and the weather—anything but the numinous, riotously exciting, dangerously unsafe, thrilling and holy God.

There is the ubiquitous handout in which the program is described, the prayer requests are listed, the pot lucks announced, the ministries described. The men will go one place for Bible study, the women another, the younger men still another, the younger women again in a separate place, and, of course, the youth scatter like shotgun pellets to various rooms.

During a lull I lean over to catch my reflection in one of the windows to see if there is a large neon sign on my forehead or hanging from my jacket pocket, blinking, which might say 'visitor'. Everyone has shaken my hand; some twice. Apparently they all are glad to see me; every one of them—such a miracle. As I descend into my typical writer's well of sorrows wherein I try to understand the reasons people do things, I find myself coming to the conclusion that they are trying to make me feel welcome. If one of them had perhaps stopped and actually talked to me, or even simply looked at me when they did shake my hand, perhaps they might have achieved their purpose. As it was, I begin to feel like a prize cow someone has brought in from the fair—with three horns.

When the men's group finished a rather insipid study on Matthew, the crowd of a hundred or so worshippers gathered for "worship", which in the lexicon of American Christianity today means that it was time to sing. The list of songs from the hymnbook is posted next to the little wooden signboard which shows how many attended this week, how many attended last week, how many were members, and how many visitors attended. I sat and wondered about the magical sprite that updated the numbers each Sunday, and where they obtained such digitally precise information—and then wondered why such things were important enough to be posted.

One of the women stood up in front of the assembly. I presumed that she was the worship (song) leader. She asks us to open our hymnbooks to a number and then indicates that she'd like everyone to stand. We stand.

"We'll all just *love* this song," she says. "It's got little movements to it that are just so *cute*." And she proceeds to educate us there before the altar on the childish hand and arm and head gestures that accompany the song we are about to sing. I stand like a rock, agog in soul, grim and poker-faced. The song begins, and I look around to see men and women made in the image of God, in their forties, fifties, and sixties, gesturing foolishly like kindergarten children before an awesomely holy God. I begin to tremble. My arms stay locked to my side, hands clenching the top of the pew in front of me like a passenger on the Titanic looking at a large iceberg on the horizon.

They finish the song and begin the next. In the middle of this next song, in which we are allegedly worshiping God, everyone suddenly stops singing—but the music, for some reason, continues. A woman with a print blouse and jeans in the pew in front of me turns around and sticks her hand in my direction, innate reticence overcome by the immense power of cultural tradition, like a Quaker draftee forced to engage in bayonet practice. "Hi," she says. Her hand is in front of me; her eyes are looking at the wall. I stand in my pew, unsuccessfully fending off more bayonet thrusts from people who grab to shake my hand but on pain of death will not look me in the eye—where is the sincerity in this? Are we not to be a true people? But the charade continues.

This is why I've stopped attending church. In America, where the Church has become suffused with wealth, it has also become polluted with the world's culture. I come to the bitter conclusion, as I do each time I visit a new church, that Christianity in our nation has become nothing but a social event. I cry out in my heart to the One who recently was burning me with fire: 'God, where are the people who cry out for reality, for Truth, for Beauty, for experiential knowledge of the God of Abraham, Isaac, and Jacob? Is this what Christianity means? Is this what you want of your people? Is this all they want of you? How can this be?' I listen to the socially-acceptable sermon, in which we are all adjured to "draw closer to Jesus", to "seek His Kingdom first", and to make sure to sign up for the men's canoe adventure next month. Pick up your paddle and follow me.

I realize that perhaps my perspective is slightly colored by what I am going through personally, but that which has been left after just a first pass by the Refiner's harrow cannot be nourished by the insipid, tasteless pabulum that today passes for spiritual food. Those who have been or are being shaped by the mighty hand of the Living God cannot process this gruel. It holds no nourishment. I escape before I am dragged to the local restaurant—which would go out of business but for Christians stopping by after church—by yet another fat lady squeezed into a dress three sizes too small.

One fall day I pull into the short dirt space that serves as a driveway for Killie's trailer. His trailer is a run-down mobile home surrounded by several buildings of assorted construction—some metal, some wood, some concrete, and some standing only by the mercy of God, all of which are stuffed to the gills with collections of infinite variety. There are more than a few (operable and non-operable) vehicles in the yard. The driveway also serves as combination dog run and security perimeter, complete with an organic minefield. I am returning a glass dish, in which three days ago Killie had given me several brook trout which he'd caught. Four days ago I'd mentioned in passing that I'd never eaten a trout. He looked at me as though I'd just admitted I was the other gunman on the grassy knoll. We finished our conversation and he must have immediately went off in his rugged little Toyota plastered with all kinds of stickers and caught maybe twenty fish in thirty minutes.

It is rumored in the neighborhood (there are many rumors) that Killie approaches a stream without fishing accoutrements—no rod, no reel, no line, no bait, no lures, no hooks. He just brings a bucket. The fish, perceiving his approach by some mysterious and deflectory aquatic vision, dash quickly to whatever fish altars there are, say their last goodbyes to their little fish gods, kiss their tadpoles and their wives goodbye, and then, taking careful aim, resignedly but with prodigious energy pop out of the water like acrobats out of a cannon into his bucket. I would not be surprised to discover that he pays his taxes this way, using money he finds in their mouths.

I knocked on the door and the sound of the two dogs barking, welcoming me, was the first thing I heard. Then Killie appeared. He is a thin man, and getting thinner—he has a severe issue with diabetes, though it has taken me four months to discover this, and not from him do I learn it. His eyes were slightly red. He sleeps strangely, and at very different times. As soon as he saw me, though, he brightened.

"Hey, young feller, whatcha doin?" which translated, means, 'Hey, young feller, I'm glad to see you! Thanks fer comin' to visit!'

I hold up the dish. "The trout were superb. Thanks for bringing them by."

"Oh, you probably hated 'em, now, didn't ya?" Disparaging his gifts is a game for him, which I've learned he plays, perhaps to downplay any overt display of generosity. But for some reason I do not follow along in these jests, perhaps because I recognize it for what it is, but also because I respect him and want him to know that I respect him, and therefore do not disregard his gifts by joshing about them.

The basement under Killie's trailer is a unique physical anomaly in the universe, known only to me and two scientists from the University of South Dakota, both of whom disappeared somewhere in this very basement in 1987. The physical space beneath his trailer is comprised of an inverted quantum matrix large enough to contain at least three Boeing 747 aircraft, but in their place Killie has instead filled every square inch with the fruit of his habit—he collects things. He collects ceramic dolls, badges, patches, toys, tools, swords, pots, pans, statues, knives, and most of all, he collects guns. He could supply Finland with all the guns they'd need to repel another invasion from the Russians...and he would, I believe, have a few boxes of ammunition remaining. Killie knows guns like Michelangelo knew paint, like Pascal knew numbers, like Helprin knows from the English language. It is from this great storehouse of stuff that he brings forth his treasures— for every trinket, every item, every physical thing in that great quantum universe inverted under his trailer is known to him, like a precious relative. And the strangest thing is that ever since I have known the man he has been engaged in the furious pursuit of giving things to people—things he think will brighten their day, or lift their spirits, or make their lives easier—and there is, as far as I can see, no diminution whatsoever in his collections. A small suspicion grows, and I gaze around for a bread basket that looks like it might hold two loaves. I'd already seen his trick with the fish.

It is raining, and Killie will not go out in the rain. I learned why from Stella, his wife, the woman with whom he fell in love in the first grade, the one whom God fashioned specifically to be his mate.

One day in January of 1966, three men lowered Killie into a tunnel in the Cu Chi province in the Iron Triangle when he was nineteen, during Operation Crimp. His company commander gave him a flashlight and a pistol. "Here," he said, shoving an old Luger in Killie's hand. "You shoot that damn 1911 in there and you'll go deaf and blind; too much muzzle blast. You got your Kbar? Good. Now git down there'n shoot whatever you see." No one knows what happened under the ground that day, not even Stella, and she knows everything about Killie. Killie came out four hours later. His company had given him up for dead and moved off to their next objective near a river bend. When Killie came out of the tunnel, it was dark, and he didn't see anyone. He was covered in blood. His eyes were not focusing well. His hands were trembling (sometimes his hands still tremble). He moved toward the next objective. He saw the river and slithered in through a bush on the bank. He needed to clean the blood from his clothes, on his hands, in his eyes. As he went into the water, he found that the more he washed, the bloodier he became. He stood still, tried very hard to focus, and then saw why. The North Vietnamese had ambushed an entire platoon from his company and left them floating in the shallow, stagnant river, which was now filled with blood, bodies, and the detritus of human beings when they are torn by automatic rifle fire and grenades.

He suddenly heard the sounds of North Vietnamese troops moving on the opposite bank. Terrified, he ducked down until only his head was above the dead water, his mouth on a level with the surface. He had to lay almost horizontal to achieve this. He hid behind the shattered bodies of his brothers for two nights and a day; it rained the entire time. On the second morning he heard the enemy move off and he walked in the opposite direction through the jungle, not knowing where he was going, not knowing what he was doing. By pure luck he came upon an American pilot who'd been shot down two days before Killie tripped over him. The man almost shot him with his revolver, but he recognized Killie as an American. The rescue helicopter picked up the pilot and a young man who would never, willingly, immerse himself in water—a pool, a lake, the ocean, a river, a bathtub, a shower, or rain—for the rest of his life.

I thought of this story, which Stella had related to me one afternoon, as I followed Killie through the labyrinthine passageways in his basement looking for a book he wanted to give me. I could never visit the man without walking out with something. He needed to give things away like other people needed to breathe. Whatever it was, the book would not be as valuable as the heart that gave it away.

"Killie, you can't keep giving me stuff. I don't come here for stuff, you know. I just come to visit."

"Now don't bother me, boy, I'm lookin' for somethin'." He puttered and fussed in a great dark pile of accumulated treasure until he emerged, like coming out of a tunnel, with an extremely old leather-bound book in his hand.

"Now here, this is what I was lookin' for," he said directly. "You g'won take this home, now...you read quite a bit, I know you like books, and I remembered I had this. Now here, g'won, take it, and don't give me any bother."

It was a first edition George MacDonald—*Castle Warlock*. This was impossible. These things...these things didn't exist.

"Where...where did you *get* this, Killie?" I was amazed, and it showed, which, I suspect, pleased him quite a bit.

"Oh, now, don't worry about that. I probably picked it up at some garage sale for three dollars a while back. Ain't nuthin to me, but I like the look of that fella there on the cover, and since yer a writer, and since that fella looks like a writer, I figured you might find it interestin'." Apparently Killie has an eye for what writers look like. George MacDonald, mentor to C.S. Lewis, was arguably the world's finest writer of Christian fiction.

"Out of God's hand through yours to mine," I breathed quietly.

Killie laughed then, a dry cackle, the first sign of the throat cancer that would try to take his life. "God's got plenty to do without Him worrying about what I buy in a garage sale."

I recall one day that fall when he and I went shooting down in the sand pit near the river. The talk ran to God somehow, and Killie felt comfortable enough with me to more fully describe his theology.

"Not sure I folla them folks at church," he said, eyeing the water from a distance. It was running slowly, shallow, over the gravel bottom. It was low then, and he could stand it—just. "Them folks tossed out Stella an' me first chance they got. We just moved inta the place we're in now, maybe it was, oh, '75 or '76, I can't remember. See, I can't work no more, and Stella's got her kids to support. Their young preacher fella come over to the house, told us we were not the kinda folk he wanted people in his church to associate with, told us not to even bother showin' up...said we wouldn't be welcome." He smiled then. "Stella's ex had a lot to do with that. He was the richest guy in town, and I 'spect the young preacher juss didn't want to part with that regular income." He shook himself and got back to his story, now thinking about Stella. "Loved that woman since I saw her in the first grade, ya know? It didn't bother me much, gittin' throwed out, but it hit Stella kinda hard, what with that waste o' manhood she married, still a member in good standing among the *faithful*." He spat out the word to display what he thought of a group of people who would permit a man to continue to beat his wife and remain in a right relationship among them. Stella's ex owned the only industry that remained in a rapidly depopulating county, and Stella's daughter had married a man who owned the largest car dealership in the largest town within fifty miles.

Hypocrisy takes its toll among so many, in so many different ways, that it must chill the very heart of God. I didn't say anything; what could I say? I just listened patiently as he talked about his childhood, about learning to shoot with an air rifle, shooting pellets at little plastic soldiers from fifty feet (Killie's eyes were still as sharp as a hungry hawk in winter). He'd grown up in this town. He'd been a boisterous, rowdy, rangy young man, always ready with a joke, racing around the little town in his beat-up truck (it was beat-up even then), strewing ruckus and roister wherever he went. He came back from the war a changed man; silent, sullen, withdrawn, moody, uncommunicative. He didn't drink, he didn't descend into drugs, but instead into that darker hole out of which the human soul cannot by itself arise—despair.

Then he found Stella one night on the side of the road, beaten and bleeding, left to freeze in the car by her husband who'd had eight too many drinks. Killie didn't know it was her at first. He had pulled over to help—

someone stopped on the side of the road in the middle of a freezing night in a Maine winter is either dead or soon to be. He approached the driver's side with his flashlight, shined it into the windows, and as the light played across the interior, he saw a pale, blonde little woman, bruised, with blood running down from her hair into her face, cowering in the passenger side of the car. He went over to the passenger side and opened the door. She cringed and tried to move away. He recognized her—after not seeing her for thirty years, in the dark, in the blinding, freezing snow with his breath coming out of him like a humidifier, he recognized her as the girl upon whom his heart had been fixed since he'd discovered it was detachable—when he was around seven. She whimpered and put up her hands in front of her face.

"Sshh, ssshhh, now, Stella, it's me, Killie. It's me, Killie, now, it's all right."

Stella, in shock, didn't recognize him. Somehow he gathered her up, got her in his car, ramped up the heat—she was frighteningly cold—and drove her to the hospital. This sounds normal, except the hospital was eighty miles away, the snow was pelting down in great flakes the size of maple leaves, and the hysterical woman was coming fully unglued as she began to warm up. He got her there, though, and he stayed there for five days and nights, camping out in the clothes he wore, sleeping in the little Toyota in the hospital parking lot in the dead of winter, until he was sure she'd pull through. On the fifth day they released her. She struggled out of the hospital on a cane, took one look at the scruffy man she recognized as the scruffy boy she knew in the first grade, got in his car and Killie dropped her off at her sister's place.

In time Stella and her husband divorced. Up here in the northern Maine woods, lawyers are scarce and the ones that do work up here work fast and cheap. Stella's 'divorce' consisted of her husband throwing her things out on the front lawn and then, with a gratuitous departing punch in the face, throwing Stella out after them. Her lawyer, with an office next to the K-mart strip mall, charged her $35 and her divorce paperwork was finished in thirty-five minutes.

In a few weeks things were back to normal in the community; Stella ended up living with her sister. Time wore on that next season and Killie and Stella eventually ended up getting married in a civil ceremony down over to Beadle Junction. They took up residence in Killie's quantum trailer.

Dogs have a thing about their chew toys—even if they're finished with them, even if they hate them with a bitter, violent hatred, they don't like other dogs coming along and chewing on them. Stella's ex was kind of like that. Once he'd thrown Stella out and divorced her, he just didn't take kindly to her getting married again, and he let it be known around town that he didn't think such things were appropriate. Since he was still a member in good standing in the fellowship, the church folk there in the town's only church tended to give Stella and Killie the cold shoulder, and that's why the young pastor came by to inform Killie that his life and character didn't measure up to God's standards. For Killie and Stella, it didn't engender much love in their hearts for the faithful.

After what he'd seen and done in the tunnels, loud-mouthed abusive husbands or disdainful church folk weren't even a blip on his emotional radar screen. What time did he have for such foolishness? So Killie went on meeting people's needs by giving them what he had of himself—sometimes trinkets, sometimes toys, sometimes money, and for each, plenty of time. Stella tried her best to make a place of sanctuary for her daughters, who were, tragically, going through the same things she endured, and neither of them gave much place or time for *religion*, as it was known in those parts. In meeting the desperate, heart-felt longings each had for safety, security, and love, they saved each other from that pit of fear and despair, and so made a life for each other. When I think about what God rescued them from, how He made for them a tiny sanctuary of peace and companionship, saving them out of the horrors that life had so brutally delivered, I wondered—was it possible, even now, that God could make something of this stew mash my life had become? Of all the things Killie gave me—of all the books and swords and knives and fish and moose and bear meat—I think I realize now that it was the gift of hope that I most treasured.

* * *

In the winter, the snow came—lots of it, more than in any year they'd recorded such things, which is something in northern Maine—and the wood pile diminished steadily. Wood smoke was everywhere, like a wraith army on the march, floating over ten feet of snow as the wind took my chimney exhaust and wafted it down the hill toward the river. The river was covered with ice now, frozen, with sticks standing near the banks like sentinels, sheathed in glinting ice, silver as the veins in angels' wings, or starkly black under snow stacked on the branches as if by infinitely patient children piling one snow flake delicately upon another until physics and the amazingly complex nature of God's creation would seem to dictate that not one more flake could be borne. Neither man nor beast moved from their dens.

Yet every evening about five or so there would come a beep from the little Toyota's horn as Killie took his dog on the circuit around the town's river. That dog loved to sit in Killie's truck and stick his head out the window, his tongue almost lapping the pavement while Killie raced around a twelve-mile loop. We suspected he went down to the sand pit near the river to smoke—the one thing he could not or would not do in the trailer—a suspicion confirmed by Stella, who relayed how Killie's doctor had remonstrated with him about the critical need to quit the habit.

"Aw, what does *he* know," Killie would rant. "God wants me, He can have me. There's way too much fuss made about all this health food business, organic this and organic that, and who knows what all else. When it's my time, I'm a-goin'."

He would rant, and Stella would fuss, and the doctor would, I'm sure, throw up his hands if he knew, but Killie went down to the sand pit every day and smoked. His dog loved him for it.

* * *

Spring came like a great rushing lion that year, and in March there was a strange hot spell that melted the river ice faster than a crazed man with a blowtorch. The water level began to rise, and the homeowners down by the bridge, the town's lowest point, began to worry. The hardware store began to stock sand bags.

One evening about five I heard the beep from the Toyota, and it sounded just a little different. That meant it was coming from the driveway. I saved the file, stopped writing, and went out.

"Hey, young fella," he said, "you ever eat bear?"

Bear meat! I'd heard about it, read about it in camping stories and wilderness stories and cookbooks, salivating, but never once thought that I'd get a chance to taste it. "Never in all my born days, Killie. Why? You kill a bear?"

"Well, now, not 'zactly." This means that there was a lengthy story to follow. The long and the short of it was that a motorist had struck a bear down by the interstate and a State Trooper friend of Killie's had put it out of its misery with his .357. So, technically, it wasn't road kill. I'd been in Maine long enough for this not to bother me.

"How can I help?" I asked.

"Well, see, I'm gonna get the critter made into a rug." Yes, he did use the word 'critter'—sane people recognize this as a perfectly acceptable noun. And it would turn out later that he would give the rug to someone who had happened to mention that they were looking for a bearskin rug to outfit their cabin.

"Now, you'll probably hate this here meat," he said.

"No, no, no, absolutely not—I've always wanted to try bear. What's it taste like?"

Thereupon followed another long diatribe about the gustatory habits of Ursus Major; basically, it depends on what the bear's been eating.

"Now, this here bear, he's probably been eatin' nuthin' but trash in some dump, so you'll probably hate it."

"No, seriously, Killie, I'd love to try it. Let me know how much it is."

So he gave me the number of the butcher where the State Trooper had dropped it off, and where I could pick up the meat in a few days.

He got back in the truck and, very strangely, smiled at me. His elbow was on the window ledge—I could see the tunnel rat patch on his shoulder.

His eyes misted a bit, and I could tell it wasn't his sugar. Something moved him deeply. "Yer writin' agin, ain't ya?" he said with a dead certainty.

I was, and looked, amazed. "How did you know?"

"Ah, young fella, it ain't that hard. You take care now." And he backed the truck out from the driveway and waved like a man possessed. "You take care now," he yelled from the road, as he drove off to the sand pit with his dog in the passenger seat, leaning out the window with his tongue just about lapping the asphalt.

The bear meat, when I got it from the butcher, was the best red meat I'd ever eaten.

Two weeks later, just as the great red ball of a sun came peeking over the hills that surrounded the valley one morning, Killie drove down to the general store. It was a small grocery store, but they had good meat—better than you could buy in the big town thirty minutes away, and with gas at ten dollars a gallon, the local store was doing business like a mortician during the plague. The store was down near the bridge, the low point in town. Stella needed some things for a dinner she was preparing for her daughters who were coming to stay the weekend.

They say that while he was checking out, everyone in the store heard a great roaring sound. Everyone in the store knew exactly what it was. Killie dropped his groceries and everyone ran out to see a rushing wall of water coming out of the north. There was no doubt in anyone's mind that it would hit the homes down by the bridge—it would wash over the banks and clean the lawns slicker than a dog licking a birthday cake—and, as everyone saw when they rushed out of the little store, no doubt wash away the three children playing on the porch of the lowest house.

"Oh sweet Jesus," someone heard Killie say, and he was off like a shot. They say he ran like a sprinter, which is strange, because I knew, because Stella told me, that he didn't have many toes left and he was in constant pain from his degenerating feet. But what was most amazing was the little fact I gathered later from the people who watched him.

"The water," they said, "was the color of blood. The sun was coming up and hitting it just right or something, but it looked like a giant moving wall of blood." Killie ran straight at it.

He managed to get two of the kids up to high ground and was headed back for the third when the water took them both. They found the little girl, washed up in those sticks along the river's edge, as if someone had hung her there, shaken but alive. We never found Killie.

There are times when I think that maybe Killie was an angel. We think that angels are great warrior beings, but we seem to forget that the real wars are fought not with physical strength but in the spirit, and what might look like a thin, reedy little man in the flesh might be a great fighter in the realm of the spirit, in disguise, sent to do one or two very particular things in a period of time that would be long to a human being, though a snap for a messenger from God. I look down into the river now each day and think about the complexity and wonder and beauty of God, and I think about my friend, the truest and kindest man I knew. I know too that there are philosophies and cultures and traditions and doctrines. I know there are men trained in seminaries to believe that things are done a certain way. I am not sure what these philosophers or seminarians would say about the heart and soul of a thin, tired old man who spent his life in the service of others, who loved and gave and suffered so that others might have a few moments of happiness, and did so because he thought that it was the right thing, and who in one last great selfless gesture emptied himself in the face of his greatest fear. Sometimes, Horatio, it gives me pause.

> *"There are more things in heaven and earth, Horatio,*
> *Than are dreamt of in your philosophy."*

Hamlet: Act 1. Scene V
William Shakespeare

RETURN TO KOIDANYEV

Alexis pressed the button on the steering wheel that answered the car's integrated hands-free cell phone. She snapped off the radio, switched lanes, and from the corner of her eye processed the sign for her exit. The skirt from Bloomingdale's rustled; her matching blazer flapped in the wind from the open sunroof.

"Monty, I'm running late, I've got to swing out on the expressway to pick up my cousin...yes, yes, I'll make it, I'll make it."

A yellow corvette flashed by, cutting her off, and she cursed like a bosun's mate.

"*Christ*, yes, I know it's important. It won't be a problem. God, the traffic out here is ridiculous...what? I have to go pick up my cousin...I don't know, she wants him to intern with the firm, I guess, but I can tell you it's not going to work...well, for one thing, he looks like a refugee from a schtetl...that's my guess...no, he's definitely not firing on all thrusters. Right, I'll see you at Pokorny's."

She punched off the phone, yanked the BMW across two lanes and smashed another selector, yanking the car around the lanes like a fighter pilot in a dogfight. A song from her iPod pounded through the car's sound system. She swirled her finger around the rotary selector to change the playlist. She glanced at her face in the rearview mirror: makeup still intact, eyebrows clean, highlighted, brown eyes deep and clear, mouth okay. Good.

Nothing too provocative; professional is as professional does. She brushed back a swirl of black hair.

Alexis pulled into the driveway of her Aunt's home, a small white clapboard affair that Alexis could have purchased with a month's salary. A rusty Volvo sat in the driveway. She honked. There was no movement, no doors opened. The house stood there, conveying an impression of stolid, seedy dissipation, as if the dust from a thousand schtetls had settled into every grain, every pore, and slowed life to a crawl.

She snapped off her seat belt, tossed it over her shoulder, popped the door, and pushed out of the car. No one was waiting outside the house; no, that would have been too much to ask. Her heels punched into the asphalt driveway like nails. She had a tight schedule. Why were these people always so...so *drifting*, so not *locked on?*

The front screen door opened as she mounted the bottom step.

"Alexis, sweetie, nice to see you! Come in, come in, sit down, have some coffee. Look, there's some—"

"I'm sorry, Sue, but I've got to get back to the city. It's kind of important. Is...is Jacob ready?" The name, once out of her mouth and hanging there between the two women, had a sound reminiscent of something foreign, something faintly Middle Eastern, something patriarchal—another distant, unpleasant, impolitic word—and it floated there in the stifling air of the dingy foyer like some tasteless, gaudy, old-world chandelier.

"Oh...oh, well, yes, let me get him." The Aunt blinked, slightly befuddled, and retreated back down what appeared to be the only hallway in the house. Alexis' nose wrinkled reflexively as she crossed the threshold.

"Jacob! Jacob! Alexis is here...come on, son, time to go to work."

"Hello, Alexis."

His voice was incredibly deep. Her six-inch heels vibrated as he spoke. His shoulders stooped. He was carrying a black book. With a shock of distaste, she realized it was something...something *biblical*. She could not believe what she was seeing; there were tzitzit poking out from under his black thigh-length coat. He was wearing a tallit underneath his white shirt.

"Is there a fiddler on the roof?" she wondered aloud. The Aunt fluttered a hand with innocent confusion. Alexis could not imagine how the firm would handle this. She began to be very uncomfortable.

"Jacob, this isn't temple we're going to...you know this, right?"

"Yeah, sure, Cousin, I know this." He was smiling at her...down at her, actually. He had to stoop down, he was so tall. He was larger than he'd looked in the hallway.

"Oh, this is who he is, Alexis...since he was thirteen, actually. We haven't been able to get him to join the real world, though believe me, we tried." Her hands flew up, wiggling. "Did we have a time trying... let me tell *you*...but such a stubborn ox! You should have such stamina! They would make you President next week!" The little white-haired lady slapped the massive young man across the hip—this was at the level of her shoulder. She was talking now a little more loudly, and slower, to Jacob, as one would speak to a particularly recalcitrant cow.

"You don't be any trouble, you hear? Alexis is doing us all a favor, taking you up to the city. This is a good deed she's doing. So you behave, and don't cause trouble."

"Okay, Momma." Steinbeck should be here, she groaned to herself. She was taking Lenny, straight from *Of Mice and Men*, into the most prestigious restaurant in New York. They would eat him alive and her name would be mud. She wouldn't be able to get a table at Burger King for the rest of her life.

The Aunt, smarter than she looked, read her mind.

"Now, Alexis, don't you worry, everything will be fine. The Uncle knows people who know people, they'll make it fine, you'll see. The Uncle talked with that good Jewish man, a...a...what was his name, Jacob?"

"Seligman, Momma." Alexis' heels vibrated again, and she steadied herself.

"Oh, right, Mr. Seligman. Alexis, your Uncle did this Seligman person a favor in the war. The war ends, what, sixty-some years ago, and does this man forget? Of course he doesn't forget. This man Seligman says it's fine to let Jacob come see what being a lawyer would be like, to make law, maybe make some things better in this country."

Her urban female soul recoiled as she stood there in the stultifying closeness of the little suburban ranchette, assaulted and vaguely offended by the doilies over the couch, the gauche furniture, the little plastic menorah on the side table—all the typical signs of New York Jewish kitsch. She listened with growing amazement to the Aunt unveil the fact that her Uncle had done some kind of favor for the President and Senior Partner of the most prestigious law firm in New York (*her* law firm, coincidentally) and began to hope that maybe her name wouldn't be mud.

Alexis looked at her watch to make sure the Aunt wouldn't open her mouth again to perhaps explain the origins of the universe. She gave a little start; it was later than she thought.

"*Christ*, Jacob, let's pack it. We've got a meeting in the city in an hour and the traffic is murder." She spun on her heels and made for the door.

Jacob looked at Alexis like a dumb calf and kissed his mother, who patted his shoulder (as high as she could reach) and by some form of legerdemain Jacob squeezed his massive frame into the passenger seat of the BMW. Alexis backed out of the driveway, shoved the accelerator to the floor, and the car rocketed out of suburbia like a bat out of Sheol.

In the car, the tzitzit was gathered in Jacob's hands; he appeared to be nodding, mouthing something to himself, his lips moving. Alexis popped ear buds out of their receptacle, punched on the iPod again, and disappeared into her world, merging with the traffic back into the city. She'd never met her cousin; she didn't know him from Adam's off ox, but they were late, and what kind of conversation could she have with a semi-Hasidic moron dressed like something out of a Cecil B. DeMille picture?

* * *

Monty Silverstein arrived at Pokorny's and ordered a preliminary round of Italian sparkling water (which at Pokorny's costs as much as the citizens of Maine spend on heating oil for a month). He looked about, executing the ritual status check to see who was sufficiently prominent to have been permitted entry into the current political holy of holies. He saw one of the young up-and-coming editors of the city's largest newspaper, Josh Berenberg. He nodded and the man smiled back gratefully. Berenberg's editorial praising the nation's brightest and youngest Presidential candidate in decades had started a media tidal wave that overwashed the entire nation, launching the Great Man's campaign and, incidentally, vaulting the paper to prominence among the Party faithful. Monty assumed (correctly) that this was why the editor now found himself dining in the upper reaches of power. As his eyes moved around the room, he saw one of the city's most prestigious litigants in a corner with two partners from the firm. They were embroiled in a case that would, if successful, crush the pro-life lobby in the state for the next twenty years. He nodded again, checking in. They acknowledged with deferential smiles behind their oversized menus.

Pokorny's was New York's most exclusive eating establishment, unobtrusively but ineluctably reserved for the city's ruling political elites. The dark wood panels, lustrous balustrades, shining brass fixtures, hushed tones, and high ceilings all spoke of wealth, prestige, and exclusivity—of having arrived. One had to be a major player in the world of New York politics, the media, the law, or entertainment in order for the reservations people to just keep you on the line, and even then, it could take a month to actually get a reservation.

Julius Mokotoff came through the entrance to Pokorny's barely two minutes short of the time appointed and saw Monty immediately. He moved through the crowd with a fluid grace, dignified and comfortable. His clothes, shoes, watch, and demeanor all exuded old-money wealth. Monty envied the man his settled position in society—and the fact that he had a few billion in the bank...what Monty could do with a billion or two. Monty stood, folded the heavy linen napkin, set it on the table with dexterity, and extended a hand.

"Julius, nice to see you, thanks for coming."

"The Senator's staff calls, Monty, and the minions leap." The men smiled. "What's cooking?"

"We want to talk strategy, Julius. I've got Mark in as well, Mark Weitzel. He should be here any minute, and Alexis Furman."

"Furman...she clerked for Ginsberg?"

"That Furman...yes."

"She just won a judgment for the state of New Hampshire, didn't she?"

"She did; the parental rights issue. She established rock-solid precedent for the ability of the State to direct how children are to be schooled. If we can apply the judgment to other states, we can effectively eliminate the home school movement throughout the country."

"God, that would be an accomplishment. Those yokels have been causing more of a problem than we need at the moment." Julius took a sip of his sparkling water.

"She's been remarkably effective. Her ability to marshal facts, her believability, her commitment—"

"And her looks have nothing to do with it, right?" Mokotoff interjected, smiling.

"Couldn't forget that, could we?" Monty said, smiling the conspiratorial male smile. Alexis was truly ravishing. Monty had a reminder on his personal Outlook calendar at home to plan a deviously-structured seduction sometime in the next month, as long as the Senator's campaign went as planned and barring any extraordinary deviations from the schedule.

"She's been incredibly useful," Monty allowed. "Hope you don't mind, but she's bringing a cousin in to lunch; apparently Seligman himself approved."

Mokotoff simply nodded gracefully—like everything else he did—and smiled. "Seligman is backing us enormously. And what, we should turn away a friend of his?"

Monty's head wagged back and forth slightly. "Glad you understand."

Mark Weitzel appeared, escorted to their table by a fawning waiter, hands wringing in anxiety to be so near the great man, the paragon of democratic virtue, the maker of kings, the deposer of fulminating traditions, the owner of so many media corporations that it could truly be said by the faithful that anything worth listening to, watching, reading, imbibing, or worshiping came from the fountain of this man's empire. Monty and Julius both stood with respectful, dignified, composed expressions of pleasure. It was rumored that Weitzel was in close partnership with some of the key—the *very* key—people working the higher agendas in Davos, Brussels, Moscow, Beijing, and Spain. Two very large men with oversized jackets detached themselves from Weitzel's wake and took places at the exits as the man himself came to the table.

"Mark, it was kind of you to come," Monty said, the rehearsed line snapped off with just the right mixture of professionalism and warmth, not giving away precedence but not assertive, either.

"Monty, how are you? How's the Senator?" Weitzel turned to Mokotoff. "Julius, a pleasant surprise; Davos, wasn't it, when we saw each other last?"

"It was, Mark. Pleasure to see you again…hope things are going well in your world?"

"Passably…passably," he replied, taking his seat. The others sat as well. Waiters breathed again.

Weitzel was a man of average height, with a most uncommon, hawk-like intensity complimented by dark eyes that constantly roamed the room, taking in everything, missing nothing—eyes that could piercingly observe and ravenously devour. The man was raw power. Monty and Julius were in awe. All heads in the restaurant were fixed on their table. For Monty, the knowledge that his stock was rising by the minute would lend enormous savor to the food. Diverting for an intellectual moment, he ruminated that perhaps this is why men craved power—it so lent savor to the senses in life. *My God, how good it tasted*, he exulted to himself, overwhelmed with the association of pure moving energy, a flow that could be controlled to direct great events, to shift the minds of men, to compel, to command. It made his blood race. At that moment he understood viscerally why men would fight wars and devastate entire nations for such a feeling.

Alexis entered the restaurant. Monty knew this because he was watching the effect Weitzel was having on the law firm partners at the far table when he saw their heads yank as if pulled by some vertiginous little boy playing with a string. He followed their gaze and there she was: tall, dark-eyed, silken-haired, buxom, moving through the restaurant like silk flows through your hand, in a beige suit from Bloomingdales that must have cost slightly more than the national budget for Rwanda. He stood. Mokotoff and Weitzel stood as well. Mokotoff's eyes were veiled, polite, but disinterested. Weitzel, who had perhaps indulged himself with more of the world's beautiful women than even he could count, did her the honor of extending a compliment.

"Sadly in our world it is not often beauty is married with intelligence, Ms. Furman, but you grace our table with both." Alexis beamed; this was a verbal scalp she could parley into enormous street cred.

The eyes of most diners were suddenly yanked away from their table by a most unusual distraction occurring at the door. A large and hulking human specimen stood, blotting out much of the light coming through the window, dressed like some orthodox Jewish refugee and looking at the tank of lobsters with a stark expression of horror. A waiter approached and cringingly requested the honor of escorting the…the gentleman… to his table. The gentleman *did* have a table, did he not? Surely at the lunch hour, here at Pokorny's, he would have…he certainly *must* have a table?

Jacob looked down at the waiter wringing his hands in great anxiety (a common trait among those who serve in close proximity to the powerful, sadly) and said, "I am here with my cousin. Are these…*shellfish?* This is not kosher. This *is* a kosher restaurant, nu?" The questions came with increasing intensity. The waiter, quailing (also a common trait), ran for the maître d', who, slightly less cringingly and with just a shade of a tyrant's reflected arrogance in his own demeanor, slightly more insistently begged the young man for the pleasure of knowing to which table he might have the honor of escorting him.

Jacob looked around wildly—this was not a good sign, the maître d' thought, a man this size looking around wildly—and fortunately for Pokorny's and the luminaries of the Party eating there that day, Jacob caught a glimpse of Alexis as she was being feted or stalked or patronized by three of the most powerful and important men in the twenty-first century.

He moved toward the table like Moses walking on dry land through the Red Sea, like Godzilla moving through Tokyo, like a monster truck crunching a line of environmentally-friendly cars. Diners gaped in shock and awe at the very size of the man. He exuded a slightly Eastern European, Hasidic air; to every deeply assimilated Jew in the restaurant, the sight of him was intensely offensive. When Jacob arrived at their table, the instinctual recoil was covered nicely by the overpowering social requirement for tolerance—although tolerance of anything smacking of the roots of Judaism was, to these utterly assimilated Jews, stretching the boundaries of tolerance to the breaking point. Alexis had a dark moment, watching her career flash before her eyes, imagining Weitzel or Mokotoff phoning each other, or worse, her firm, wondering what among all that was holy in the Party were they doing, letting a loose cannon like that Furman woman bring a refugee from Fiddler on the Roof into their restaurant. Didn't she have the least degree of appreciation for the dignity, the authority, the *gravitas* of those who required a quiet place of solitude in the midst of the hurly-burly? Didn't she have the faintest idea of the kinds of things that went on in such places?

Her downward-spiraling reverie was interrupted before she self-destructed upon the cliffs of her own imaginings.

"How is Seligman, Alexis? Doing well, we hope?" This conversational sortie came from Weitzel—the wise, the gracious—reminding her that he knew, as did everyone else, why this hulking excuse for a human being was taking up their time and a chair at Pokorny's. Seligman's prestige was such that any disapprobation would be dismissed immediately—or, at least, it wouldn't fall on her slender shoulders.

"In excellent health, thank you, Mark, for asking," she replied hurriedly, and too relieved to worry about how it sounded. A waiter appeared magically behind her, hands wringing on the back of her chair, indicating that the deepest purpose of his life would be fulfilled if she were to be seated comfortably. She sat, smoothing her skirt. The men sat, and Jacob, hesitatingly, sat, wondering if the floor would open up and swallow him. He glanced around quickly to see if there was a golden calf being fashioned. The assembled crowd, eyes agog, held their breath—there was an audible intake as Jacob descended upon the chair—and just as audibly the crowd exhaled as the pride of Pokorny's was upheld. Apparently the chairs were stouter than the waiters' hearts.

Weitzel, after lifting his water glass, gave a discreet nod to Monty, who took the cue.

"Gentlemen, Alexis, permit me to get right down to things. You know that the Party's candidate for President will be elected. This is a given," Monty began, launching upon the conversational mission of the luncheon. "Another four years of the opposition's hooliganism, with political strategies worked out at...at *barbecues*, for God's sake...will simply not be permitted. And we simply will no longer tolerate *any* interference in the political arena from those 'of faith'".

"Unless it's ours, of course," Julius inserted dryly. They all smiled.

But having the great man elected was not enough, Monty went on to say. "We need to put certain programs in place—programs that will convince the people that the hope of the Party, the hope of the nation, the hope of mankind, will truly be the answer to everyone's problem." Weitzel smiled at this bit of political foolishness, recognizing, like one shark circling another around blood in the water, the real objective—power, pure power. Monty continued. "These programs need to ensure that the state controls everything there is to control for the good of the people—their money, their children, their property, their employment, even the exercise of what faith we consider appropriate." Everyone there at the table recognized how damaging and divisive misguided fundamentalists had been to the philosophical tapestry their Party had attempted to weave into the social conscience in decades past. They were also aware how successful their efforts and the efforts of their predecessors had been to almost completely eliminate any influence from such inappropriate sources—sources which might stand in the way of the golden highway to Utopia they were going to build.

"The tapestry of hope needs to be strengthened," Monty emphasized. "The threads that will build a new, incredibly ordered society, structured on the basis of intelligent, far-seeing men and women need to be crafted *now*, before the Senator takes office, so that in the first hundred days these new policies would rock the world. The Senator is completely confident that the policies your people can devise will be more than satisfactory, and he is demonstrating that confidence by providing unlimited access."

"And he calls upon us to demonstrate our willingness to exercise these policies by providing unlimited funds," Weitzel stated astutely.

"Yes sir," Monty answered, meeting the bald statement head-on. "Your people," and here he nodded his head toward Julius as well, while in reality embracing the truly global elite in whose circles Weitzel moved, "have more than enough...*assets*...to implement the strategies you have in mind. You just need access. The Senator is providing that."

"We are not sure access to America is as critical as it once was," Julius intoned slowly.

Weitzel, not wanting the truth of the statement to unnecessarily pinion the brash and aggressive Senator's aide to the conversational mat, intervened.

"It may be, Julius, but nonetheless access at this time would enable things to proceed in a more...well, in perhaps a more *seemly* fashion."

Weitzel looked slowly at Alexis; Julius did as well. Monty took these gestures as a question: What, then, is *she* doing here? He took this unspoken question head-on as well. He would enjoy the reaction.

"Alexis is going to be leaving her law firm shortly," he said. Alexis, despite her attempt at composure, looked sharply at Silverstein.

"Like bloody hell I am," she exploded. The men laughed at her discomfiture.

"Senator"—and here he used the Great Name itself, suitably impressing everyone, stifling even Alexis' outburst—"will call for Alexis to fill the post of Special Counsel to the President. She'll be working on these policy issues directly with the future President." He smiled, looking at Alexis to test her reaction.

She was stunned. Her bright brown eyes were wide open, flashing, the fires of ambition stoked to white heat. Weitzel saw it and duly congratulated himself on his foresight to extend a little grace about the hulking oaf sitting next to her. Amidst the general distraction, Julius let his eyes stray over Monty's shoulders.

"My God, Monty, you know how to surprise a girl!"

The men laughed. It was not often one could catch a hard-boiled, razor-sharp New York lady lawyer by surprise. The shell of cynicism and disdain was a requirement for entry to law school, one supposed, or maybe something that happened to New York lawyers while in the womb, when their mothers perhaps smoked some particularly bitter herb.

"And by God, you'll pay for it!" she said, quick as a whip. Her eyes, however, as everyone could see, indicated that she had other plans.

The laughter was louder this time. Julius began to consider alternatives. Apparently Monty's calendar would be occupied shortly. He lifted his glass of Chablis, subtly toasting Monty's future success in a gesture that only the two men caught.

"I...do...not...like...that...man."

The words, rolled out slowly and unobtrusively just below the noisy garble of conversation at Pokorny's like a bowling ball under the tables, seemed to come from the tree that sat quietly at the table with them. Diners near the windows looked to see if perhaps a thunderstorm was approaching. No one at first knew that Jacob had spoken. If it had not been for the way the water rippled in the glasses, or the vibration they felt in their shoes or in their elbows as they leaned on the heavy tablecloth, they would not have known anything out of the ordinary had occurred.

The laughter at the table began to dwindle slightly, the altered atmosphere absorbing it like a sponge absorbs liquid. The palpitation of the waiters—who had indeed caught the fact that Jacob had spoken and did in fact hear very clearly what he'd said—was like watching a class of suicide bombers on a practice range.

"I...do...not...like...that...man."

This time the words shook the table like a small earthquake; they struck a harmonious resonance and forks sang as though being tuned. Alexis started, irritated, yanked rudely away from considering the bright new direction her life had taken.

She could tell it was Jacob speaking because her heels were vibrating again. She shook her head slightly. "Jacob...Jacob, it's fine," she hissed. "Don't worry about a thing, now, eat, please, and don't interrupt. We're speaking about important things here. Don't cause any trouble." She smiled to cover her embarrassment.

"That...man," Jacob proclaimed, and pointed with a large hand that stretched like the hand of doom across the table, level with her eyes, pointing over Julius' right shoulder. She turned and saw a very large, strange-looking man sitting in a chair over which hung a faded green overcoat—like a trench-coat, she thought, discordantly. The man was sitting by himself at a table across the room, plainly staring at them, mechanically lifting a spoon back and forth to his mouth. She could tell from here that he was slurping. What struck Alexis immediately was the size of the man's hands—thick, beefy fingers like sausages, fists the size of small hams—resting on the table in front of him. He was consuming a plate of soup. The spoon was like a toothpick in his fist. Arms the size of a sewer culvert stretched the seams of his jacket.

The man saw Alexis looking at him and the fleshy mass of his face rearranged itself into a smile. Alexis could not believe it. She was she seeing a man in Pokorny's—yes, *Pokorny's*—actually *drool*. It had to be something else. She looked away, disgusted.

"Just ignore him," Alexis hissed at Jacob. "He's disgusting, yes, but ignore him." Jacob did not reply, but continued to stare sullenly at the man. Weitzel caught the exchange.

"Strange fellow," he remarked, his head inclining toward the large man still staring at their table.

Julius turned in his chair, looking in the man's direction. The man lifted a great ham-like fist in which was, barely noticeable, the spoon, and waved it at them, smiling moronically. He could see soup dripping on the man's chin.

"Yes, he does seem a bit...odd," he remarked.

Alexis began to form the idea that this is just what he was—a moron, perhaps some lunatic escaped from Bellevue—but my *God*, how *could* the establishment let someone like that in here? Someone's head was going to roll, she thought. There would be lists made even as they sat there being offended—lists of waiters, reservation agents, and suppliers to be fired. What *is* it, she thought to herself, about monstrous men today? God, I can't get *away* from them, they're everywhere.

"I do not like him," Jacob reiterated, encouraged by Julius' expressed opinion.

"Don't blame you a bit, dear boy," Julius replied, looking up at Jacob, hoping to take Jacob's mind of the offending man. "Tell me young man, are you looking forward to practicing law?"

Jacob's eyes snapped down and away from the large man eating soup and took in Julius.

"I am not going to practice law," he replied in the same measured tone. "I am going to be a Rabbi." The voice penetrated deeply into Julius' chest; he could feel his ribs vibrate.

"A Rabbi! Seligman will be so pleased!" Julius exclaimed, almost laughing. He wondered if Seligman realized that his protégé was planning such a career. He wondered if there were any gay Rabbis. And then he realized that of course Seligman would know his protégé's plans, and this was the reason the young man was at the table; so that they could begin to shape him. No doubt he would become a very influential Rabbi in the City—shaped and molded along the lines of their policies and philosophies, as they had done so many times to so many, many other influential (and subtly influenced) rabbis. Those who birthed the philosophies so much embraced by everyone there at Pokorny's never tempted so successfully as when they were closest to the altar. Mokotoff realized again, with deep appreciation, the depth and power of Seligman's genius.

"Have you picked out a congregation in the city yet?" he asked.

Jacob looked at him as though he was seeing him for the first time, his mouth slightly open, a look of incomprehension plastered on his face. "New York? No, not New York...Russia...I am going to be a Rabbi in Russia...like my Grandfather."

"Your Grandfather?" Julius said, trying to conceal his amusement— Russia! What was Seligman thinking? "Was he a Rabbi in Russia?"

"No," Jacob replied, "he just visited there. I am going back to where he visited."

"To where, Jacob?" asked Weitzel, trying to diminish the embarrassment that might get back to Seligman if the incident was not handled correctly, "I know Russia well. Where did your Grandfather visit?"

"Koidanyev," he said. "Much needs doing there. Perhaps it is too late, but nonetheless..." and Jacob's words trailed off, fortunately, before the drinking glasses shattered.

Weitzel had never heard of Koidanyev—men like him wouldn't have—and was about to ask Jacob where this strange place was when the conversation was interrupted by several things happening at once.

Jacob became agitated; diners' heads were turning like puppets on strings. Weitzel sat back, set down his glass of wine, and exhibited the strangest sense of disquiet. Alexis looked up to see that the hulking moron, like a walking side of beef, was moving toward their table. The two large men in unobtrusive jackets bulging obtrusively began to move to intercept the man, but they didn't have the angles to intercept him before he got to the table.

Monty watched in horror as the strange man with arms like great steel beams stumbled to their table. The man appeared to be chuckling, if the rumbling they heard could be interpreted correctly by matching the moronic smile that accompanied it. Monty felt only a slight degree of danger. The man himself didn't appear to be dangerous but the situation—not planned, not scripted, not controlled by him—therefore warranted an elevated sense of awareness. And, it must be admitted, Monty was a coward.

The waiters, cringing, did not know what to do. Imagine their perplexity—here was a diner at Pokorny's interrupting other diners at

Pokorny's. Unfortunately the waiters did not have immediate access to the protocol list, and so did not know whether to interdict this boorish gentleman or thank their lucky stars that they had the opportunity to clean the dust from the floor whereupon he had walked after he finished gracing this other table with his wisdom. This was a process problem that the managers would later fix by implanting tiny audio chips in the ear canals of every waiter.

The large beefy man stumbled and wound his way through the maze of some of the most important personages in the Party of the Future until he came to the table around which sat four of the most influential Jews in the country. He smacked his forearms down like a butcher bringing home the bacon and knelt, shoving himself in a friendly sort of way between Alexis and Monty. He smelled of something; Alexis couldn't place it, but the fact that he smelled was enough to wrinkle her nose. The man's jacket brushed against her Bloomingdale creation. She felt soiled. Jacob was standing now, alarmed, which alarmed the rest of the diners. Policemen in the precincts felt a fluttering in their guts for some unexplained reason. Clouds began to form outside, above the restaurant. Waiters fainted.

"Jews," said the large, ham-like man, rumbling deeply, chuckling, pleased with himself, speaking with what was obviously some type of Eastern European accent. He pronounced it *Juice*. "Juice...I like Juice." He opened his hands wide, obviously meaning to include the entire table with his complimentary epithet, and then slapped his hands down on the table between the wine bottle and the four kinds of water glasses. The bottles and glasses (and Monty) jumped like dilatory soldiers caught standing around by a furious adjutant.

"By *Got*," he said, now apparently speaking to the entire restaurant, judging by the adjustment in volume, "by *Got*, I love dease Juice!" He spread his arms to embrace both Monty and Alexis. He was no longer smiling, but serious, his face contorted in moronic passion. There was a bit of drool, or soup, staining his jacket. Alexis began to be afraid.

The two men detailed to protect Weitzel arrived at the table and quickly assessed the situation. They looked at their principal, who appeared to be upset, unsure of the situation, and backing away slightly without trying to appear frightened (the security people see this thing in their principals all the time, and are taught what to look for). They moved quickly behind the strange man. One grabbed a wrist, the other grabbed the other, and with a quick motion twisted each behind the man's back and away from the threat of touching the diners at the Table of the August. Alexis felt a flash of appreciation (and some attraction) for the bold move by the security man protecting her.

But the large moronic man, finding himself with both arms now behind his back, became inordinately frightened. Something flashed across his face and in a paroxysm of fear, he twisted his hands somehow, grabbed the security men's wrists, one in each of his ham-like fists, squeezed, and snapped bones like twigs. The men went to their knees, trying to grimace unobtrusively. Weitzel began to seriously think about running, and Monty struggled manfully to keep from crying. Diners gasped, several lifted from their chairs with eyes searching for the closest exit. It was becoming an extremely distasteful incident. Pokorny's would never live this down.

The man dropped the arms of the security guards like discarded bones. They'd been apparently forgotten in a moment, and then looked back at the people at table—his friends, the 'Juice'—and smiled again. "You are *goot* Juice," he said.

One of the security guards, the one with the functional gun-hand wrist, was pulling his gun from the unobtrusive bulge under the unobtrusive jacket. He could not ratchet the slide back, however. He looked to his compatriot, who understood immediately, and grabbed the slide with his teeth and held on. The first guard shoved it forward, the slide slammed a round into the chamber with a resounding click that sounded like…well, it was a sound no one in that restaurant had ever heard, for no one in the Party of the Faithful would ever have anything to do with guns (it was against everyone's religion). The security guard struggled to stand. As he did so, he pointed the weapon at the large beefy man who had easily snapped the bones in his left forearm.

"Now...back *away* from the table, sir," he said, firmly but (as always) politely.

Silence reigned in the restaurant like an unbroken plate of glass. It was shattered suddenly by a woman's strident, commanding voice with just a touch of upper-class English accent. "Stop! My *God*, please, *stop!*"

Upon hearing this voice, the strange man suddenly straightened and looked around, eyes rolling somewhat, as though caught with his hand in a cookie jar.

"Uncle! Uncle, *do* come along now! Omigod, I'm *so* sorry...he *never* does this...*never*! What are you *thinking*, Uncle! I mean, *honestly!*" The woman's strident tones and high-flying, clearly British accent were unmistakably familiar to the large beefy intruder. He began to chuckle again, a laugh that implied close camaraderie with his new special friends. The security man lowered the gun.

"My leetle niece," he explained gently, looking over at the diminutive woman, waving a hand with the palm down, up and down, so as to put any fears she might have at rest. "My dear, relax, relax, I vas just tellink my frentz—dease nice Juice—how *much* I like dem. I luf to see all de nice Juice here in dis place."

"Uncle, please, *please*, come along now, don't bother the nice Juice." The woman unthinkingly mimicked the old hulk's ancient Eastern European accent. She was tugging at the man's sleeve. It was like watching a mouse try to pull a Mack truck. The man leaned down again on the table and whispered conspiratorially to the strategic planners of the coming Utopia.

"I vill tell you," he said with a wink, "vy I like Juice." The niece was still pulling at his arm; she wasn't even affecting his gravitational field.

Alexis recoiled from such a blatant, distasteful reminder of things foreign, of Eastern Europe and all the backward, primitive...*religious* things such a place represented. The thought of listening to a biography of the man's entire life repulsed her. By God, she had *things* to do, programs to plan, strategies to formulate, policies to implant in the mind of the Great Man himself. She was going to be the Special Counsel to the President. By God, who *was* this idiot to be taking up her time?

"Ven I vas foorteen," he began, "I lived in leetle village in Pohlunt... Przebrno, near Krynica Morska. Och, it vas such a nice place, near de Vistula Bay, you know? I vas poor. Ve didn't haf much to eat, and den vun day I got job. It voot saife my family, I am tellink you. Dey make me hangman, you see. No vun else in de village voot do it, you know? Dey gaife me hood. Ven you hang somevun, you know, dey gif you hood because dey don't vant any vun to know it's you, but efry vun knowse." The man began to choke up, and lines of tears dripped down into blubbery crevasses. "But I vas no goot, you see...I vas no goot, it vas difficult, because I coot never tie de noose. I voot alvays make a mistake. De hands," and here he held his massive fists before his face and looked at them like traitors, "dey voot not go vere dey shoot go to make de knot in de right vay."

Jacob was trembling now, but standing stock still, rooted to the ground. A great black swirling mass of cloud rose above the restaurant, threatening to become a tornado. It would be the first in history to occur within the city limits of New York. Police everywhere in the city were calling emergency numbers, wondering about their ulcer medications. Fireman awoke and dressed, wondering if there was a massive unreported conflagration they hadn't heard about.

"Ah, but de Juice," the man said, now smiling again, "de Juice safed me." The mousy niece was making some progress; the man's arm had moved about a centimeter. The man leaned forward and shook one large sausage-like forefinger at each of them. "Efry time de Chormans brought a Jew to be hanged, de Jew *himself* voot tie de noose for me. Andt efery time it voot vork. *Dis* is vy I love dease Juice!" He was crying, barely able to get the last words out.

The man sniffed in remembrance, wiped one arm across his eyes, and stood, finally allowing his niece to lead him away.

Suddenly there was a flood of waiters (miraculously revived), swirling about, clearing glasses and upset bottles. They removed the silk tablecloth stained by the beefy man's unsavory interruption and reset a fresh table, complete with eighteen forks at each setting. The two security men were trundled off to hospital; two more magically appeared, taking their place, looking just like those they replaced (they are stamped out of a mold at a secret base in North Carolina). Alexis, Monty, Weitzel, and Julius were speechless. Jacob returned again to his chair and the tornado dissipated (amazing meteorologists for the next decade, some would write doctoral theses on the phenomena that would come to be known as 'Pokorny's Tornado'). Diners resumed their sedate luncheon in a tense atmosphere of thankfully-recovered dignity.

The maître d' arrived with his dignity slightly burnished, all profuse apologies, all fluttering fuss, as though someone had offended the natural laws of the universe. The luncheon would be on the house, the guests were assured—it was nothing, nothing to the horrendous inconvenience they had experienced. No one answered him.

"My God, who *was* that man?" Alexis asked of no one in particular. No one answered her, either. The maître d' bustled and hovered and snapped his fingers, waiters trembling to respond. She got the impression, if it was possible in a place like Pokorny's, that the waiters and the maître d' were actually trying to ignore her...or ignore the question, perhaps. And then Alexis saw a strange thing.

Her widening eyes caught the attention of the others in her Party, and they all stared, shocked to see the young niece lead the strange moronic slab of a man *back to his seat* at the table from whence he'd come, and sit him down, where he resumed eating his soup. He even looked back at them and lifted his spoon gently in acknowledgement of the brief moment they had all shared together.

"By *God*, this is too much," Weitzel exploded, losing his dignity. "You there, man," he snapped his fingers at a waiter, who collapsed on the spot. The maître d' appeared in his place, instantly responsive.

"By *God*, I'll see that man tossed out of this establishment or I'll make sure that you, your family, your relatives, any children you'll ever have, and anyone who's ever met you in your miserable existence spends the rest of their lives scraping out a living on a dirt farm in Missouri!"

This fact seemed to cause the maître d' to quail; apparently farming was only slightly less abominable than hell to the denizens of New York City restaurants. His knees shook, he trembled like he had the palsy, but he alone knew what every other waiter did not. He put his hands together in supplication. "P-p-p-please, Mr. Wi-Wi-Wi-Weitzel, p-please, I *can't* throw him out, sir. That's Mr. Pokorny, sir. He *owns* the restaurant."

WAGON OF FOOLS

23 Ya'ir Stern
Haifa, Israel
June, 2009

My Dearest Pyotr;

I live in Haifa now. I have a very nice apartment that looks out over the sea. There are oranges always on the table, with a white cloth, and there are candles on Shabbat. I am old now, in the very last days, and there is an indescribable peace that is beginning to settle upon my spirit as I consider what is to come. I sit on my balcony and look at the ocean and think of a bottle, thrown far out from the beach. I imagine the water filling the bottle while the bottle is completely immersed in the sea—the water in the bottle, the bottle in the water—and can understand in this way how He can be in us while we are in Him. My throat closes with longing and emotion, and there are always tears, and I must not go out on the balcony and look at the ocean and wish for such things without my handkerchief, which I have kept close to me for the last sixty-some years. O God, I so wish to see your face; may it be soon.

My great granddaughter Areli comes to visit on Sundays, in the afternoons mostly, when the sun begins to set, and the sky is painted with all the colors that God has made in one vast and continuously renewing array of jubilation and ever-changing beauty. Areli is a strong young girl who will, if God so chooses, grow to become a vibrant and beautiful woman. She is kind to look after her old great grand Mama as she does. She is tall for an Israeli woman, with jet black hair and striking green eyes, and long, strong arms and legs. She leaps back and forth in my little apartment like a playful, mischievous cat, pouncing on a cup for tea or a lump of sugar or a shawl to keep me warm, or pretending to drop a bowl of apples when in fact she shows off to me by juggling them—a trick learned from her father. And yet I worry for her spirit, Pyotr. I worry that she may never see and understand and then experience the truth which has always been so hard to encounter, living where we do, in such times. Like many Israelis—and perhaps like all of us the world over—she has a deep, almost intense antipathy, an opposition to searching out who God really is and what He is like. It is difficult for those of her generation to get beyond law and tradition and sacrifice and our own history. She knows not the depth and breadth of His compassion and love and mercy and kindness. I suppose all this is to be expected—she has not yet been broken (may the day come soon). As I look beyond the fields and on into the horizons of her life, I worry that there may be little chance for her to encounter an opportunity to hear about this most important, most life-changing truth—the piercing sweetness that comes with an experiential knowledge of He who enfolds and swallows up all truth and all beauty; He who is in fact Truth and Beauty. And so when she comes this Sunday I will tell her this story. Much of it you know, Pyotr, but there is much you do not.

* * *

You know that I was twenty-three years old when the Germans crossed the border and invaded Russia. I lived on my family's small farm about one hundred thirty kilometers southwest of Minsk, near Baranovichi. Areli knows that I came from Russia but she knows little of my life there. I was very happy on our farm. My mother and father were good people; strong peasants who loved the land, loved the people in our village, and who had never a thought of anything other than those things which passed through our small sphere of life.

Areli does not know this but she gets her height from my father, who was very tall for a Russian Jew. He had a rich black beard and bright green eyes and he smelled of earth and horse and leather, and the rich, yeasty smell of grain before it has been hulled. My father loved of all things to sit in the barn with the animals and the smell of the land and its fruit and read Torah. He said it was the search for wisdom that drew a man closest to God, since God was wisdom Himself. He had little time for the comments and impressions and extrusions from other people—even learned Rabbis and commentators. These things, he would rail, were forced on people by others. He had the strange notion that God could make Himself clear to a man if that man simply desired to know what it was God asked of him and was willing to do it. You and he would have liked each other, Pyotr.

My father taught me the secret of how to know what God asks of us. He said one day while I sat on his knee in the barn when I was young, "Daughter, to know what God wants of us, we must simply have the heart to do what He tells us to do. And when He comes to us—as He will, most assuredly—we must do what He says *on that day*. And then we will know, *that day*, what it is He wants us to do. It is in the will, Daughter," he emphasized, holding up one rough and calloused forefinger and tapping his heart to make the point. I held his one finger in my two tiny fists; I remember this now—I can, even as I write to you, feel his calluses in my hands. "It is the *heart*, my child," he would always say. "If we have the *heart* to do His will, He will make known to us what that will is."

My mother was a short woman, thin but hearty, shorter by far than father, but just as determined, firm, and committed. Her life revolved around making a safe home for her children. I remember that she always moved deliberately but with grace. My father said that she had once been a ballet dancer, but she never spoke of this. She had lovely blue eyes and blond hair, and I remember my father looking at her with intensity and passion. It made the heart of a young girl very secure, knowing her parents were in love. She would sit on our small porch in the evening, knitting, while father read to everyone. There was Misha, my oldest brother; Alexi and Dmitri, the twins; then Yurik, and finally me, the youngest. My mother would say to me often that I was God's gift to her after four boys.

I did not get the chance to tell you about my parents when we knew each other, my dear, but perhaps there will be time later.

It was at dawn on a morning in late June of 1941 when thunder in the western sky woke me. I remember this because we were late getting the hay in that year and a day that began with rain meant that we would be gathering the hay later still. Two days prior my father had scythed the fields and the hay was aground; cut, raked, and almost dry. Rain on newly-mown hay would most assuredly concern my father, who worried so that our horses would not have enough to eat through the winter. I leapt out of bed, hurriedly threw on my working clothes, and ran down the stairs from the loft where I slept alone. Misha had gone to school to become a doctor, married a girl from a good Jewish family in Minsk, had settled there with his own medical practice, and was blessed with two lovely daughters. Alexi and Dmitri had both gone to join the Army two years ago, conscripted. We never saw any of them again. You know better than I what happened to the Jews in Minsk, and I think we heard from a relative that Alexi and Misha had both died at Stalingrad. Yurik too had gone, but south…very, very far south. Yurik had always wanted to go to Palestine, but he was not the first in our family to arrive in the Promised Land, my dear.

Father was standing on the porch that morning with my mother at his side, an arm draped across her shoulders. The light was just beginning in the east, but our porch faced to the south, and so I could only see the light on my parents' backs as they stood facing west, wondering about the thunder. I sensed their anxiety from the way they stood. My mother clasped my father's hand over her shoulder in both of hers, and he held her tightly.

I must have made a noise. "Stasy," my mother cried, almost too loudly, surprised, "you startled me."

"The thunder woke me, Mama," I said. "We should get in the hay before it is ruined."

My father turned and smiled at me, strong white teeth showing through his beard. There were flecks of gray in it now, streaked in a way I had not seen when I had sat upon his knee in the barn so long ago. "You should know," he said gently. "You will be running the farm when I am gone."

"Well, you are not gone yet, Poppa, and we need the hay gathered before it is wet. Should I hitch the team?"

My father looked again to the west. "There will be no rain today," he said, gazing into the far distance. "It is the sound of guns that has disturbed you, my daughter, not thunder. The Germans are coming."

Five days later, on the 26th of June, after we had gotten in our hay safely, we saw vehicles in the west. I would later learn that they were from the 66th Panzer Corps, and the history books will tell you that on that day they captured Baranovichi with little effort. What the history books do not say is that the Germans were given instructions to lay waste to everything in their path. I am brought to the stone step of despair and yet lifted to the highest cliffs of hope when I realize how very little effort the Germans exerted that day, to release the hold my parents had on life and send them into a far better field, and what significant impact such effort had on my life.

We were in the fields that morning when the motorcycles appeared a few kilometers away. My father, peering into the distance, turned to me and spoke in an odd, uncharacteristically harsh voice. "Stasy, run to the cellar; they will want food, and perhaps if we can put out some potatoes and onions...yes, and get out the wheel of cheese from last fall too, they will like that. Perhaps they will take those and leave us alone." He lifted an arm to point toward the house. "Go now, run!"

I gathered up my skirts and flew across the field, not thinking, just wishing to do my father's bidding. The motorcycles were advance elements of a larger force, and they raced up the road toward our farm. There was the unforgettable sound of clanking behind them, a sound of metal moving as though it was alive; a sound I would later learn came from tanks, striking fear in the hearts of soldiers on foot. They were Panzer Kampf Wagon light tanks, the PzKw III model, used for reconnaissance, and I would learn in the days to come just where to put a sticky bomb on their treads to disable them, and how to kill the men that fought in them.

But just then I did not stop to gaze. I got to the house, ran into the kitchen and darted down the stairs into the cellar just as a sound like popping corn came across the fields. Then there was a single great boom and suddenly there was a crash in the house above me. Dust cascaded down through the floorboards. I dropped the potato bucket I'd been carrying and ran back up the stairs. The door was slightly jammed, and I tried to shove against it, and there came another great noise and I lost my ability to perceive my surroundings. My teeth ached for some reason, and my eyes could not focus. And then the door flew back, struck me in the face, and I knew no more.

It was dark when I awoke. I was lying on my back, covered by smoking potatoes. I was not sure what time it was. I was not sure what day it was. I sat up, painfully. I reached up and touched my cheek; there was a stickiness on one side of my face. My feet eventually steadied upon the hard dirt floor and I was able to stand. There was a smell of smoke and burnt potatoes. The cellar door was shut, or blocked, I could not tell which. I walked unsteadily up the stairs and pushed with all my might against the door, and eventually it fell to one side. No light flooded down, no sunshine, no fresh air; nothing but darkness, the acrid smell of smoke, and a stench… an indescribable stench which I hope I shall never again experience. Light was in the east, and I realized that I had slept the entire day in the cellar. Something was not right; my parents would surely have come to get me, and then I remembered, and began to run toward the field.

In the dim light I saw clumps on the ground, and there I found my mother and father sprawled in the rich soil of their own land, land upon which they'd worked and sweated and from which they'd drawn sustenance enough to raise five children, land which had given them its blood but which had now taken back theirs into its embrace. I imagined them standing together, my father's arm still around my mother's shoulder, both bravely facing the Germans. I imagined I heard the shots, and saw them fall, my father seeking to protect my mother as life drained from them. I suddenly realized why my father had sent me for potatoes and onions, and I put my face in my hands, fell to my knees, and my soul flowed out in anguish into the dark loam.

I awoke when the rain began to fall. I had collapsed there beside the bodies of my mother and father, my head on my father's cold chest. The rain spattered against my face. My hair was tangled and dirty. My skirts were stained with the ashes of my house, which I had run through on my way to the field. The Germans had shelled our home; it was the shelling that had knocked me back down into the cellar and falling into the potatoes saved my life as my house and my life burned and fell to pieces above me.

As the rain came, it helped clear my mind. I stood, fearful to see two large vultures standing on the ground not ten meters away. I picked up a clod of dirt and threw it in anger, and they rustled their wings and darted their heads in arrogant indignation and flew away. I ran after them, yelling, screaming, throwing what dirt or stones I could find. I then went to the barn for a shovel to dig my parents' grave. The Germans had burned the barn to the ground. I cast about the ashes, but everything we'd owned besides our clothes and the furniture in our house and our kitchen things had been stored in the barn—our tools, our harnesses, our seed, our straw, our oats, our livestock. With that thought I started, remembering our horses, and looked in the pasture. There was no sign of them. The Germans had taken them, as they had taken our cows and our sheep and our geese. They'd left nothing but two bodies and two spires of smoke.

I tell you, Pyotr, that as I sit here on this hill in Haifa looking out over the ocean, waiting to join my parents, I can think of stepping into His great eternal sea with clarity and eagerness, but then...O, then, my dear love, then my heart was filled with nothing but rage, and anger, and a sick despairing, and I remember thinking that I would never see my parents again and that the finality of death was so utterly crushing. It is strange how not knowing about things is the cause of so much pain. I did not know then what I know now, my dear.

So…so I walked to where our kitchen had once been, scrabbled among the blackened timbers and crumbled stones until I found our cast iron skillet, still warm, and then marched back to where my parents lay, and for hours I dug there in the field and scraped a grave out of the mud. I laid the shells of their souls in the ground to rest together, covered them in the shallow depression, and then knelt and bowed my head, for what reason I know not, since at the time I knew nothing of He Who best comforts those in grief. It was perhaps grief itself that prostrated me, and in that remembrance, I also recalled that my lack of belief in God, or any semblance of obedience to the dictates of His heart, was the cause of much of my parents' grief.

The rain was falling in great heavy droplets shaped like tears as I finished. I stood, brushed the soil from my parents' farm from my hands, and began to walk east, following the tracks of the panzers toward Minsk, toward Misha and what family I could find. The Germans got there before me.

* * *

I wonder what Areli would say if she knew that her great-grandmother once lived for a year as a partisan in the Russian forest. Would she be surprised to know that this ancient, doddering, fragile old woman once ran through snow and mud and field and hedge, catching and killing rabbits and then men, at first dodging and then hunting German patrols, joining with bands of Russian Jews hiding in the woods, fighting the Germans?

I tried to find my brother in Minsk. The Germans arrived on the 28th of June, 1941—two days after they had murdered my father and mother, and several weeks before I could stumble one hundred and thirty kilometers over a raped and ravaged countryside. Within hours after their arrival in Minsk the Germans promptly rounded up almost forty thousand men: Jews, Russian soldiers, and non-Jewish males. They put them in a large field surrounded by barbed wire and floodlights. I do not know if Misha was there. German officials appeared shortly after putting everyone into this enclosure. They had a list (the Germans always have lists, Pyotr, dear). They called out the intelligentsia, the professionals, the educated class. Perhaps Misha stepped forward, perhaps not; I don't know…many did. Almost two thousand came forward, thinking quite logically that perhaps they would be set apart to do some particularly delicate work, perhaps be engaged in the administrative effort that the Germans certainly must undertake to manage so many prisoners. I do not know what they thought. We did not know then that reason, logic, and humanity had fled the world as light flees when a candle is extinguished.

The Germans led these men out of the wire prison, took them into the forest outside Minsk, and promptly shot them all. I do not know what ever happened to Misha, or his wife, or his children. I cherished a hope that perhaps they escaped into the woods to join the resistance. I have never heard a thing from him or about him…but I will soon learn all there is to know, dear Pyotr, never fear.

I arrived at the outskirts of Minsk in early September of 1941. It was God's intervention that kept me from entering the city; had I done so, I most certainly would have been arrested and shot immediately, for I would have tried to cut the eyes out of the first German soldier I encountered. No, it was God's mercy that kept me out of the city. I was staggering toward its skyline when I was intercepted by three men, a picket patrol for the fledgling resistance.

I spent a few weeks with this band, my dear. We never spoke of it when we knew each other, but I know you saw the effects. I could feel your eyes upon me at times when the unbearable hardness of my soul would shine like Krupp steel through what little veneer was left to a Russian peasant girl who had endured the murder of her family and watched both Russians and Germans die in inconceivable agony for unfathomable reasons. I never told you about my best friend I made there in the woods, Katerina Damaskova. She wasn't in the resistance, you know. She was just a young girl from a farm where our teams would occasionally go to sleep. We would braid each other's hair now and again. Her parents had a nice barn and many horses. The Germans came one day and they hanged her in the barnyard, along with three partisans they caught sleeping in the barn. Twenty grim-faced, butchering Germans stood and laughed while Katerina died slowly. We watched through binoculars two hundred meters from the farm, hidden in the trees with no weapons, helpless. I cried for two days and then went out with this band of partisans and dynamited a German supply convoy.

I come now to the time just before we met. You do not know this part of our story, my dear, so perhaps it is time now for you to know, before I see you again. There was something, some urge, which would not let me stay near Minsk. I had to be away, to search, to look for something, and truthfully, at the time I knew not what it was. Perhaps it was simply fear that drove me; fear of the Germans, fear that if I stayed in any one spot, they would catch me. So I donned pants, diminished my figure under a bulky field jacket, tucked my hair under a man's cap, shouldered my submachine gun, and walked alone into the depths of Russia, looking for peace in the forgetfulness and pain of wandering.

Sometime in the second week after leaving that first group of fighters, as I stumbled around the steppes trying to avoid anything that sounded remotely of engines or machines or gunfire, I came across another small band of partisans. They saw me and somehow knew immediately I was a wandering comrade. This was a stroke of unimaginable luck, you see. Perhaps you did not know, Pyotr, that the Germans had begun infiltrating partisan bands with Russian-speaking Germans disguised as partisans. They would use Russians by paying them to inform on their countrymen. With the majority of the Red Army streaming eastward before the conquering German blitzkrieg, there was confusion and chaos everywhere. In those days, in those times, in those places, a person's life was not worth the clothes on their back. That these partisans would recognize me as one of their own instead of shooting me outright was lucky, as some would say.

On the fourth day after I met them I went on patrol with a small squad to their designated sector of the forest, where we hoped to set up a mortar and disrupt the Germans in their night lagers as they tried to sleep. We did this occasionally, and I read in history books that it helped to make their lives miserable. I am glad of it.

As night approached we found a bunker in the old Stalin line set back from a row of truncated pine trees, hidden well by the trees. We approached the bunker with tactics learned from months of bloody mistakes, made sure it was safe, and the rest of the patrol entered after it was cleared. At the door, just as I was about to enter, a strange thing happened. I found that I couldn't go in. Something held me back. I thought it was fear, but I had had too much recent experience burying my fear, so I just pushed this strange sensation down and strode into the bunker behind my comrades. But there would be something stranger still.

A man named Grigori had the watch before me. Grigori was a Jew from Vilna who had lost his family when one of the Einsatzgruppen came through his village. You do not need me to tell you of these special squads, Pyotr—not in this letter, please. Grigori was in the woods when they came that day, and he has lived in the woods ever since.

After Grigori finished his watch, he woke me quietly and I stood, took up my submachine gun, and walked to a place just outside the bunker entrance, a guard spot positioned well in a small clearing behind a thick clump of trees that covered the entrance and offered a good field of view to its approach. We were to set up the mortar later, in the early hours of the morning. The moon was high that night, and full. It reflected all its silver glory upon the frost-covered fields. The trees covered the entrance with shadows, but the shadows were not as deep or as dark as usual because of the brightness of the moon. They called it a hunter's moon. I was grateful for its brightness as I sat there in the cold clearing. I thought it would give me good warning of any approaching danger…such was my ignorance of reality then.

Pyotr, my dear, I know that you thought me callous and harsh when we met, and you did not understand my fears. Perhaps what I tell you now will explain.

The Germans came flooding across Russia like a plague, like an invading army of locusts, like a virus—but, Pyotr, more than anything, and I cringe even now to write what I write—there was trailing in their wake such an attendant stench of demonic activity that the half of it cannot even be imagined in today's world that denies even the existence of such things. But those who would deny such things did not see what I saw in the forests of Russia in those years, Pyotr, things that made strong men's blood run cold. And the state of men's souls in Russia at the time was such, my dear, that there was but little defense against such an onslaught.

Settling in on my watch that night, I looked up to find the North Star. I noticed that there was a strange blackness, like a stain in the sky, and the stars in one portion of the sky were blotted out. I looked down again at the path leading to the bunker. It was clear and easily seen in the moonlight flooding down through the trees, for the stain had not covered the moon. I started suddenly. There was some sort of shadow descending into the wood. In my years in the forest, I saw many strange things, but nothing compared to what I saw that night. I remember that when I first saw it, I did not immediately sense any threat, but thought simply that it was a trick of the light. But no, the night sky was clear; stars could be seen outside the brilliant silver roundness of the moon, and this shadow was following a winding path. And then I noticed that the forest had become exceedingly quiet. There was no wind where a moment ago the wind had gently stirred the trees. There were no sounds of animals, or creaking branches, or anything possessing the breath of life.

This shadow, a moving dimness, seemed to be coming through the forest, traversing the path which led to the bunker's entrance. It appeared as an utter negation of the natural forest God made; an attempted negation, therefore, of God's nature, a slash across the portrait of His creation. It possessed no form or solidity. I could see the foliage and trees behind it.

As this thing stained the ground on the path that would bypass my position, I remember…I remember that the hair on my neck stood, and my flesh crawled. I remember—and I will never forget this, Pyotr—that I became, in a moment, extremely agitated in my spirit, and my physical body was affected powerfully, as if I'd eaten too many tea leaves. I began to tremble, not with cold, but with an unimaginable and unknowing fear. My mind became blank. I could not think. I could not cry out or speak or whisper; my throat was paralyzed as surely as if a powerful man had clamped his hand around my neck. I know now what this was, but did not know at the time. At the time, all I knew was mind-numbing terror.

As this thing came between me and the entrance to the bunker, it paused, and I could sense—though do not ask me how—that it turned and considered me. It was then that I heard in my mind a word.

Today, Pyotr, people believe that we give words to things—things are first, and then words come later as a name to things. But this is not so, my dear. In truth words come first, the names of things, and the word—the name—then enables the emergence into reality of that which is so named—words are first, then things. There in the forest that night, a word was spoken into my soul. I could tell it emanated from this shadow, and I felt my soul falling into a chasm of despair; blackening, burning, curling unbidden like paper dropped into a furnace. Yet just before my very essence dissipated, another word was spoken, or formed; a word of clarity and wholeness and sanity and piercing sweetness, and I felt...restored, whole, and very, very tender, like newly-grown skin after it has been burned.

Almost in response to this cleansing word, I was then strikingly, sickeningly overpowered with such a blast of hate and malice that nothing I could write would convey the half of it. With every ounce of strength and courage I possessed I looked up and saw (or felt, I am not sure) pure malevolence—unadulterated, intense hatred. But for some reason—and even at the time, my dear, I was aware of it—there was a boundary, a fence, or some type of restraint that kept it from me. I will always believe that it had something to do with that spoken word of clarity and wholeness. The evil was restrained from physically harming me, and I could tell that this restraint greatly angered it, but alas it seemed to realize that it could yet assault my spirit and it did so with such violence that I was rocked backward and fell to the ground.

And then came the stench...O, God, there came then such an overpowering infusion of spoilage and death that went beyond the sense of smell to assault the very soul. This shadow exuded a billowing train of such pure ordure that my stomach heaved on the spot and I bent over, sick, at the foot of a tree. And so I crouched there, incapacitated with fear, trembling uncontrollably, on my hands and knees. Then…then came a sudden chilling rush of cold, and I knew somehow with a vile certainty it was Death itself, flowing into the bunker like a knife flows into flesh. I collapsed onto the soiled forest floor, curling into myself, terrified beyond all reason, oppressed by a supernatural terror which cannot be explained, but which, to those who've experienced it, requires no explanation.

I came to myself as the first streaks of light banished the stars and the wind was again moving in the trees. I picked up my weapon and stumbled to the entrance of the bunker. No power on earth would have compelled me to move beyond that doorway, but I tripped over something and fell, clumsily, into the center of the bunker nonetheless, hands and arms splayed into a dark, sticky, dirty substance. I looked up in the dim light and saw my five comrades, tossed around the room as though they had been caught in some gruesome harvesting machine…but I will not describe it further. They were dead, all of them, killed like stock in a slaughterhouse, and I knew that no human power had done such a thing. The horror was such that I bolted to my feet and ran from the entrance screaming in pure terror. The screaming was the last thing I can remember of that day.

✳ ✳ ✳

The next thing I remember was the piercing, triumphant neighing of a horse. This was a strange thing to hear in the forest. Arkady—he was the one who would run around the wagon much of the time, hands in the air, leaping and crying out, in case you do not remember, my dear—Arkady told me later that it was actually Afanasy who first saw me. Apparently I was nothing but a ragged form crumpled upon the side of the road.

"Afanasy let out one of his great stallion calls, you know, Stasy, and then Bogdan joined to confirm it. Bogdan was always doing what Afanasy wanted, anyway, and they were both pulling the lead wagon that day, like they do every day, of course. Pyotr could do nothing but look around, because these two horses, they spoke to him, you know, and it was then that he saw you…Oh yes, Pyotr, he saw you, yes he did." Arkady did like to go on so, Pyotr, do you remember?

You and your wagon of fools came upon me there on the side of the road, a shattered wraith in a blood-covered field jacket, no hat or scarf, no weapon, wearing men's pants that were unspeakably ripped and torn. I do not remember how long I had been out of my mind. It could have been a day or a month; I have no recollection of that time. It is as if my life was divided into two very distinct parts—the time before the bunker, and the time after. I do remember, though, that from the earliest days of my memory, every day on my farm in the bosom of my family, from the day that I left my murdered parents buried under the soil of that farm, on the day that I went into that bunker, and up to the very hour when I left that bunker to take up my guard post, my hair had been a thick, rich, deep, chestnut brown. And I know dear Pyotr, that when you found me sitting in the mud by the side of the road, mindlessly pounding the ground with a rock, my hair was an utterly stark white; a shocked, unruly, swirling mass from petrified roots to its bitter ends.

You know of what followed after we met, dear Pyotr, but I should write it anyway. It helps if you know how your wagon of fools looked to my eyes, it may help others understand about the things you did in the war, and it helps me to remember. It is in the particular blossom of remembrance that the aging flower of gratefulness gives forth its penultimate fragrance.

* * *

You stopped the wagon and got down, resting the reins on the seat. You first went to Afanasy's head and spoke to him and then walked in front of the team and came to where I sat in the mud. I remember then that there was the sound of a man, running about beyond my field of vision, exclaiming nonsensically. I could hear his footsteps in the mud like small slaps. You knelt down to stare at me and looked directly into my eyes. I can remember this because your face is that which called me out of the horror of my memory and it is your face which is upon page one of my life after... after the bunker. I have not forgotten your face, Pyotr. You looked at me and the terror in my soul began to diminish.

Slowly, softly at first, you wiped my face with a handkerchief. With this first human touch I awoke, and I put my hand to yours—you told me all this later; I didn't remember any of this at the time, except your face. I gripped your hand and that cloth with a fierce intensity and would not let go. You told me later that I would not release that small handkerchief for ten days. No, my dear, I have not yet released that little handkerchief and it has been more than sixty years.

As my consciousness returned dimly through a bitter and poisonous fog, there was gradually the absence of what I had come to believe was the central reality of life; the rhythmic, sequential sound upon which I'd focused since becoming conscious. I had stopped hitting the ground with the rock.

There was a different noise then, and more running feet, and for the first time I heard your voice, commanding men to do things, and another voice, softer, more difficult to hear, insistent but laced with tenderness. I felt myself lifted gently and you and your friends carried me into the first wagon. I could hear horses snorting; I felt their power and their presence as I was carried past them like a person who is carried on a stretcher close to a fireplace feels the heat, and inexplicably I felt my terror drain away like filthy water draining from a basin.

I was laid in the back of the wagon and I remember looking up to see a wizened old man with leathery skin in a Red Army uniform with thin, bony hands moving amidst a pile of rags, talking to himself with an impossibly soft voice. I was shaking, and I could not hear well enough to understand what he said, but I do remember that he looked at me as my head turned toward him, and he leaned over the pile of rags and then I realized that in fact he was talking to me, saying, "You sleep now, Daughter…you sleep now." He spoke to me in Hebrew, which I thought strange. And then I went to sleep with the old man's soft voice in my ears along with the rustling as he rummaged in the rag pile.

When I awoke, the wagon was rocking gently. I heard the sound of the horses' hooves on the road, plodding gently. The old man, whose name I would learn was Dukhi, was still there, muttering. He was staring forward, through the opening, watching the road. There were rags around my hands.

"The crazed woman is awake." A deadpan monotone, devoid of any emotion, came from the back of the wagon. I lifted my head to see a Russian soldier's cap at the back edge of the wagon. There was another voice then. "She's awake, she's awake, she's awake." The voice ran around the wagon toward the driver.

"I see that she is awake, Arkady," I heard you say. "Thank you. Dukhi will look after her."

The monotone voice came again. "You be careful of this Dukhi, Lieutenant, he is not to be trusted." The old man looked slightly grieved, but otherwise gave no sign that he'd heard the insinuation from the emotionless voice.

"I am always careful, Svoboda," the lieutenant replied slowly. I realized that the voice of the lieutenant was that voice which had called me out of my horror, and it was then I surmised that I had been picked up by Russian soldiers.

"Are you...are you Red Army?" I asked of Dukhi.

With no break in flow or tone, no increase in volume, Dukhi just kept talking.

I extended one of my rag-covered hands to catch his attention. "Excuse me...but are you soldiers? Russian soldiers?"

Dukhi paused, then began to speak again, this time looking at me. I tried to rise but could not, and so he leaned closer and spoke to me in Russian.

"We are; you are safe. I am Sergeant Dushkovic. I am called Dukhi. I cannot speak too loudly. A German shot me in the throat three months ago and so if you wish to speak with me you must stay close and be quiet and then you can hear what I am saying to you. Do you understand?"

I nodded. He was a strange old man, with a rough, lined face but kind eyes. His beard, spotty and grizzled, short in some places, stubbled in others, was gray.

"Where are we going?" I asked.

He shrugged. "We pick up Jews," he replied quietly, whispering. "It is what we do."

"Jews!" I exclaimed, all breath gone from my body. Was I a rabbit who escaped from a fox only to find itself in the jaws of a wolf? "What...what happens to them when you...when you pick them up? Do you...do you shoot them?"

Dukhi made a quiet sound, much like that which my mother would make to calm me after a frightening storm, and patted me on the head and smiled with his eyes. The old man's eyes twinkled, and in them it seemed to me then that all the light and life of stars were made manifest. I began to breathe again.

"We are not going to shoot you, Daughter. We go round to the villages in Russia to warn the Jews about the Germans, to help them get away. The Germans have come across much of Russia this year, you know, and it seems they are everywhere. There is a great evil that follows their armies, and they are seeking to kill as many Jews as they can, along with every Russian that gets in their way. So we go to villages and tell the Jews that there will be Germans coming to kill them and we help them to run away and hide."

My eyes widened with fright when he used the words 'great evil', but I would not speak of it. I wondered about the truth of what he was telling me. In my time in the forest I had not heard of such a unit. "What does the Red Army care about Jews?" I asked suspiciously.

"The Red Army cares nothing for the Jews. The Lieutenant, he is the one who cares for the Jews. Are you hungry? You have not yet eaten, and you do not look well. Here, eat this." He handed me a small piece of black bread softened in milk, and I took it. I heard a horse whinny. Dukhi went on speaking, but I could not hear.

I laid back again onto the bed they had made for me, confused and fearful. While Russia was not barbaric to its Jewish population, to conceive of a Red Army unit detailed to specifically seek out and protect Jews was... was beyond comprehension.

"Who is the Lieutenant in charge of the unit?"

Dukhi simply nodded toward you, my dear, with your broad back a few meters away, sitting straight, arms bent holding the reins, talking softly to the horses as you drove. I saw that it was beginning to snow.

"Where are we going now? What do his orders say?"

Dukhi shook his head. "You do not understand, Daughter. The Army doesn't care where we go or what we do. The Lieutenant decides where we go, if the horses agree. He pays more attention to the horses than to the Commissars or the Army commanders…and he is wise do so."

I ate the rest of my bread in silence and went back to sleep, rocking in the slow and peaceful embrace of a conveyance drawn by living creatures.

In the days to come, I realized that I could not sleep without Dukhi or you, Pyotr, in the same wagon. If you or Dukhi were not close by, I would awake screaming, dreaming of fire. I realized that I was not whole, then, and within me began to gnaw the fear that perhaps I never would be. That word…that destructive *word* that had been spoken and which had threatened to consume my soul still haunted much of my conscious awareness and prowled unfettered when I slept, unless Dukhi or you were there—you driving, or Dukhi rooting around in the back of the wagon constantly talking in that still, small voice.

I asked Dukhi about you one day, soon after you picked me up. I had to listen very carefully.

"The Lieutenant was with a tank company in June, near Bialystok with an advance armor element of the 10th Army, when the Germans invaded. They were overrun and almost everyone was killed, but he escaped and came back to 10th Army headquarters. They assigned him to drive a wagon instead of a tank, and here we are." It was not until several weeks later, when they let me out of the back of the wagon, that I could talk with you to learn the entire story. Do you remember telling me this? I will write what you told me, Pyotr, so that we can both remember.

* * *

You were raised in a good home on a farm near Leningrad. Your parents were strong, hard-working farmers. You had a productive parcel of land with a few cows and some pigs and a large timber lot, which you and your father and your brothers worked to provide lumber for your village. You were ten, and the Revolution had occurred thirteen years ago.

When you were eighteen, you had a close friend—Mikhail Kutosov—whom you had known since boyhood. You and he would go everywhere together, true brothers. He would work in the lumber yard with you and your family, and he was the hardest worker. He was very strong, you said, and could lift trees others could not. Some would marvel, others would be jealous, but you thought it wonderful. You both had made plans, you said; you two were going to become the greatest warriors in Russian history. You were very martial then, and both dreamed of becoming soldiers in the glorious Red Army to protect the motherland.

But as the days went by and the nature of Lenin's government emerged, holding Christ in disdain, and subjugating Christians (as is the nature of tyranny everywhere), Mikhail could no longer look forward to serving in the Red Army. His heart was closer to his God than to his country. Alas, you could not understand this. As the days went by and as Lenin consolidated power, there were unmistakable signs that Mikhail was becoming more disturbed.

"These men taking over the country," he would say as you and he sawed logs into planks, "have no conception of the God of Abraham, Isaac, and Jacob. Their godlessness will ruin this country, mark my words. No nation survives the removal of God." You looked around nervously, for the Cheka were everywhere.

Mikhail's constant reference to God, as though Mikhail had a very close relationship with Him, as though he could know who God was and what He wanted, was the only irritating thing between the two of you. You and your family were faithful attendants at the Russian Orthodox Church, but Mikhail and his father would worship privately, in their home, even when the local priest would come to their house and rail against their godlessness and heresy. But in the very core of Mikhail's nature you saw a great difference.

There was an emphasis on not just reading but living the Scriptures, and Mikhail not only knew *about* God, you felt that he *knew* God. You told me that he would speak of God as he spoke of a friend, as a person he knew, as a person who ruled his life. In Mikhail there was nobility and peace and intensity and…and a sense of 'aliveness', you told me, that made Mikhail so different from others. You felt proud to be associated with such a man, and, you said with tears in your eyes one evening as our wagon moved along under a bright moon, you secretly hoped that when people saw you together, they would assume your character to be as strong and sterling and lofty as his. It was one of the reasons you remained his friend.

One day on the streets of Leningrad you saw a notice announcing that the Red Army was accepting recruits for a prestigious training academy to supply officers for the new forces they were building, and your blood raced to think of such a career! You rushed to Mikhail to share this great news with him. Here was a chance for you both to fulfill your destinies. But Mikhail's reaction shocked you.

"Why do you want to spend your life's blood defending a bunch of Bolsheviks, Pyotr?" he asked. "I have no fear of death, but to be found supporting those who oppose my God fills me with fear." He leaned close and spoke with a quiet, intense passion. "Come with me and my father. We are leaving this God-forsaken land," he said, spitting the words, describing the new government with disdain. "It is godless. We can no longer support the things they do. We are going to Finland; we have some cousins there. God would not have us lift up arms and defend such evil, I do not care what the priests say." You argued with him throughout the night, with him and his father, whom you respected and revered, but they would not acquiesce, and you left broken-hearted, but too with the beginnings of bitterness growing in your heart. They had cast a shadow across your greatest dream.

On the announced day you reported to the center where officers of the Red Army were taking applicants—without Mikhail. There was a large table covered with a cloth, and cakes, and fruit, and a band was playing. Young men moved through the crowd with boldness. Young women swirled around the room as if enraptured, talking excitedly with officers in dashing uniforms, leather boots and belts gleaming, moustaches bristling with martial vigor. You were dazzled.

The applicants queued to speak with the officers at various tables. You desperately wanted to join the tank corps, but this was the longest line. And so you waited; nothing would put you off from your destiny! You saw Father Alexi from the Orthodox Church eating a pastry, and you spoke with him for several moments while you waited in line. He was full of praise for the government, for Lenin's reforms, for the new place the Church would have, side by side with the ruling classes. You listened respectfully.

When your time came, you stepped up bravely to face the man behind the table. He wore a splendid uniform, and you could barely breathe as you imagined yourself in such splendor. He looked up at you with a hard face, for it had been a long day. There was a grim set to his features and you remembered that his moustache was short, with sharp black hairs, and he had not shaved well that morning, for stubble was to be seen around the bristles. He had black eyes.

"Name?"

"Pyotr Federoskiya."

"Town or village?"

"Leningrad." You hoped that the officer would be impressed, but he made no indication.

"Age?"

"Twenty."

The man looked up at you; perhaps he did not like what he saw. "Why do you want to join the armor?" he asked. You felt that his question was asked in a tone as hard as the armor on his tanks.

You stammered, and told him that you thought that perhaps history could be, or would be, made with this new weapon, and that you wanted to be part of such a great and glorious future. Apparently this did not impress the officer.

"We hear this all the time, young man. Are you aware that this is the hardest and most demanding branch of service for the People's Army? And of all things, you must be politically reliable." He looked again at you with a sharp eye. "You are politically reliable, are you not?"

You gulped and nodded. The man behind the table was again not impressed, and after a short pause, made a note in his book.

"We have too many applicants for the tank corps, Pyotr Federoskiya. You should consider applying to the infantry. Next!"

You were crushed, and as you turned from the table to leave, your eye caught the form of Father Alexi, moving through the crowd, his huge belly before him like the prow of a ship, shoving cake into his mouth with one hand, waving the other in the air as if to fan the flames of good feeling in the room. The thought flashed, and you acted without thinking—either with your head or your heart.

"Wait!" you said, and turned back to the hard man. "I *am* politically reliable. I can prove this to you. I love this country, and I can prove this to you as well." Your mouth was dry, you told me later, and you were ignoring an aching bitterness that suddenly sprouted in your chest that made it hard to breathe, but you pressed it down like a dying man reaches for any hope and spoke hurriedly to the tank officer.

"I know a man, here, in this city, who has spoken against the...against the party. He and his father are planning to betray the country. They are going to run away. They...they are not reliable, and they are a danger to the motherland." There. You said it, and there was no way to turn time around and withdraw the words. There was a stone in your chest.

"Who is this man and his father to you?" the officer asked sharply. Another man, standing behind the row of officers taking applications, moved closer to listen to the exchange. He was a tall, thin, cadaverous officer with a crawling white scar across his face and a black cap.

"He was a friend of my youth," you said with strident, almost brash assertion, and you told me that when you said this you stuck out your chin and hardened your eyes and clenched your fists. "He and his father have worked with my family since I was young. We had been friends, until I learned that he is planning to betray...betray the party. This is unacceptable. I learned this just yesterday," you added, thinking quickly. The eyes of the other man, the thin, lethal one, eased, for he had been poised to ask the very question you answered. This man gave an indecipherable signal to the tank officer seated behind the desk.

"What is this man's name and address?" You told him, sealing the fate of Mikhail and his father.

The officer spoke with a deadened voice that would ring in your ears like acid for years to come. "You are accepted, Pyotr Federoskiya. You will make a good officer in the people's struggle. Take this application, complete it, and then report to the Commandant in the building across the street. You will be marshaled for transport to the academy in three days." The man handed you a sheaf of papers and you moved away to the tables with cake and fruit and you sat and wondered that you did not feel wicked or unrighteous. There was that nagging sensation in your chest, but the prospect of rolling across the Russian steppes in the cupola of a tank, the dust flying behind you, the banners waving, the crack of the main gun and the smoke and excitement of armored warfare, all served to diminish what pangs of conscience might have remained. You looked up from contemplating your future to see Father Alexi speaking conspiratorially with the thin man wearing the black cap, and they were looking at you. Father Alexi at least was smiling, holding up a piece of cake.

* * *

In the summer of 1940 you reported to the armor academy and finished with a good record. They posted you to a tank company in the occupied territory that had once been Poland. You thought this was a wonderful opportunity, since they only put the finest officers forward. The others were sent to rear-area battalions and supply centers for logistics duty. The Germans had invaded Poland and Stalin had pushed the Red Army into what remained of the victimized nation, carving up great huge chunks of some of the best farmland in Europe under cover of the non-aggression pact signed by Ribbentrop and Molotov. The Poles had no armed force left to them, casualties among the invading Russians were negligible, and morale was high. You were on your way to your dream.

Your unit was equipped with the BT-8 tank, a light, maneuverable vehicle built on an American chassis. You were in command of a platoon, trained to maneuver eight tanks in support of the infantry. You were esteemed by your Company Commander for your quick thinking, your bravery, and your willingness to sweat and labor and join with your men to do the hard things. Your efficiency reports were glowing. You were proud of your men, your unit, and, most of all, yourself.

One day in late June of 1941, very early in the morning, the sound of artillery exploding awoke you and your fellow officers in barracks. The rail line leading north out of your bivouac was destroyed, and you could see explosions marching toward the parking area where your unit's tanks were stored. You yelled to the others, ran to the enlisted barracks, rounded up your crews, and moved your unit out of the tank park just as artillery shells began to explode nearby. You looked up with alarm; Stukas were falling on the fuel depot, and it went up with great gouts of orange and blank flame, smoke writhing in anger. And then the Panzers came rolling over the horizon.

The German tanks were slower than yours but much better armored, with a better main gun and better optics. Soon your platoon had only one tank remaining—yours. And then suddenly a German shell found your tank, your loader and gunner and driver were screaming, and you were blown out of the hatch, lying on the ground, your uniform smoking but otherwise unhurt. The ammunition in your tank began to explode, and you ran, not to rescue your men but away, into the woods, away from the Panzers. The machine guns from the Panzers followed, cutting down your fellow tank crews as they too fled.

A Red Army infantry company came from nowhere, arriving in trucks. You could have stepped out of the woods and joined them to attack the Panzers that had decimated your own unit, but you were shaking, you told me, and you were afraid, and you were under cover and desperately wished to stay safe. You watched as the infantry dismounted and began to form up in units, their officers barking orders under a blazing sun, the tension rising as ammunition and tanks and fuel storage bunkers exploded in the distance, soldiers looking over their shoulders with eyes widening in fear. The Panzers found them at long range and the trucks began to explode, scattering the infantry like ants in an overturned anthill. Men ran everywhere and then the Stukas came out of the sky again. Bombs fell among them, slaughtering. You watched from the woods. Some of the infantry tried to run to where you stood under the thick cover of the forest. You watched them die under the guns of the Panzers and the Stukas, and then you turned and ran into the forest.

It was there in the forest, as you faced your failure while making your way back to units of the Red Army, when God began to refine you. He had prepared the ground of your heart, had ploughed it, and was now ready to plant His seed of the Spirit in you so that it would bear fruit.

Thousands of Red Army soldiers were fleeing the Germans. Many were caught and shot out of hand. One day you found yourself in a swamp, surrounded by a company of German infantry as it sought to eliminate Red Army soldiers caught in one of their encirclement pockets. You hadn't eaten in four days. You were tired, hungry, weak, but most of all, terrified. You knew what the Germans would do when they caught you. Suddenly you saw another soldier, incredibly, hiding just meters from your position. He had seen you as well, and was motioning for you to come closer. You slid on your belly and moved closer to him. He was just a boy, you saw, also suffering, with sunken cheeks in a thin face, dark eyes, the beginnings of a wispy, youthful beard, and a tattered uniform that hung from him like a sheet. He had lost his boots but still had his rifle. You had nothing but your sidearm. He was an infantryman, a soldier from the ranks.

"Lieutenant," he whispered in a raspy voice, "I have been watching these Germans. When they find someone, they all rush at him. They are closing the circle like hunters around a trapped deer. One of us can escape, though. Now listen."

And this man whom you'd never met, this soldier from the ranks, proceeded to describe to you, a Lieutenant, a Red Army officer, his plan. "When they get close, I will run, in that direction," he pointed with one hand while the other was flat on his chest, "and the Germans close to us in the closing circle will chase me. You hide here, let them pass, and then move in the other direction. You will be out of the trap. But you must wait for me... you must not—you *cannot*—do anything until I act, do you understand?"

"But wait," you whispered, putting a hand on his arm. You were confused and frightened. "Why...who are you? What is your name?" You were speaking quickly; you wanted to know who this man was but there wasn't much time. You told me later that you realized then that as an officer you could have ordered this man to stay and chosen yourself to run, that you could have sacrificed for him...but in tacit acceptance of his sacrifice, in agreeing to a plan that would have him give up his life to save yours, all you said was "Why would you do such a thing?"

The man turned to face you and looked directly into your eyes and I remember that when you were telling me about this part of your story you paused and could not speak for a moment. There must have been in the boy's look something that struck deep within your heart, something you could not explain then, but I think I know what it was now. The young man said a strange thing.

"I am Davidovitch," he said softly, with an intense passion, "remember my people. Now get ready; there is no time."

The sound of German soldiers moving in the swamp was close, and all too soon the young boy leapt up and sprinted through the low brush, splashing in the muddy water, his left arm held out, parallel to the ground for balance, the other arm holding the rifle high to keep it dry, clearly visible. In a moment, Germans began shouting for him to halt. Shots were fired; the boy still ran. You heard several Germans splashing through the water close to your hiding place and then they ran past you, intent on the fleeing figure before them. More shots came. The Germans were yelling now, angry, tense, in their fear lusting for blood. And then there were no more shots, only loud, male baying and relieved and triumphant laughter, and you moved off slowly out of the trap and into the forest again...saved.

You told me later that this was the worst part of your entire life, and when you first told me this I thought to myself how strange it was that one man would find himself in the pit of despair after another willingly sacrificed himself so that he should live. But this is an eternal dynamic, unalterable, and I had not yet come to that point in my life that you had in the woods then. For some reason Davidovitch's sacrifice called to your mind your own betrayal—your betrayal of Mikhail and his father—in the same way that only in a clean mirror can we see truthfully our own mire-smeared faces. The shame of what you had done, the blatant brutality and horror and selfishness of the act, was borne in upon you by another man's sacrifice and nobility. As you stumbled and starved your way back to the Russian lines, all that you were, all that you'd done throughout your life, was set clearly in its right and true perspective. In seeing these things you realized truly who and what you were, and more importantly, finally came to admit to yourself these truths. You were not the admirable, righteous, bold, courageous, unflinching, compassionate man of your imagination. No, you were a traitorous, prideful, selfish man who had, all his life, positioned himself to best advantage, and done things for people so as simply to reflect well upon yourself, and who thought only and ever always of himself. It had taken one selfless act by a truly admirable, righteous, bold, courageous, unflinching, compassionate man for you to see and admit to yourself this ultimate truth.

There were times in the next few days when you wished that the Germans would find you and put you out of your misery. The true depth of your treachery—not only toward Mikhail and his father but toward others in your life—struck home, for upon seeing your one act of selfishness with clarity, you came to easily recognize the many others throughout your life. You realized you'd been selfish, prideful, ambitious, and arrogant, and as one grows habits, so grows one's character. What selfless acts you'd performed had been calculated simply to position yourself more favorably in the eyes of those who might further your ambitions. What deeds of bravery you accomplished were only those designed to improve perceptions of yourself in the eyes of others. As these truths were hammered home to you day after day, night after night in forest and swamp and steppe, your hard heart was melted down into something that God could shape. And God wasted no time.

You made it back to your lines. Pavlov's 10th Army had been routed but you found a Divisional command post and reported to an officer, who took you to the Division Adjutant. There was still much of the old man left in you, Pyotr, as you said, and you were expecting them to give you a medal for surviving. Instead, they thought seriously of shooting you as a deserter, but before they carried out this intention others from your unit arrived and reported the same thing that you had, that the tank unit had been overrun, the infantry slaughtered, men cut down like wheat with the passing of a scythe.

The Divisional Commander did not like to hear such things, and he knew that Pavlov, the Army Commander, would like them even less, for it would reflect poorly on his own leadership, but he needed every able-bodied soldier he could find, and he didn't have any ammunition to waste shooting prisoners. But he had taken a special dislike to you, Pyotr, and at the time you could not fathom it, for then you were not familiar with God's method of justice, in that a man will reap what he sows; you became instead bitter.

The Adjutant came out of the headquarters tent and walked carefully through the mud to the stockade they had hastily rigged to hold prisoners. "You can all go," he said through the wire, "and you will report to Major Rishtenko here. He will assign you to your new units. Go and do not disgrace the motherland again, do you hear me? Die first." The gate was opened and the men stumbled out, numb, wondering what new horrors were in store.

"Federoskiya, not you; you come here." The Adjutant moved to the side of the column of men leaving the stockade and you stepped through the mud to stand near him.

He looked at you with an intense disdain. "I do not like you, Federoskiya; there is something about you, something that makes me think we are making a mistake letting you live, but there is nothing I can do about this now." He stepped closer to you then, until you could smell him, and spoke very quietly, so that only you could hear him. "You are a disgrace to the Red Army, Federoskiya; do not let me find you on the battlefield. I will shoot you where you stand, because you do not deserve to put one foot on the same sacred earth where true soldiers fight and die. You were a combat unit commander, and you fled when your men died. You do not deserve to live, and you certainly don't deserve to be in the presence of men honored to fight for the motherland. You will not be assigned to a combat unit. You will be assigned to this headquarters unit here, where you will empty the drums of waste from the latrines into pits, where you will burn it. This is your duty. Now go."

And so, numb like the rest of the men released from the stockade, but with much less hope, you marched over to where the latrines stood, and reported to the sergeant, a coarse, brutal man. You began a time of humiliation and privation such as you'd never known.

You did your job, you said. From what you did not tell me, I realize that God was having His way in you, for as you burned the waste of the latrines there in the forest, God was burning the waste of the old man out of you. It was during this time, a time when some would be most prone to completely despair and lose hope, that you thought of something—or, as you would have said, God brought the thought to you.

'Why', the thought queried, 'would this man Davidovitch give up his life for you if your life was useless, worthy enough only to empty waste and filth? If God put this man in your path to save you, then perhaps God desired you to be saved, and to learn what you can do for Him.' This thought was your only light, your only hope, and it was this thought, which you told me later as we drove through the woods, that enabled you to survive that time in the miry pits of clay. You would say to yourself day after day, when you were too exhausted to carry on, that if only God would not give up on you, you could survive; you could carry on through hell with hope. I remembered how I had felt when I came upon my parents in the field, and when I killed my first German, and when I met pure Evil in the forest that night, and understood your heart.

You said that one day soon after being relegated to the pit, it became intensely hot, and the heat from the flames in the pit combined with the brutal sun beating down upon you as you carried bucket after bucket of filth wore down your spirit more than your body, and you sensed that you were coming to the end of yourself, that you could go no further, and you would soon drop in agony as your heart died; your body was past caring.

A thin scarecrow of a man approached as you climbed out of the pit and were trudging back to the latrines for another barrel of waste. His head was bowed and he walked slowly, like an old man, and you saw that indeed he was—very old. He was talking to himself. A group of boisterous soldiers passed him and one bumped into the man and knocked him aside roughly. There was laughter, and with harsh words the young men expressed their disdain. The older man, almost swallowed by his greatcoat, stumbled and resumed his path. You shook your head at all the cruelty in the world, but then you remembered the cruelty that you had brought down upon Mikhail and his father. You looked at the slime in the bucket and saw your filth-encrusted hands around the handle and were still.

You heard his voice before you saw him. You heard words, spoken softly, below the range of hearing, and then they became louder, and you looked around, and there was the old man, with a thin, leathery face, and you realized that the words he was speaking were actually directed to you, and he was saying something to you, and holding something in his hand.

"Here," the man said, almost too softly to make out. He was standing next to you, his boots in the same filth wherein you stood. "Take this. Read it. In it are words that lead out of this pit."

You looked down. The man held out an incredibly worn, brown, leather-covered book. On the cover in Cyrillic you saw the words *Holy Bible*.

You looked up; the man had already turned and was hobbling up out of the pit. You looked again at the book in your hands. You thought to yourself, 'Here I am, a filthy Russian traitor—traitor to my country, a traitor to my friends, to the ones I loved, and...and yes, a traitor to my God—standing in this sea of filth, and this man gives me a book to read.' That one simple act of love smote your heart, so much so that you would cherish the written word of God for the rest of your life. You put the book into your pocket and went back to your task. You did not know it then but you had been rescued.

* * *

One day a few weeks later there was a commotion in the camp. New orders had come down from Moscow. There would be a new attack. They brought in horse-drawn wagons to support this new attack, scavenged from the Far East, from the Siberian units poised along the frontier waiting in vain for the crazed Japanese to strike into Russia from the east as the Germans struck from the west. The Division Adjutant stripped the wagon trains of almost every man to staff the infantry units, but he knew that the wagons would also be needed to supply the troops during and after the attack. He strode through the muddy camp and came to the pit where you were burning the most recent quantity of human detritus.

"Federoskiya," he yelled harshly, "come up out of that pit. We have a job for you." The Adjutant stood above the pit with Major Rishtenko. They were both trying to contain their disgust at the sight of you, covered in human waste. You dropped the half-barrel, wiped your hands on your pants, climbed out of the pit, and stood before them at attention.

"You realize, Federoskiya, that I would rather simply shoot you and dump you in the pit there, but it would be a waste of a bullet. So…instead you are going to serve the motherland in a different way now. You have stated that you once drove tanks. Is this true?"

Hope leapt up like a hart; hope, you said later, that you recognized soon thereafter as simply a remnant of the old pride resurgent. You thought these men were going to restore you to the position you once held. You thought that God works on a transactional basis, and that you had performed sufficient penance for your selfishness and betrayal with your own suffering. You told me later that God does not work in any such way, that He is always doing the best He can for us, that His thoughts toward us, His plans, are as complex and multitudinous as the stars in the sky, that He does not desire sacrifice as much as obedience, and our meager conceptions of transactional exchanges with the God of the Universe are laughable at best, tragic at worst. This truth was burned into your soul as you as you stood there at the edge of the burning pit with the Adjutant's next words.

"So…we have no tanks here, Federoskiya…at least no tanks we would want you to command. But we do have something else you can drive.

Follow us." And they led you to a wagon—three wagons, actually, gathered in a line—with the teams tied to trees nearby.

"This is your new command," Rishtenko said, in a gruff voice. You realized then that the Major had taken to himself the Adjutant's dislike for you, and you would find no mercy in this camp.

You looked around. "There are no men, Comrade Adjutant" you said, in a raspy voice. You had not been fed well, your health was broken, and you were but a shell of the young man who had proudly commanded tanks that morning in late June, but they paid such things no heed.

They laughed, and you thought then that such a laugh bode ill for your prospects. "You'll have men assigned to you," Rishtenko said, chuckling grimly. He walked away.

"You will take these wagons and roam the rear area," the Adjutant said, harshly, looking away from you at the camp swarming with Russian soldiers, "keeping the Regimental and Battalion headquarters of the Division supplied. You will return here to stock the wagons and Major Rishtenko will then tell you which headquarters unit you are to supply, and where they are located." He looked back at you with disdain. "Do you understand, Federoskiya? Do you think that you can do this without getting your people killed?"

Shamed, you bowed your head. "Yes, Comrade Adjutant."

"See that you do," he directed, with a seething dislike. "Now see to your command. Your...*men*...will be sent to you shortly." The Adjutant left and you turned to look at the three supply wagons. Such a far different picture they made than what you had envisioned for yourself. You could hear the sound of the engines belonging to the great war machines—they were reinforcing the tank brigades with the T34, the world's best tank at the time—in another part of the camp, and there you stood, smelling of excrement, preparing to drive horses. "Just another layer to shed", you would tell me later, "of repentance. There was still so much of the old man in me that God was working to remove. But He always has a plan," you said, your eyes smiling as you shared this with me. "He always has a plan. Never forget this, Stasy." You would touch my face when you said this, your eyes so filled with hope that I would one day understand. O, Pyotr, O how I wish you could know that I understand now. I understand, my love.

Dukhi was the first one they brought to you. Old even then, he was hunched over, a skeleton in a Red Army greatcoat, mumbling constantly in whispered tones. Two soldiers brought him to you, one on each side. You suddenly recognized the old man who had brought you the Bible in the pit.

"Here," they said, and they shoved Dukhi at you. "This old man never stops talking, but he never says anything loud enough for anyone to hear. He's crazy. He's your sergeant." They laughed and walked away. Dukhi stood there mumbling softly, whispering words that were immediately overcome and trampled into the mud by the noise of men marching, the sound of tank engines ripping the turf as they formed for the attack, the clank of treads and shouts of commands and the sound of distant gunfire—the cacophony which always attends industrial man preparing to slaughter his fellows.

You walked over to him and strangely, the cacophony of confusion dissipated for just one moment and you were able to catch a few of the words Dukhi was saying. "Welcome...you will do well...you are where you should be...will help...begin..." You drew back as the old man looked up at you. Was he talking to you? Did he know who you were? Did he know what you'd done?

"Thank you for the book," you said, your voice cracking with emotion. Tears formed in your eyes. The old man smiled at you with his eyes and patted you on the arm and went to see to the wagons.

They brought Arkady next. It took three men to hold Arkady still and walk him over to your area of the camp, but still he tried to leap, and would constantly look around, looking everywhere and at anything but you. By then you had untied each team and, with Dukhi's help, moved them to some grass where they grazed. The sun was shining and it was a warm day, as you recalled to me.

When the soldiers released him, Arkady would bound here and there, leaping and jumping up and down for no reason whatsoever, arms upraised constantly, sometimes turning cartwheels in the grass, laughing hysterically, never still. He was a big man, which is why it took three burly soldiers to bring him to you.

"Here," they said, breathless. "This idiot won't stop moving. He's in your command now," and they left, relieved. Arkady hooted and then began to sing an old Russian folk song. Your first concern was how you would be able to move through the countryside in safety with this human alarm bell sounding constantly.

It was then that you realized that the Adjutant and the Major were skimming men from combat units who were damaged or unbalanced or deranged and dumping them into your unit. But God had not been idle; what faith you had was beginning to grow, trusting that God knew what He was doing.

Mooskov arrived next. Mooskov was a bear of a man, very large, with rich Slavic features plastered across a fearsome countenance. This was deceptive, you were to learn. Mooskov was as docile as a lamb. No soldier brought him; someone had directed him to report to you, and he simply obeyed the order and reported. As he approached the wagon area, you watched him suddenly pause by a stretch of mud in the pasture, and then he knelt down and rolled over onto his back and flapped his arms in the mud, covering himself with mire and dung. Then he stood up, shook himself, and walked toward your command. He stopped once more at another muddy spot in the path and did the same thing, and you realized that the big man was not normal. With the beginnings of humor you remarked to yourself that he would fit in nicely.

They brought you Isay, a young, thin, fragile boy with long eyelashes and frightened eyes who had grown up in the city, in a cultured environment. The soldier bringing him to you shoved the boy at you with disdain.

"He is disgusting," he said. "He is like a woman; he cries constantly. He is useless. Get him out of my sight." The soldier spat at the boy, who stood with tears coursing down upon his cheeks, sobbing quietly. He put his face in his hands as the words of the soldier struck into his heart, and it was as though you could see the physical impact of those words as his shoulders shook. You took the boy gently by the elbow and led him to the wagons.

Another was brought to you, pushed ahead of two soldiers on the points of their bayonets. "Kazimir is yours," one of them said. "Keep him away from us. He comes near us again, we'll shoot him, we don't care what the Commissars say. He is cursed."

The young man they pushed looked normal to you, although despondent. This was to be expected, being threatened with bayonets. He walked over to the wagons dismally, shoulders hunched, while you turned to talk to the men who had brought him.

"What...what has he done?" you asked.

You recalled to me the emotions of disgust and horror and, perhaps, fear, that wrapped their souls and which then could be seen upon their faces. "He cannot leave the dead," one whispered hoarsely, with a tinge of dread. "They picked him up after the Germans overran our defenses south of here, sitting by the dead bodies, talking to them. He is unholy," they said, crossing themselves, and moved away quickly.

There was another man they brought—morose, with a heavy, curling moustache and long, calloused hands. At first you thought he was a gypsy, but they did not recruit or permit gypsies in the Red Army. The man stared straight ahead, mouth slightly open. He looked moronic but then you revised your estimate; not moronic, just devoid of emotion.

"Who is this?" you asked the soldier who brought him to you. You were leaning against one of the horses, checking his foot.

"They call him Svoboda," the soldier said. "No one knows anything about him. He hasn't said ten words since he reported here. The men don't like him; they think he is...that he is not quite right...you know," and the soldier tapped his head.

You stood up and looked at the man. "Can you speak?"

The man looked back at you and replied in a deadpan monotone. "I can. There is not much to say. We are put here on the earth, we eat, we live, we die, we go into the ground. We are resurrected to life everlasting or we burn forever for our sins—the choice has been made long ago, we have nothing to say about it."

The soldier nodded. "See what I mean?"

You nodded and called for Sergeant Dukhi. "This is Sergeant Dukhi," you told the man. "You will obey his instructions. He is the sergeant of our unit." The man looked at Dukhi but appeared not to see him.

"Who are you speaking of?" he asked, though Dukhi was standing before his eyes.

"Sergeant Dukhi," you answered, perturbed, pointing to the old man in the oversized greatcoat "This man, right here, in the coat."

Svoboda narrowed his eyes. "Perhaps that is a man...yes, perhaps so, perhaps not." He turned again to you and said, "And what is he to me? He looks dangerously unstable."

You were about to berate the man severely when Dukhi made a shushing gesture toward you and just took the man by the sleeve and led him over to the wagons. The man appeared not to notice the sergeant, but went toward the wagons nonetheless. The soldier smiled at you, tapped his head once more, and departed.

Later in the fourth day after being given your command they brought to you another man, a middle-aged soldier, escorted by a sergeant. As they approached you could see the two engaged in conversation, the sergeant angry, the other man nonchalant, almost smug. The sergeant suddenly made a quick motion with his rifle and butted the other soldier, who stumbled and then continued on, still talking constantly.

They approached the wagons and the sergeant shoved the man toward you with his rifle. "Get this cancer out of my sight," he said. "He disgusts me." The sergeant turned on his heel and left, trailing his rifle through the mud, weary and despondent.

You looked at this man and could see nothing, on the surface, to warrant his inclusion in the group that you were coming to think of as your wagon of fools.

"You know," the man said, looking over and pointing at your wagons where the others of your unit were reposing, such as they were, "that large man is filthy. He's been flopping around in mud holes since I've been here; he's disgusting. And that other boy, the snot-nosed kid who can't stop crying...doesn't he realize how foolish he looks? And for all that's holy, what is that fool of a man doing, shouting and doing handstands like that? Doesn't he know the Germans are only twelve kilometers north of us? Is he an idiot? Oh, look, they've given you some bag of bones in an oversized coat who looks older than Methuselah. What job will he do, carry three grains of oats at a time? He looks as if he'll drop dead if he lifted a twig!" The man went on for several minutes, selecting and disparaging various qualities of the men he observed while you stood there, amazed at his ability to find fault with each of the men in your unit, men for whom you were coming to feel some affection. He then went on to find fault with the sergeant who'd delivered him, and the captain of his company, and the Division Adjutant, and General Pavlov.

"This is all very well, but what is your name?" you asked, interrupting him.

"Berestichslovski," he replied. "It's a good name, but sometimes too complicated. Some people—"

You held up your hand. "Fine, Berestichslovski, join the others...but you are ordered not to speak unless I am there as well. Do you understand?" You leaned closely toward him and made your eyes into slits. "If you speak without my permission I'll have you shot."

Berestichslovski drew back, eyes wide with shock, and saw that you were serious. Unit commanders in the Red Army had such authority. "I...I understand, Lieutenant."

"Good. Now the water hole is over there about a kilometer. Take this bucket and water the horses for me."

"Of course, Lieutenant," the man said warily, with suspicion. You did not trust that he would obey you for long. He took the bucket and went to water the horses.

They delivered another soldier the next day. He came walking toward the wagons by himself, carrying a flower in one hand and his knapsack in the other, dropped his knapsack on the ground and then saluted you.

"Comrade Lieutenant, Private Silvestovic reporting for duty, for as long as we're here at least, which shouldn't be long, since the Germans will surrender soon and our brave and glorious soldiers will enjoy the sunshine of peace in paradise after this bitter darkness of war and gloom."

You were surprised and somewhat bemused. You looked around the camp. The 'glorious soldiers' were trudging through mud turned into black sludge, some carrying boxes of ammunition, some carrying stretchers, some with bloody bandages, some hobbling on crutches, many missing limbs, some fighting with each other over scraps of food. The sound of German artillery was in your ears.

"Have you come from the command tent, Private? Is there something you know that hasn't been announced yet?"

"Oh, no sir, it is just that, well...everything is so plain. Of course the Germans will surrender, you know; what else could happen? Even if the war continues, *we* will certainly not be involved." He waved his arms as he said this, taking in the entire picture of men and horses and tanks and armies preparing for war. "We'll soon be done with this foolishness. Stalin will come, Zhukov will come, the Generals will come—it could be at any moment, Comrade Lieutenant, and we'll be rescued and there will be no more Germans and no need to fight any longer. I look at those men over there, getting ready to attack, and shake my head. Why worry, I say to myself, we will be whisked from this battlefield before things get too difficult."

You nodded; you understood now. The boy had completely detached himself from reality; you had seen this before, in some men who, when circumstances so threatened or frightened them, somehow reconstructed their perceptive organs such that they could only see what they wished to see rather than the reality before their eyes. It was a form of denial. You wondered of what use in combat such a man would be who could not see the reality around him. But you also realized that he was just another man out of his senses—another fool—whom they had detailed to you, and so you directed him to report to Sergeant Dukhi and the rest of the unit.

* * *

They brought others to you; those feeble or frail, some embittered or crushed by the cacophony of war and hate, some deranged, some dangerous. You sent each of them to Sergeant Dukhi, who, strangely, was able to get them to pay attention, assign them to a specific duty, and instruct them in the performance of that duty. It was a strange thing to see the frail old man, bent over, looking up at Mooskov and telling him in that quiet, whispery voice that he must carry those bags of oats to the horses three times before he could roll once in the mud. There was struggle on the hulking man's face, but determination as well, and he did what the sergeant asked of him. Dukhi assigned the crying city boy to drive the second wagon, and, in an assignment that surprised you, directed Berestichslovski to drive the third wagon. You asked Sergeant Dukhi about this and were only able to catch part of his reply. "The horses...heal..." he said, "and ... words ... bounce ... from them."

The horses! At first you cursed the humiliating assignment, for there was nothing less prestigious in the eyes of the new Red Army than driving wagons, especially when compared to the power and speed of tanks, but you later came to love the horses. They were all Russian heavy drafts, a sturdy breed, with presence and power, not as large as some draft breeds, more economical than the larger horses when it came to feed, but powerful and able to pull a wagon all day. When they assigned you to the unit, you did not know their names. You had no idea even that horses would have names, your mind being so inundated with the mechanical thought processes of the industrial lie which besmirches all of nature.

Dukhi came to you one day, just before your first mission, and quietly pointed out to you that the gray and the bay were the lead horses and should always be placed pulling the lead wagon; the gray was the dominant stallion. Strangely, the Red Army had forgotten to cut these horses, and they had somehow let six stallions slip through and assigned them to pull wagons. Dukhi said that the gray's name was Afanasy, and Afanasy's harness-mate, the bay, was Bogdan. There was Leonid and Feofilakt, whom he called just Leo and Feo, and Yakim and Yerik.

"How do you know such things?" you asked the sergeant in surprise.

The old man smiled and tapped himself on the chest and shook his head. "I gave them these names," he said, holding up a finger at you. "Why shouldn't I know them?" And he went to see to their feeding.

Major Rishtenko came to you one day, striding through the grass in gleaming boots while you were currying Afanasy. The horse shook his massive shoulder muscles under your comb and you stopped, curious, and then saw the animal with his head turned, looking across the pasture. You followed his gaze to see the major approaching. He had a map in his hand.

"Lieutenant, gather your men. We have been ordered to resupply a battalion of the reconstituted 4th Army. They have pushed the Germans out of the salient and your unit must resupply them immediately. They are here." The major showed you the location on the map; it was a few days' travel with the horses.

"We will leave immediately, sir." The major's face showed surprise, some ridicule, and not a little disgust as he looked around at your unit. Arkady was cartwheeling across the grass; Mooskov, dripping with mud, was arising from a particularly loathsome hole, and Isay wept uncontrollably under a tree, watched over dolefully by Leo and Feo.

The major simply shook his head. "You will pick up the supplies there," and he pointed toward a large stack of boxes and crates that had been brought in by trucks the night prior. "Get loaded and on the road by this afternoon. The headquarters element is relocating. Here," and he again showed you the map, "here is where you will return to find us." He pointed to a different location. By the juxtaposition of the references given, you understood that the Red Army was still in a confused retreat, but you chose not to make this observation.

"Yes, Comrade Major. We'll begin loading right away." The major left and you turned and called to Sergeant Dukhi and gave him the order to harness the horses and load the wagons. The old man turned and began to walk toward the other wagons. He lifted one frail arm and, seemingly at random, some of the men, in their mindless arcing around the pasture, would find that their orbit intersected with his, and he caught their attention and they ceased their peregrinations and listened to him. Others came from where they were engaged elsewhere and he gave these men direction as well. Soon the horses were harnessed, the wagons loaded, and you, driving Afanasy and Bogdan, were leading the procession along the main camp road and toward your resupply point.

You shared with me the recollection of how soldiers laughed at your 'wagon of fools', and I remember both the pain and the irony in your eyes as you told me about this first drive through the camp. Arkady was running alongside the wagons, twirling and jumping and hooting. Mooskov would fall into every muddy hole along the way, even before you left the headquarters area. Isay was holding the reins to the second wagon, driving Leo and Feo, crying. Berestichslovski was remonstrating with Kazimir about something, waving his arms, forgetting to control his team, and they would wander back and forth about the center of the road. Others would drool or yell or grasp at unseen butterflies, meandering along with the wagon train. Your humiliation was complete.

* * *

The second day after leaving headquarters your wagons came to a crossroads. The resupply point was only a few kilometers straight ahead, but suddenly Afanasy turned to take the road that led to the right. You tried to haul him back, but he simply stopped. Bogdan would not go either; they both refused to move further. There was no shuffling, no sidestepping to indicate they were nervous—they simply stood there with their legs solidly planted, extending down from their stocky barrel bodies straight into the ground like small trees, and would not move forward. You yelled at them in a moment of brief frustration and shook the reins, the thin straps of leather slapping their great broad rumps, but still they would not move. The sun filled the sky; the wheat in the fields hung their heads in the heat, and you could hear the voices of Berestichslovski and Kazimir arguing, Arkady laughing, and Isay crying. You hung your head in shame. You could hear Dukhi in the back of your own wagon, sorting through the supplies, murmuring in a low voice; you could just make out a few words—'horse' … 'trust' … 'patient'. You got down from the wagon as the other wagons came up and stopped.

"What is it?" Mooskov asked, mud caked on his uniform.

"The horses have stopped," you replied, and turned to see what might be in the road. Perhaps a snake or a coyote had put them out of countenance. You came to where they stood, looked up and down the road ahead, and spoke softly to Afanasy. "What is it, Papa?" you asked quietly. You called Afanasy your Papa because he reminded you of a good father, and in Russian, the meaning of this word is much like the Hebrew word 'Abba', the English word for one's Daddy. As well, 'Afanasy' meant 'immortal' in Russian, and you felt that the horse somehow was much, much older than you; that he possessed the wisdom of the ages. And you were learning, or were being taught by the horses themselves, that gentleness was more quickly understood than harshness, and with it you achieved much better communication. The horse turned his head and nosed you in the chest: 'What do *you* want?' he seemed to ask. You did not understand.

"Lieutenant! Lieutenant, there are trucks behind us!" You took up your submachine gun before running back to the last wagon, where Berestichslovski had called out in alarm. If they were Germans, you and your unit would be slaughtered, caught out in the open.

"Oh, they're ours, I'm sure," Silvestovic shouted, jumping down from the running board on the second wagon to join you. "Maybe we're being sent to the Italian front!" You were not so sure, and assurances from a man who could not see reality were not comforting. Kazimir stared off into the distance with dead eyes. You stood there with the others and watched the dust cloud forming. You had seen this type of dust cloud before…when the Panzers struck your tank park near Bialystok.

But no, this time Silvestovic was correct; they were Russian. The trucks slowed to pass the wagons on the left, and the lead truck stopped when they saw you were an officer.

"What are you doing on the side of the road, Lieutenant?" asked the man in the passenger seat of the lead truck; he was a Captain, apparently, commanding the mobile infantry unit in the trucks behind him.

"The horses will not go forward," you replied, in your perplexity not thinking about the reaction this statement would create. The burst of laughter from the men in the trucks inflamed your cheeks. They tossed down jibes from their benches.

"Press on the starter, you imbeciles, maybe they'll get going that way!"

"Did you not put petrol in their water?"

"They are stopping to do their business; they'll get going soon, you wait and see!"

"They smell Germans; they're smarter than you are!"

"Maybe they're tired of lugging around a wagonload of idiots!"

The Captain laughed and waved to the driver and they moved on and passed the lead wagon. Afanasy and Bogdan stood like stone statues, watching with great deep brown eyes as the mechanized infantry trundled past in a cloud of dust and laughter. You trudged disconsolately back up to your team and put your arm over Afanasy's broad back and watched the last truck in the column pass through the crossroads. You could still just see the first, almost obscured by the fine Russian dust, when it exploded. The truck flipped up completely off the ground, overturned, men tumbling through the air, and the fuel in the truck exploded into a ball of orange flame that blossomed from orange to red to black, consumed everything within its circumference, and then disappeared as quickly as it erupted, leaving behind a thick, oily grayish-black pillar of smoke. Another truck, the third in line, blew up seconds later, throwing the cab straight up and backwards, crushing the men riding behind on the benches in the bed: minefield.

You ran toward the infantry as they leapt from the trucks, yelling at them to stay where they were, but they emptied out of the truck beds like lemmings leaping from cliffs, and soon soldiers were detonating anti-personnel mines, sowed in the field by the Germans along with the anti-tank mines on the road. It was a thickly-sown field, and you could do nothing but watch in horror as men tried to walk back toward the crossroad junction where the horses and wagons were waiting and were blown up, sometimes killed by a mine set off by a comrade a few feet away. An entire company was thrown into confusion. Dozens were killed, hundreds wounded, most horribly maimed. A few hours later more trucks came and took what remained of the company back to an aid station. The pillars of smoke were still rising from the destroyed vehicles when you soberly remounted your wagons and started along the road that ran to the right. Afanasy and Bogdan moved out easily under your hands, and you arrived at the battalion's location the next day only to find that it had been completely overrun by the Germans.

* * *

You stayed there for a day and a night, scavenging whatever supplies, arms, and ammunition you thought would be helpful to return to headquarters. You directed Sergeant Dukhi to detail a man to see that Kazimir did not bother the dead. He had a disturbing habit of trying to put on dead men's clothes or shoes. You made sure that Mooskov was kept out of mud holes here; typhus or other diseases bred quickly in the hot sun and you did not know how long these dead bodies had lain in the open, bleeding into the water. Dukhi was able to control the men well enough so that they loaded the wagons with a large amount of arms, ammunition, food, and priceless clothing and blankets—winter was approaching, and you did not wish to leave anything for the Germans.

As you mounted your wagon the next morning to leave, you saw Isay wandering near a pile of dead bodies. He took a boot from the body of a dead Russian, and a blood-stained coat from a dead German, tugging at the sleeves, sobbing. You were about to call out to him harshly when Dukhi appeared by your side. "This is the task given to him, Lieutenant. Watch and let him be."

Isay, still crying, took the boot and the bloody cloak and wrapped them together, soaked them in some petrol, and put a match to them. They flamed up instantly. He tossed the burning mass onto the bodies and stood watching until the dead began to burn. He walked back to his wagon, took up his reins, and waited for you to give the signal to move, shoulders shaking.

Headquarters had relocated, so you took a different road to return. On the second day after leaving the slaughtered battalion's location, placidly moving along a solid dirt road that ran through a swamp which itself was bordered by a thick wood, you came upon a Russian infantry column moving in the opposite direction. The column split into two marching lines, one on either side of your wagons as you drove in the center of the road. Some of the soldiers waved, some laughed, and others threw insults at you, your horses, or your wagon of fools. Still others began to shout out in fear, afraid that Arkady or Mooskov were haunted because of their behavior. The soldiers avoided Kazimir with an instinct that made you shudder. They laughed and tossed harsh and jagged taunts at Isay as he drove the second wagon, tears on his young, boyish face. Dukhi would move back and forth among your men, calming them, keeping them focused, helping them to do their duty as the infantry column wound past the wagons.

Afanasy and Bogdan suddenly bolted. You were shocked; you had no experience with such behavior. The horses paid no attention to your commands, either as you shouted at them or as you tried to yank back on the now-useless reins. They galloped in their traces. Soldiers leapt out of the way, cursing, as the wagons careened along the road. Your shouts were taken by the wind and dropped behind the wagon like so many useless clods of dirt falling into the dust, mingling with the soldier's epithets. The other two wagons were rocketing along behind you as well, Isay and Berestichslovski unable to control their teams. Mooskov and Arkady just managed to leap and grab a rope on either side of the second wagon as it went by. They were dragged through the dust. The wagons barreled along the road with the two fools hanging on for dear life, the others inside the wagons being shaken unmercifully, everyone along for the ride, wondering if the wagons would shatter. They were loaded with supplies and equipment and food and you marveled in the midst of your fear that two horses could pull so much so fast.

As the wagons barreled through the column, a break in the line of men on the right appeared and Afanasy ran through it. There was a small path through the swamp—otherwise the wagons would surely have come to grief as they were pulled so rapidly through the muck—and the horses ran down the path a few hundred meters into a particularly thick wood. The two lead stallions took the first wagon onto the path that soon turned to parallel the road and they could see the marching column of infantry, pointing at them in the trees, laughing at their terror or cursing them for their recklessness. Arkady, his taste for motion temporarily satiated, stood still, almost as shocking to see as the recent scare of watching draft horses gallop in traces. Mooskov, covered in mud and dust from being dragged along at the side of the wagon, did not look as satisfied as one would have expected. He was somber; muted somehow, as he took stock of his condition. Perhaps being dragged through filth had a different effect than wallowing in it oneself.

As the wagons came to a halt, the horses panting, they could hear the derisive laughter of the infantry, still out on the open road, marching in the sun.

You got down from the wagon and went to Afanasy. You were shaking. It was an effort to remain calm.

"What...were...you...thinking, Papa? What in the world were you—"

You stopped as you heard a sound like a banshee wailing. You knew that sound. Every Russian who fought in the Great War knew that sound: Stukas. The officer in command of the column had time enough to simply look upward before the first bomb fell. Other Stukas appeared low, hopping over the trees, surprising the column, strafing the men as they ran in terror for the woods. It was clear that it had been a planned ambush. The infantry could not run as fast as the horses. Many were killed in the swampy ground or as they tried to take the path into the wood as the Stukas took their time, going back and forth over the killing ground the way an angry housekeeper sweeps a filthy floor. The Stukas slaughtered most of the column—hundreds of men, within minutes—using just a few machines.

* * *

Three days later your wagon of fools arrived at the spot on the map that marked where the headquarters would be. You found them; but once again you saw the unmistakable signs that the Germans had been there before you. The ground was ripped by tank tracks; tentage and field desks and canteens and dead bodies lay strewn about, mangled by heavy iron machines. Bodies lay sprawled everywhere...too many Russians, not enough Germans. As you surveyed the carnage, you wandered over to the headquarters tent and saw the bodies of the Division Adjutant and Major Rishtenko. You brushed the flies from their face, closed their eyes, and walked out.

You had almost a regiment's worth of supplies. You were one lieutenant in the midst of a front overrun by the enemy, your own forces in headlong, bungled retreat, all sense of command and control blown away into smoke and ash. You were in command of three wagons, an enormous amount of food, weapons, ammunition, and supplies, and a motley assortment of semi-functional, mentally deranged soldiers. As you surveyed the situation, you told me later that you were actually encouraged—you remember being grateful that you had what appeared at the time, after dodging a minefield and an attack by dive bombers, to be six *very* intelligent horses.

Your unit spent three nights at the headquarters location, dragging bodies of former comrades into piles to be burned, chasing away birds and other animals that sought to desecrate the remains, and gathering even more food, ammunition, weapons, and other supplies. You could not carry any more on the wagons so you had Sergeant Dukhi detail men to dig trenches and bury all the equipment so that, should you need it in the future, you could return and dig it up.

On what proved to be the last night before you moved away from the position, you were sitting on a hill overlooking the small valley in which the Division had placed its headquarters; the valley of death, you so aptly named it later in your descriptions to me. You were wondering what to do next. No one had given you any orders; you were part of no existing Red Army unit that you were aware of, and no one was expecting you to report.

As you sat there you sensed that Dukhi had approached and you could hear him speaking softly outside the range of hearing. As he came closer you realized he was talking to you, listing your assets and your options. It surprised you, and the thought swept into your consciousness that perhaps he was always talking but people were too busy or too loud or too drowned by the noise of the war to listen to what the sergeant was saying.

"...and you have some very intelligent horses. So what will you do now, Lieutenant?" he was asking. "Where will you go?"

You turned to him and moved slightly, inviting him to sit on the ground next to you, and he did, lowering his aged frame very slowly, as the old do whose liquidity of limb has long since flowed into the past.

"I suppose I should try to find an Army unit," you replied. "I am not sure." You looked over the remains of 10th Army headquarters and wondered what else the Germans had destroyed, and how far their path of destruction had carried into Russia, and wondered where your duty lay.

"Tell me about how the war started for you," he said unexpectedly, and you found yourself telling him about the tank academy and the assignment to Bialystok and then the German assault in late June that shattered everything you'd known, and the brutal march back to your own lines, only to be treated as a deserter or, worse, a coward.

Dukhi was nodding his head slowly. "Yes," he said softly, "and there is but one thing worse than either of those—a traitor." The words were spoken almost under the range of hearing but they pierced your heart to the very quick, and tears of remorse—deeper, richer, ever more saltier tears than any you'd shed before—began to flow, and you realized that like layers of an onion drawn from the rich Russian soil, so is the quality of repentance. In a quiet voice, tears falling steadily, you spoke to Dukhi about Mikhail and your betrayal. When you finished, you hid your face in your hands.

Dukhi was quiet for a moment, and then made a small shushing sound and laid his hand on your shoulder gently. "There was a man who saved you; tell me about him."

Without thinking how Dukhi had known about this, you described your episode in the swamp when the man Davidovitch sacrificed his life so you could live.

"Did he say anything to you, give you any direction or command?" Dukhi asked quietly.

You shook your head, and your voice in reply was just as soft and rasped and broken as Dukhi's. "No, I don't think so...I can't remember. He told me what he was going to do and where he was going to run, and told me that I should wait until the Germans passed my position and then move beyond them, out of the circle."

Dukhi waited.

"There was one thing," you said, hesitantly. "When he told me his name...he said his name was Davidovitch, and then he told me to remember his people. Yes...he told me to remember his people. What do you think such a thing means?"

Dukhi looked off into the distance, into the great Russia forest, and then turned to you again. "It is clear," Dukhi replied, voice rasping but clear, barely heard above the night noises from the woods. "Davidovitch is a Jewish name. When the God of the Jews was called upon to remember His people, He was in truth being asked to protect and defend them."

You and the wagons and the fools departed the headquarters valley the next day under a threatening sky. The weather was becoming colder, the ground easier to move upon, the swamps firmer but deadlier as the colder water would more quickly chill the body. Mooskov was finding the mud not as easy to wallow in as it was in summer. Arkady was more careful now that the ground was firmer. Before you left the decimated headquarters area, Isay again pulled the boots from a dead German and took the greatcoat from a dead Russian, rolled the coat in blood, then set fire to it and used that to burn the pile of bodies they'd made. The smoke pyre marked just one spot among many where Death played that year across the steppes of Russia, and they none of them looked back as you all rode into the vast Russian wilderness.

* * *

The wagon convoy wound its way along behind the advancing German lines, somehow miraculously avoiding being strafed by Stukas or surprised by German patrols. Occasionally you would see a Sturmovik fly over, one or two, never very many. The Russian Air Force had been shattered, and the replacements were only now just daring to make appearances over the battlefield. For some reason—and you never learned why—the horses would not run from Russian aircraft. It was as if they knew they were not a threat. It made no sense, but you were becoming increasingly confident in the ability of your horses to move across a dangerous battlefield, sensing things that you could not. Your confidence in them, and your affection, was transmitted through your hands on the reins, in direct touch with their soft mouths, and in your tone of voice as you spoke to them from the wagon, comforting them, telling them stories, speaking to them as you would to a friend. Perhaps you spoke with the horses more often because you found it difficult to hold a conversation with Arkady as he was cartwheeling along the side of the convoy, or with Mooskov flopping in a mud hole, or Svoboda, dead and without any spark of life or passion, or any of the others. You found yourself conversing with Dukhi more frequently.

It was in early September when you came across the first village. There was a synagogue in the center of the village which the Germans had burned to the ground. The bodies of men, women, and children were lying in the streets, in the fields, in clumps along the road leading into the village. The horses would pass these bodies and become agitated, but they nonetheless took your direction and your unit moved steadily into the village square. You stopped the wagons and decamped. The others got out of the wagons in shock; there was no noise, not even birds. You were all speechless. Even Arkady was subdued. Mooskov was stilled, awed. The butchery was soul-numbing.

The Star of David was drawn in red—presumably blood—upon the stone wall of one of the village homes, with the words *"Tod den Juden"*— Death to the Jews—written underneath the symbol in German. Men lay crumpled against walls in alleys, fallen where they had been lined up and shot. Kazimir stumbled toward the rubble that marked what had once been the synagogue walls and stood, gasping, dumbfounded at the carnage before him. The Germans had rounded up the women and children and burned them to death within the synagogue. There were hundreds of bodies frozen in the last rictus of agony. Kazimir could not look upon them any longer, and he ran from the edge of the ruins and was sick. From that day forward Kazimir could not look upon death without becoming ill, and you wondered later if somehow, in some small way, death had been used to heal death as sin is sometimes used to kill sin.

Silvestovic too could not process what he saw. The experience so contradicted what he believed so deeply about the world that he began to go into shock, until Dukhi came alongside and took him by the arm and set him to work, preparing the bodies for burial.

The next day after you had gathered the bodies of the villagers and placed them in the ground, Dukhi, who, you were surprised to learn, was Jewish, said the Chevra Kadisha over them. It was the first time you heard Dukhi's true voice. Everyone—all the fools from every wagon—stood at the grave enraptured as Dukhi's words of agony and heartbreak and joy and hope lamented the remnants of souls.

It was perhaps the high, ringing quality of his clear, cold cry echoing against the trees above the graves, standing like shocked and muted sentinels, which brought the survivors out of hiding. There were eighteen of them—some men, a few women, mostly children. They had watched you and the fools while they wept or were sick. They watched as your unit gathered their dead and buried them, but they had not trusted you until they heard the words of the holy prayer wafting into the wood through the cold morning air. No enemy would, or could, say such words.

They came up to each of you and each fool in turn saw in their eyes a picture of the death of humanity. These survivors could not believe, they could not process in their minds, what had happened. One of the men came forward and spoke to you. He told you that special units, called *Einsatzgruppen*, were following the German Army with explicit instructions to slaughter all Russian Jews wherever they were found.

He was grabbing at your shirt with trembling hands, and his voice trembled as well. "This...this is not possible, but I heard them. I saw them. I hid in a cellar for three days while they shot and burned my people...and they laughed...they *laughed*..." The man broke down and wept in your arms. You held him while his body shook. You thought of Davidovitch and what he had asked of you.

You had learned by now that to try and command the fools yourself was fruitless; they would not or could not follow your instructions. For some reason only Dukhi could get them to do what was required. "Dukhi," you cried, and the sergeant appeared at your side, "get these people loaded into the wagons. We are going to resettle them."

Dukhi quietly issued instructions and the men began to respond. Arkady was subdued still; he seemed to sense that his hysterical, mindless jocularity and capering would offend the very fabric of creation in that place, and was therefore submitted to a more natural order of behavior. Mooskov, recognizing that there was something in this small clearing in the woods so much darker and more evil and filthy than he could possibly imagine, refrained from soiling himself with its dirt, and kept his shirt clean enough to be able to lift the smaller children into the wagon without staining their clothes.

Berestichslovski complained to Kazimir in a voice loud enough for you to hear. "Where are we going to take them that the German won't find them again?" It angered you for a moment, but then you realized that his question was practical, not a complaint. It was something you had to consider.

You loaded the survivors into the wagons and the horses, with an emotion you suspected to be satisfaction and eagerness, turned quickly and retraced their steps out of the village and back onto the main road. Where to take them, you thought...where could you put them that the Germans would not find them again? You had driven for two hours along the same road when Afanasy and Bogdan suddenly turned and made their way across a level field of grass and wild flowers. You thought about yanking them back toward the road with the reins, but experience had taught you to rely on these animals, so you gave them their head. And go they did—it was if they knew exactly where they were going. They crossed the field and came upon a little-used road in a forest, overgrown with grass but solid and level, and the horses began to canter in their traces.

They cantered for an hour, towing all the supplies and equipment and ammunition and food and eighteen extra people, and Arkady and Mooskov, who both, once they'd departed from the road, immediately hoisted themselves back up into the wagon. You never once touched the reins.

The horses came to a stop in a clearing that was deep, deep in the forest. There were a few small huts made of stone surrounding the clearing, each with its own chimney and thick, thatched roof. They seemed to be in good condition, but abandoned. The horses, blowing from their run, stood still, and Afanasy turned to look at you while still in harness, waiting. He stamped his front foot once, and held it up, bent at the knee. You did not need to be told twice.

You leapt down from the wagon and ordered the Jews to be brought off gently. You directed Dukhi to have the men get the people settled in their new quarters. You had more than enough food and equipment and blankets to keep them warm and fed for the remainder of the winter.

Your unit stayed with the Jews throughout that first night, to keep them safe and provide what they might need from your wagons. Around a fire in the center of the small circle of stone huts, a strange thing occurred. Kazimir brought out a guitar, and Svoboda a balalaika from their personal effects, and the two of them sat around the fire and began to play. No one had had any idea that these men could rub two sticks together, much less play musical instruments.

The piece started with a slow, conventional introduction, seeming to meander, and then it paused and, slowly at first, a theme repeated itself and began to gather force and passion through the silent and suspenseful mystery within the music, leading the listener to expect that something powerful portended. It then began a different approach: questioning, wondering, and plaintive, as though the music expressed the heart of the listener, wondering why there was this horror and mystery and death; why there were so many unanswered questions. This theme was expanded as they played, each complementing the other as if they'd played together for decades. The music flowed up and down again, softly, rhythmically, like the peaceful rocking of a wagon, taking the men and women and children around the fire back to earlier days of serenity and wonder...and then another pause, a declension into the mystery again, and then it quieted. There followed almost a digression into a responding theme rich in passion, like the backdrop to a play or the background in a painting, highlighting what the mystery had before simply suggested, or perhaps providing an answer. There were echoes, and strident primary melodies, and harmonies that wound together like closely-woven threads in a tapestry. Kazimir looked up once and in the gleam of the firelight you saw that he was playing with tears running down his face, which made you think of Isay, and for one shocked space of time you saw that Isay was not crying; he was instead sitting, smiling peacefully, enraptured by the music. Svoboda had such a look of intense passion that you felt that your heart would break, and Silvestovic, deeply moved, had what could only be described as a look of deep confusion. They ruffled the strings and there was a frisson in a new melody, expressing hope and the richness of life and the depth of the human soul, and then a background that spoke of that spirit in which all lives are lived, the richness of God's holy and ever-present love, and the piece came to an end in a sweet, subtle, poignant, majestic musical expression of awe. When the music stopped they felt as if they had been laid down to rest in a bed of clouds by the hand of God Himself.

The Jews wept.

Svoboda and Kazimir played other songs then, and though perhaps you were imagining it, there appeared to be a spark of life returning to the dead eyes of the Jews you'd rescued, and it was here in this small clearing in the forest that you first learned that there may be times when only through the most complex language of creation—music—can the damage perpetrated upon the soul by the brutal, soul-killing, de-constructing anti-language spewed by men who hate be restored.

The next day before you and your unit departed, you took aside the man who had cried in your arms. He was the surviving village elder. "You will take these," you said with a measure of firmness, pointing to a stack of boxes that Mooskov and Isay had unloaded. Dukhi was standing by your side. "They are guns, with ammunition. Sergeant Dukhi here will teach you how to use them and how to keep them clean. If the Germans come again," you said, and paused, placing both your hands on his shoulders and looking directly into his eyes. "If the Germans come again, use them."

The man looked down at the boxes at his feet, looked back up at you, and you could see his train of thought like newsprint in his eyes. He had wanted to live a peaceful life on a farm, raising chickens and a few cows, maybe growing some hay, raising his children, reading Torah, meditating joyously upon the wonders and mystery surrounding the God of Abraham, Isaac, and Jacob...that was all, nothing more. There was no thought of killing, of taking up arms, pushing bullets through a metal barrel and out into the bodies of other men to slay them. And then you saw pass across his visage the remembrance of what the Germans had done, and the realization that when confronted by such evil, to do nothing was perhaps just as much a horrible sin against the God who put him on this earth than that which the Germans had done. The existence of evil was a problem that God would solve; what to do when faced with such implacable evil, an evil that threatened to eradicate all trace of anything God loved, this man solved there on the spot, and you saw the answer appear in his eyes like the blaze of a falling star as it flashes across a darkening sky.

"I will take them, Lieutenant...and I will use them if the need arises."

Once the horses had delivered the men and women of the village to the sanctuary that apparently only they had known about, they permitted you and Isay and Berestichslovski to drive them back out of the forest. There were times when you came to a halt and did not know where to go. You would then drop the reins and say, somewhat loudly so Afanasy could hear, 'Where to now, Papa?' The horse would pick up his feet and Bogdan would whinny and Afanasy would choose a direction. It was after one such occurrence that you and your wagon of fools came upon a demented young girl with shocking white hair, sitting by the side of the road, pounding the ground with a rock.

* * *

About ten or fifteen days after you had come upon me in the mud, we were camped in the forest in a clearing, waiting to go on. It had begun to snow in the afternoon, a deep, quiet, steady release of thick flakes from the vast storehouse in mid-heaven. Afanasy and Bogdan had refused to move any further along the road that afternoon, and while Arkady and Mooskov and even Svoboda, displaying a rare flash of personality, expressed a strong desire to get moving to find the next village of Jews, you would hear none of it. If the horses would not move, you would not move. So you tried to see if they would turn aside into the forest from the road, and they did so easily enough. Fine, you decided; you would camp for the night. The matter was settled.

As it darkened—and it was beginning to darken earlier in the afternoon as winter approached—we heard, far off in the distance, the sounds of rumbling and thunder, which, we all knew, was not thunder but the sound of armor advancing. We could hear artillery too, accompanying the armor in its attack, and we realized that not far up the road the Germans were moving through the country along one of their main axes of advance, and I closed my eyes that night wondering about your trust in the horses, and wondered about the fact that they had refused to move further north along the road. The sounds we heard were coming unmistakably from the north.

I was awakened by the sounds of shouting. The horses had gotten loose and were racing through the woods. I could feel the ground shake as they passed my wagon, their great hooves pounding into the forest floor, shadows cast by the fire racing behind or before them and up and off into the dark arboreal abyss. I threw off my blanket and leapt to the ground in time to see Arkady and Mooskov racing through the snow after them, waving blankets, and Kazimir, running without shoes, chasing the two men, brandishing a rope. Svoboda too ran, a look of intense concentration on his face—concentration and fear, worried that we would be abandoned in this dark forest. The horses easily outdistanced them all and thundered off into the blackening night.

I ran through our camp, furious in my own fear, hair flying in the wind and snow, looking for you. You were standing with Dukhi near the fire with a look of wonder and a strange, crooked smile on your face. I wanted to smack it away.

"What do you think of your precious creatures now?" I yelled, fear spurring my rage. "Who will pull the wagons tomorrow? Do you think Arkady or Mooskov or…or me," I smacked my chest, "do you think *we* will pull them? What are you thinking? What are you *doing*, standing there? You must go and get them back!"

You looked at me with quiet eyes and said, almost as softly as Dukhi, "They will come back, Stasy, do not worry." Dukhi was making that shushing sound that he made which always, in spite of myself, seemed to calm my spirit. But I was still angry, for I had not learned to trust, and I have learned since that it is in the lack of trust that fear flourishes.

I began to cry then, which for some reason upset them all, and you and Dukhi were soon busy calming everyone and telling them not to worry, the crazy woman would be well again, and happy, and they were not to worry. Arkady began to leap and jump and hoot. Mooskov sought ground near the watering trough where we had watered the horses and rolled in the freezing slush, which clung to his coat like sin clings to us all. Kazimir retreated into himself, staring out again at the night from dead eyes. Silvestovic began to make noises that I was not to be sad or disturbed, that everything would be fine, that the Red Army would appear out of the snow, they could appear at any moment, we were not to worry, and this would all be a dream, and we would be rescued.

You came out of the snow and took me by the arm, but I collapsed, so you picked me up in your arms and took me back to the wagon and set me down, where I fell quickly into a turbulent and fretful sleep. There were no dreams of fire that night—you or Dukhi or both of you, perhaps, stayed close. Dukhi rounded the others up and had them bed down. He had trouble with Svoboda, who was again tending to ignore him.

The morning dawned bright and clear, with the clean, pure, white silence of snow surrounding us. There was a slight rushing sound, like a gentle wind whispering over water, and there was upon the camp a strange peace. I pulled back the curtain and peered out. There, tied and placidly chewing their morning rations, stood the six stallions. Leo and Feo looked around at me as I gazed from the wagon, as if to let me know that they were, in a respectful way, deploring my lack of faith. I snapped the curtain closed again and sat back, abashed and amazed and then surprised at myself for being so, thinking then that it was beyond the realm of possibility that they had any sense of my disappointment in their nocturnal departure. I knew little of horses then.

There was the rattle of tin and the sound of sizzling, and your face appeared at the front of the wagon and you held up a plate of fried mushrooms and potatoes. My mouth watered and I ate gratefully. You were kind enough, as you stood there in the cold air, not to mention that the horses were back, and I think this is when I began to notice the reality of you; it was then that I first became attracted to your soul, for it was your soul's similarity to God's own true gentleness and compassion which first called to my heart. It is ever so with any true love, for a true heart loves best that which most reflects God's own heart.

We harnessed the horses after breakfast and with a snap of the reins you led us out of the clearing and back upon a winding path through the forest toward the main road. I sat next to you as we drove, with Dukhi in the back, rooting as ever among the supplies. As we moved I saw a patch of disturbed snow. My eyes, my dear, were better then than they are now, and with a gasp I recognized patches of red. You heard me gasp and reined in the horses. They pulled up, reluctantly, and Afanasy looked round quickly as if to remonstrate, but he perhaps saw my look of anxiety and hung his head in a position of resignation or submission, accepting the fact that he would have to wait until we examined what was ahead before proceeding. You jumped down from the wagon and motioned to Svoboda and Dukhi to follow. You took your submachine gun and I came too, following behind, at a trot. You paused to speak with Afanasy, and he rubbed your head again, marking you with his scent, a sign of contentment. I could see your tension slip away and flow down and out of your arms and shoulders, and you shifted the submachine gun into your left hand, letting it drop by your side. We trudged through the crisp morning snow and came upon what had been a camp where men had stayed. By the heat of the ground near some blackened wood, it appeared they too had had a small fire; most probably, it had been last night. We could not ask them, although they were there. They were dead.

There were six of them; Germans, specially outfitted with winter camouflage and parkas, boots, and snow pants of exceptional quality. Their tents, crumpled and splayed into the mud and slush, were made of a light fabric which nonetheless felt smooth and warm. Dukhi found one of their rifles, a very complicated, very dangerous sniper rifle. The camp appeared to have been overrun by armored vehicles in the night. Such things happened more than armies cared to admit when the front is fluid and men bivouac away from their platoon's lines. There was no sign that they had fought or tried to escape. They had all been killed in their tents under their blankets, crushed by some massive force. We couldn't understand it, though; the tanks would have awakened one or two and given them time to at least step out of their tents and run. It was a mystery to me. I did not get too close to the bodies—such things still frightened me. As I walked away from the scene of the camp, I looked back into the forest in the direction from which we'd come, and then down in the snow. The sun sparkled upon footprints; no, *hoof* prints; hundreds of hoof prints in a line from where we'd camped last night to this spot, the ice shining with reflections from the morning light upon every curve. Some were edged in a pinkish tinge. I followed them to the edge of the German hunter's camp—for this is what they had been, Dukhi confirmed; specially-trained Germans hunting for important Russian military personnel, snipers trained to identify and then kill commanders, commissars, and other necessary battlefield leaders. I realized that we would have come upon them, or they us, either last night or this morning. The hoof prints were scattered profusely throughout their camp, especially near the tents.

You called to the rest of us; it was time to go. Svoboda and Dukhi picked up the rifles—you said they might be important, and we left the camp as we found it. As we trudged back through the snow, I saw you pause and caress Afanasy's face with a special tenderness, and as I passed them I looked behind our wagon and saw that their hoofs left traces of red in the clean white snow.

Arkady and Kazimir helped me into the wagon, the horses stepped up, and as we passed the camp, there was a shout, and Isay stopped his wagon. The others pulled in their teams and the horses waited patiently, breathing steam into the cold morning air. Isay dismounted, stepped slowly through the snow, removed a boot from one soldier, a parka from another, rolled the parka in the man's frozen blood, placed them where the Germans had set a circle of rocks, and put them to the match. He stood back and watched for a moment as they burned and then turned his back to the bodies and got back in his wagon and we moved out again toward the road. He was not crying.

We came to another village two days later. We could tell this was a Jewish village. I would have known this even if I had not known that for the past day and a half you had simply let the reins drop. Afanasy was the one deciding where we traveled. I was surprised that we had come upon this village; you were not.

Remembering the last experience, Arkady was subdued, Mooskov clean in one of the dead German's expensive winter parkas, and Silvestovic solemn and watchful. Dukhi was in the back of the wagon and I was on the seat at your side. My hair was under one of the dead German's winter caps. With my cap and Mooskov's parka, it is perhaps no surprise that the village seemed still as we entered. People stared at us until I spoke to them in Russian and then in Hebrew, asking for a blessing from their elders.

There were smiles then, and an older, prosperous-looking man with a thick gray beard appeared in the doorway of the main building in the center of the village. He had a watch on a chain across a deep black velvet vest, and he wore a gray coat. I looked at the other people on the streets and they too seemed unusually prosperous. I smiled at them, and they smiled back, free of concern. I warmed to them. Perhaps there was still an oasis of peace in this land that had otherwise become a nightmare, I thought.

You stopped the horses, who for some reason appeared anxious, and you patted Afanasy and Bogdan before you turned to address the older man in the doorway. You motioned for Sergeant Dukhi, who as usual appeared quickly at your side, and you both ascended the steps of the building and shook hands with the well-dressed man. After a few words you looked around and motioned for me to join you. I leapt from the wagon in a flash and strode up the steps, careful not to slip on the snowy stone.

"Yes, Lieutenant?" I asked, eyes downward.

You looked at me quickly and then turned to the Rabbi. "Stasy, this is Rabbi Blumenthal. He is the village Rabbi. He is also the village authority." Next to the Rabbi stood a young man, tall, thin, with the beginnings of a beard. He was dressed richly, like his father.

"Welcome to the village of Gudensk-Smilivich," the Rabbi said with dignity. I nodded to him respectfully and he smiled at me in a formal way. He had a round, florid face; bright, intelligent gray eyes; a thick neck that seemed to be stiffened somehow, as if he had difficulty turning it separately from his head; and a moustache that curled at the ends. He did not reach out to shake my hand, which would have been most improper. "This is my son, Benjamin," he said, nodding toward the young man at his side.

"Rabbi, we have space in the wagons to take your people away from this place. The Germans will be here shortly, and everyone is in great danger." You spoke with earnest intensity, but for some reason I felt that your words were simply bouncing off the man's vest.

"Yes, yes, Lieutenant, we understand your concern, but really, there is no cause for alarm." I saw you look up sharply at him in surprise.

"But Rabbi Blumenthal, there is…there is most certainly cause for alarm. The Germans are moving through the countryside, killing every Jew they can find. No Jew is safe."

"Come inside, Lieutenant, and you will see what I am talking about."

You looked at Dukhi, who only shrugged, and then you looked at me, but I would not argue with a Rabbi, so you followed him into the town hall, and we followed you. Benjamin remained at the entrance, hands folded; he seemed timid to me, as though overshadowed by some monumental, massive force, and somewhat sad.

. The Rabbi led us down a marbled hallway. His shoes clicked loudly on the floor; ours made different sounds, more like the dim echo of soft leather upon stone. He turned with a flourish and I could tell that he was preparing to impress us with something. I sensed that he was quite impressed with himself. He opened large double doors and we walked into what seemed to be a hall of records. I could hear Arkady hooting outside, and Berestichslovski yelling at him to be quiet, shouting imprecations that he not make them appear like fools before the entire village. They sounded like squabbling children. I saw you cringe. Dukhi closed his eyes briefly and shook his head.

The Rabbi went to a large cabinet, opened its doors, and pulled out a drawer lined in green felt. He searched through the documents and pulled a large one from the drawer. It was on cream-colored paper, with a gold seal embossed upon the top corner with a blue ribbon under the seal that flapped noiselessly in the room as he set the document down upon the large mahogany table.

"Now, Lieutenant, you will see why there is no cause for alarm. Read this." He made a gesture with his hand toward the rich, gleaming paper on the polished wooden table—a gesture that combined significance with dignity and not a small amount of pride, as if to say, 'Here, you ignorant soldier, will you see what real power and prestige and connections can provide.'

I saw you lean down and begin to read the document. Dukhi was standing in his greatcoat with his hands clasped behind him, head down, muttering to himself. I saw you pick up your head and pay close attention, as though Dukhi was talking to you. You nodded.

"Rabbi, this paper seems to be simply a document testifying that you have worked at one time for the Krupp steel company. I do not understand."

With exasperation, the Rabbi took the document and turned it so he could read it more easily, pulled out a set of reading glasses from a vest pocket with some ceremony, and leaned over the paper. "See here," he said, standing up again and pointing to a line on the document. "Do you see this name? This man was my employer; I worked directly for him."

I leaned over your shoulder and read the name to which he pointed. You read the name out loud. "Gustav Krupp von Bohlen und Halbach," and turned again to the Rabbi. "So you worked for the Krupp family. I still do not see what…"

"Young man, you are perhaps not as wise in the ways of the world as you should be, but permit me to tell you that when men of a certain class make connections at this level, in this way, there is a…there is an understanding that transcends politics, that surpasses mere nationalistic or even religious differences. We are men united together in a greater cause. There is a transcendent movement in the world, young man, a cause of which I suspect you are not aware. This is the cause of linking the world together via business and the great and transforming power of technology. We here, with this paper, have no fear that the subterranean passions you speak of will stain our world. I grant you," he said in a contrived, patronizing tone, holding up a hand, "that perhaps others might. Other Jewish communities should perhaps be concerned—at least those which have not aggressively pursued relationships and dialogue with the people who will most significantly contribute to the world's future." As he spoke with such dignity and grace I could not help but see concealed beneath his façade the stench of overwhelming pride in his positional relationship with the famous Krupp.

At this, strangely enough, Dukhi turned from staring out the window and snapped at the man with a voice I had not yet heard from him; it was silent, sibilant, yet laced with silken, righteous anger. "You are a *fool*, Blumenthal. You think this…this *relationship* you have with this *German* will keep you and your people off the butcher's block?" He spat the words with disdain and intensity. "You have no idea; you are besotted with your own imagined position, power, and possessions, which you clutch to you like some shield. You have *no idea* what evil is coming this way…and what is worse, your arrogance will condemn those who look to you for leadership to a fate you cannot even imagine."

You and I were taken aback by Dukhi's outburst. I certainly had no idea he felt such intensity, and was surprised to hear him express himself so passionately.

You looked from Dukhi to the Rabbi and then spoke. "Rabbi, I wish to tell you that…"

"No need to apologize, Lieutenant," Blumenthal replied. "The man is a sergeant; what can one expect? No…there is no need for apologies. You should understand that—"

"Sir, I was not going to apologize. I was going to tell you that if Sergeant Dukhi tells you something in this way, it would be wise to act upon it immediately." You hesitated for just a moment, looking around the room, trying to find a way to express yourself. Finally you said, "He…he knows things."

The Rabbi drew his bulk even more firmly into himself and turned his stiff neck in his collar as though it was irritating him. I was reminded of the Russian fairy tale my mother would tell me of the wolf that would huff and puff and blow down pigs' houses.

"You may think what you like, Lieutenant." He snatched the document from the table, set it back down in the drawer as though it was some holy relic, closed the drawer with precision, and then turned back to you, face mottled with rage. "You will oblige me by taking your filthy wagons and your troop of idiots out of my village, or you will be reported to the local constabulary." Dukhi's eyes went wide and then he dropped his head and shook it. The edges of his eyes began to glisten. This was not normal for Dukhi.

You did not give up; I like this about you, Pyotr, and it gives me such hope, especially in our present circumstance. No, you did not give up in the face of this man's monstrous arrogance. "Rabbi Blumenthal, please, listen to me. We have come from a village not fifty kilometers from here. They were Jews; they were slaughtered by the Germans. The Germans have special squads that travel behind their armies, and these squads are designed solely for one thing...to kill Jews wherever they can be found. Do you understand? They shot the men and gathered the women and children into the village synagogue and burned it to the ground. We buried them, and..."

"Lieutenant, Lieutenant, enough, I have already told you that we have no reason to fear in this village." He pointed back at the drawer, where his precious document resided, and turned to face you. "Did they have one of those? Did the elder in *that* village work personally for the world's greatest industrialist? Did *their* Rabbi make crucial contributions to the chemical processes necessary for a great nation to grow even greater, to build great cannons, to fashion the world's greatest and strongest steel? *Did they?* Did they have such bonds, such connections, such networks to the great and the powerful?" He was shouting, and you just stood there, agog, wondering that a man could be so foolish.

"But Rabbi Blumenthal, there are women and children here. You and your people here are Jews...the Germans...you have a son—"

"The Germans will do what I tell them to do!" the Rabbi thundered, red-faced with a tumultuous and pharisaical anger. "Now get *out!* People like you, you and your Red Army vermin, only increase the risk of bringing to this village the dangers you are simply imagining. Get out! Get out!" He thrust a fat arm with sausage-like fingers in the direction of the doorway, toward which Dukhi was already moving. You and I followed, shocked and saddened beyond reckoning. I had seen what the Germans did to my father and mother, but had not yet come across any evidence of what Germans were doing to the Jews in Russia. I could see, though, the shock and horror on your face and upon Dukhi's countenance as we left the hall and descended the steps. You and Dukhi knew better than I what the Germans were capable of doing—had done—and were appalled at the man's turgidity and sickened by what it would mean to those who depended upon him for security.

Your men had heard the shouting; a silence and a solemn fear had descended upon them as the argument had begun, like children who hear their parents arguing in another room. Everyone had already mounted the wagons, ready for a quick departure. The horses were restless and agitated. Mooskov handed me up to the seat and you climbed in afterward, took up the reins, waited for Dukhi to slowly, painfully climb into the back of the wagon, and then before you could even snap the reins the horses leapt into the traces and we were off. Dukhi tumbled into his pile of rags at the precipitous departure. As the horses took their first few steps I looked back to make sure the other wagons were following, and I saw Isay with the reins in his hand, staring down at a little girl standing in the street, holding her mother's hand. Tears flowed down his cheeks and fell like diamonds onto the reins.

* * *

There was an event which followed shortly after our visit to Gudensk-Smilivich, an event which since then I have researched in specific detail, Pyotr, and while I do not think you will be surprised to read of it, I think I should mention it, for it builds upon the wonder of our story together.

A man named Artur Nebe commanded Einsatzgruppe B. His unit was directed by Himmler to follow Army Group Center during the invasion. Their records were recently found when a small guest house in Germany was demolished, and in the cellar there were documents related to activities of the German police during the war. I found them on the internet—it is a new technology, my dear, and not important—and searched specifically for details about their movements in Belarus when we traveled there with your wagon unit.

It was upon the first of December that this event occurred, and I remember this specifically because it was two days after we had left Gudensk-Smilivich, and I specifically remember that we had been there on Shabbat, because there was a calendar in the room where we argued with that stiff-necked Blumenthal person, with the days marked out, and the last day marked was the 29th of November, 1941.

I saw in the records that a unit of Einsatzgruppe B was in a town just to the north of Gudensk-Smilivich in late November, and they have an interesting entry in their combat diary—if you do not consider the word 'combat' to be too offensive, my dear, to describe their cowardly activities— for the first of December.

You remember that we had traveled forward, again letting Afanasy lead the convoy, and as the morning of the first of December dawned, cold and clear, we were just coming into another Jewish village. Children ran out to greet us, and their parents and others in the town came to their doorways to see. The horses pranced and flung their manes and arched their necks and walked carefully so as not to frighten the little ones or step on the braver ones who ran down to greet us in the dirt street which ran through the village. Arkady and Mooskov behaved themselves. I was sitting on the seat with you, wrapped in a blanket Dukhi had found for me, and was surprised as you sought to halt the horses there in the center of the village—but they would not stop. You yanked back on the reins, but tentatively, because you were always sensitive to their instincts and you trusted them; it was one of the things I found hard to understand at the time, but I understand now so much more about so many things that happened then.

But to continue; the horses would not stop and the children ran only a little further and pulled up short, staring at us with disappointed faces as the three wagons moved through their little village and departed northward up along a winding road and into the forest.

I looked at you and you looked at me and shrugged; such a thing had never happened before.

"Lieutenant, surely we are going to stop," I asked with hesitation, not as sure of myself as I had once been.

You shrugged your shoulders slightly. "Afanasy knows what he is doing," you said, ever the archetypical Russian fatalist, with a resigned confidence I could not share. "And Stasy, you may call me Pyotr, you know. You are not in the Army."

We were not thirty minutes away from the village when the wagons broke out of the wood onto a wide and flat, open plain stretching off into the distance to the east, with what appeared to be a cut in the ground, forming a cliff to the west, to our left. The road ran out of the wood and along the cliff. It was about eight or nine in the morning, and the sun sparkled on the untouched field of snow. As we moved down this road only a little, the woods on our flank disappeared and we found ourselves completely in the open and moving along where the road came close to the cliff. It was then that we saw the vast cloud of snow and ice particles to our front and heard the sound of vehicles. We could tell this easily, since a horse and a wagon makes little or no noise, especially when hooves are muffled in snow, compared to the grinding, clashing, clanking sound of armor and wheels and engines and the stink of burning petrol.

You were startled for just a moment, and then reached back into the wagon for your binoculars and stood on the seat. Afanasy simply plodded along, head down, walking slowly. You put the binoculars to your eyes and stared for what seemed like an hour. "They are Germans," you said grimly, seconds later, "armored cars, some Kübelwagons, a few motorcycles… no tanks." My heart leapt into my throat. The horses, inexplicably, kept plodding along; you had dropped the reins some time ago, and I began to be afraid.

Suddenly Dukhi poked his head out from the middle of the wagon, something he almost never did. "What is that?" he whispered, though we both heard him clearly in the cold morning air.

"Germans," you answered, "coming this way."

"No," Dukhi said, "*that!*" It was as if his words were coated in wonder, suffused with an expectation of the numinous. He stepped onto the seat and leapt down into the snow, tumbling, and then was up and running sideways, away from the wagon, running east, away from the cliff, looking behind us.

It was then that we heard what sounded like a waterfall. It started as a soft, gentle rushing, like a small river, but grew to become a swirling, tumultuous rush of wind that came from behind us. I leaned out over the side of the wagon to look back and gasped; the entire field behind us was like a great wall of snow, leaping as if a hundred tornadoes were following us, but slowly, as if a supernatural painter with artistic flourishes was twirling his brush laden with white paint across the canvas of the sky. This vast celestial canvas was coming toward the wagons at what I can only describe as a majestic pace; unhurried, stately, complex, like an army of ballerinas all in white, arms held high in swanlike arcs, twirling with beatific grace as they moved across a stage in time with the most rhythmic and beautiful music one could imagine.

In wonder I spoke, calling you to look behind us, and you did, and I heard you draw in your breath. "My God," you said, and I shall never forget what you said then, for it was because of those words that I knew I would love you forever, "My God," you said, "it is so beautiful!"

Dukhi was dancing in the snow, enraptured, davening, his arms spread wide, a look on his face that would outshine a thousand stars...but no, more truthfully, I should write that the light of a thousand stars shone forth from his eyes.

The horses stopped then, all of them at once, as the great swirling mass approached. I gasped again when I looked at them. Before my eyes each horse became larger, luminous, suffused with a brightness that seemed to come from within them, the contours of their every muscle etched by rippling, living light shining outward from their hearts. Their heads were up, necks arched and regal, their manes streaming like capes. They began to prance in their traces with what was clearly joy as the white curtain of dancing snow approached. I saw that day what true and real horses look like. Others I have seen since then seem simply dull substitutes; dull, lifeless imitations of what Afanasy and Bogdan became as they stood there illuminated from within by a pure and noble argent light.

The curtain stopped as it covered us, and steadied, hovering, suspended in the sky just above and slightly behind the rear wagon. The rushing noise conveyed depth in a dimension beyond sound, beyond our awareness, and we all stood staring up at pure white beauty, fully covered and immersed, with time and Germans all but forgotten.

The white curtain of joy—for this is what I will call it forever—gradually diminished and descended slowly with a poignant dignity and grace into the snow, there to lay, all the ballerinas settled and chaste and demur, and then there was nothing behind us but the bright blue sky and the sound of a light wind blowing across the surface of the snow.

We shook ourselves. We felt as if we had been given just a glimpse of something that was beyond description, something not of this world, and that we would ache for something of its nature for the rest of our life. Dukhi was in the snow, crumpled, tears of joy on his face, once again an old man in an oversized greatcoat. You and I jumped down and managed to get him back in the wagon and then at the same time we both remembered the Germans. You grabbed for the binoculars.

"My God," you said in a hushed and reverent voice, the glasses to your face.

"What? *What!*"

You lowered the binoculars and turned to face me; you were awestruck, but you were smiling. "They're running away. They're running away."

You looked again. "Wait," you said, "something is happening. They're falling," you said then, more slowly, "the cliff is...is crumbling. No, wait... they're *driving* off the cliff. They're driving into..." Then you suddenly jumped down again from the wagon and ran to the edge of the cliff. I followed you and looked down and beheld a wide rushing river just beginning to be choked with ice; black and wildly tumultuous and wickedly cold. You looked down into the water and then downriver to where the Germans were floundering and put the binoculars to your eyes again. "They're drowning," you said, with a finality that spoke of steel under your gentleness, and we both walked back to the wagon, wondering.

As soon as we mounted, the wagon jerked and you fell onto the seat roughly. Afanasy had decided that we would turn around and return to the village. I sat with eyes wide in wonder, relief flooding through me along with gratefulness and wonder, and it was then that I first began to conceive of the possibility that perhaps God was larger in Truth than what my narrow conception of Him had been, and that perhaps He was a God of wonder and beauty and fearsome power, a God that so far exceeded the tiny sphere of my own small concepts of laws and legalisms and ritual and rules, and I thought that perhaps I should get to know this God. I felt as if we had experienced just a tiny portion of His glory there on the road under the white curtain of joy, as did Moses when God covered him with His hand as He made His glory to pass by. O Pyotr, people today talk and write and argue and contend with all manner of contentions, and they wrestle over doctrines and treatises and theories and interpretations. But once a human soul has *experienced* the living God, once a human heart has tasted the very essence of joy and heartbreak and seen, with the eyes of their heart, who God is, there is no longer any question, there is no longer any argument or conviction or pressure or political party or philosophy that will stand against that one blinding, crystal moment of pure understanding and awareness; that one instant of fiery, passionate, intense fusing heat of complete sublimation into the great I Am, He who is Truth and Love and Beauty and Goodness and Joy. Every word of Scripture I have ever read from that day forward has taken on an added intensity of meaning. It is backlit by a numinous illumination—in the same way I saw the horses that day—that would not have been possible had I not experienced first the terror and the fear in the forest, and then the utterly beautiful and dramatic redemption by God in that vast field of snow.

We did return to that village, Pyotr, as you recall, and we did evacuate all the Jews there, and we settled them deeply in the forest and supplied them with everything they needed to survive the winter. I still get letters from their grandchildren, you know, my dear.

But the point of this vignette, my love, was what I learned in the records recently discovered about Einsatzgruppe B. In their unit log for the first of December in 1941, it records that they packed up and moved out of a bivouac in a town and were deploying along a long curving road on a cliff that ran along the edge of a river at about eight or nine in the morning when they encountered a massive formation of T34 tanks in the distance directly to their front, spread out on a vast plain of snow, coming directly toward them at high speed. The Commander of the Einsatzgruppen unit realized that his small group of police and volunteers in thin-skinned armored cars and motorcycles stood no chance at all, with every possibility of being slaughtered, and so they turned around and raced back the way they had come. But in the blowing snow and the confusion, they came too close to the cliff, which had suffered apparently from erosion, and the motorcycles and armored cars and Kubelwagons all drove off the cliff and into the river, and the military police and hired murderers on foot all stumbled and fell into the cold, swirling water and were drowned. A single survivor returned and reported the loss of the entire unit.

It was then recorded that another Einsatzgruppe Commander took another unit back down the road two days later and into the village just hours after we departed with everyone loaded on the wagons or following us on foot. They burned the village to the ground, including the synagogue, but did not kill one soul or even threaten one Jew in that place, and as they moved on into the Russian steppe to look for other victims, Afanasy took us all deeper into the forest.

* * *

Russia—and the unfortunate invading German Army—experienced its coldest winter in one hundred and forty years that year. The bitter winds leaping across the vast territory, the snow, and the cold certainly helped the Red Army as the Germans pounded into the depths of the vast Russian steppes, attacking Leningrad and Moscow and capturing many less-fortunate Russian cities and towns and villages, all the while stuffing newsprint into their uniforms to keep warm, since they had neglected to bring winter clothes. We spent the winter roaming behind the German front line as it advanced, staying one step ahead of the Einsatzgruppen, trying to save as many Jews as we could.

One day, under a mottled gray sky that was clearing after a January storm, the wind was resting and the wagons were moving along a road that wound comfortably through a dense forest. We had forty Jews in our train that morning. The women and children were in the wagons, the men walking. It was strange but do you remember, Pyotr, that whenever we had Jews in our train, Arkady would never misbehave? He seemed instead settled and sane. Mooskov would scrupulously avoid even the semblance of enjoying mud or filth; he kept himself meticulously clean. It was if the others too were both sobered and restored to health as they discharged the duties attendant to rescuing the Jews…as if they were only then fully sane. And too, ever since we encountered, or were met by, the numinous cloud of white dancing joy, no one remained as they had been.

We saw a crossroads ahead and first Afanasy and then Bogdan lifted their heads, as though they had seen something, and you sensed their heightened alertness through the reins in your hands.

"What is it, Papa?" you asked, soothing them. "Whisht, whisht, it is good, now, hush, Papa, what is it?"

You felt them pause for just a moment; they snorted once and shook their heads, as if angry or irritated. They paused for just another moment and then they put their shoulders with renewed confidence into their collars and the chains pulled the cross bar of the wagon again and we jerked slightly as they in some way rectified that which had concerned them, and we were again pressing forward without concern or fear.

We came to the crossroads. There was a man sitting on a log, and below him there was stacked a pile of books and a thick blue velvet duffel bag trimmed with gold and silver thread. He was stocky, well-dressed in a black coat, a soft gray vest, a gleaming white shirt, and dark woolen trousers. He wore a long, rich, soft gray overcoat which, from my seat on the wagon where I sat shivering in a thin German Army blanket, looked exceedingly warm. He wore dress shoes, which was strange. We had not seen a village all morning; perhaps we were approaching a more populated area. This man certainly did not seem to be dressed appropriately for the Russian forest in the dead of winter.

The horses stopped of their own accord and Afanasy snorted once and swung his great noble head and looked directly at the man sitting on the log. He blew from his nostrils, steam puffing forth like a dragon. The man, strangely enough, did not look up, but kept paging through a book he held on his lap. The great gray stallion lifted one foot and pawed the ground and let forth a stallion's low, rumbling noise that was at once and all together a combination of warning, an announcement of status, and an expression of disapproval. You sat there, holding the reins in your hands, looking down curiously.

Finally the man closed the book, looked up at you with what could only be described as an impatient air, and somewhat brusquely, placed his hands down flat on the book as though he was ready now, from the goodness of his heart, to condescend to speak to you. "Good morning. I am Professor Rosenbaum," he said, "What can I do for you?"

He had a short, bristly black moustache and a sharp manner, and Dukhi, in the back of the wagon, stopped talking for a quick moment. I heard him draw in his breath and felt his presence over my shoulder as he poked his head through the canvas flap.

"Good morning, Professor Rosenbaum; how are you today?" Both of us were surprised to hear Dukhi's voice so strident and clear. Dukhi had greeted the man in Hebrew, and the man had most certainly heard the greeting.

"Yes, yes, very nice," the professor replied, in Russian, waving his hand, making it clear he had no wish to speak Hebrew. "Well, what is it? I'm a busy man, you know." He crossed his legs and flicked a speck of lint from his knee.

"Professor Rosenbaum," you said, picking up the conversation from Dukhi, "there are Germans in the woods, you know, and it is not safe for Jews to be alone."

"I know this full well," Rosenbaum replied. You were surprised. He picked up the duffle bag and pulled from it a worn volume bound in soft green leather. "Here," he said, holding it up, "is my book on what the Germans will do when they invade Russia. It is the definitive argument which, if I may say so, will stand against whatever counterpoints might be brought to oppose it."

"What do you mean?" you asked, curious.

"There are Rabbis and teachers and village elders scattered all over this district," he answered, "who are completely unaware that the Germans are devils who will strive to their utmost to completely and utterly eliminate the Jewish race from the earth. Some argue that the Germans are simply misunderstood; others put their faith in their position or in some particular skill they may have which they think the Germans will prize. You do not know him, I am sure, but there is a Rabbi Blumenthal of…"

"We know this man," I blurted, taken completely by surprise that he would know of the Rabbi of Gudensk-Smilivich. I was then so surprised by my temerity in speaking to such a great and important person as this professor before us that I reflexively popped a hand up to cover my mouth.

"Then you will know what I am talking about," he went on, with undiminished confidence. "Blumenthal thinks that his lavish and ornate document alleging that he worked with Krupp will save him when the Germans come. Ridiculous! I argued this very point with him last month in the debates held in the great hall in Greboynk-Bialensk."

"We are glad to…"

"And here," he said, interrupting you, lifting another book from the duffel, "is another of my books which shows definitively that it is only in the hope of Yeshua, the Messiah of Israel, that the Jews will be saved."

You raised your eyebrows at this, curious to meet a Jew who thought Yeshua was the Messiah.

"You believe in Yeshua, then? You, a learned man of the Jews?"

"Of course I believe in Yeshua. I've conducted an exhaustive study of the Scriptures; there can be no mistake. This man Jesus was the Son of God and will come again to rule and reign on the earth. And mark me," he pronounced ominously, with great dignity and portent, "He is coming soon." He waved his hand around to embrace the entire forest, the entire earth. "All of this…all of this war, this death, this oppression by ungodly men and hate-filled nations will one day come to a dramatic and bloody end when the Son of David comes back to claim His own."

You sat there with a look of surprise on your face, and then Dukhi spoke from over my shoulder.

"Nu…so come with us, Professor Rosenbaum. We are going about the land, picking up Jews and hiding them from the Germans. You can help us. Jews respect wisdom; they will respect a well-educated man like yourself."

The professor's eyes clouded for a moment, as though to convey the picture of a great man gripped in the throes of deep contemplation.

"I agree with your assertion," he replied, nodding sagely, with gravity appropriate to his station, "that the Jews will be oppressed. The Jews will be hunted down and killed, as will anyone who helps them. But I see no grounds for your second point, alleging that we should therefore attempt to hide them. Why, that would be foolish, putting all the Jews in one place... it would be easier for the Germans to find them. And I see nowhere in Scripture that indicates that Jews should be hidden from Germans. Now, there is some allusion to the Jews in Israel being remanded to the wilderness of Judea, but nothing which would give me any reason to undertake any effort to actually try and hide Jews here in Russia. You perhaps may not be aware that the German Army is a massively powerful and comprehensive force that will race through Russia and much of Europe—it is all here in my book—and there will be nothing for it. No one will be able to hide, and, therefore, any attempt to try and do so would be foolish."

Being impressed with the Professor's clothes and his richly appointed baggage, I was not able to immediately grasp the horrific discontinuity in his logic, but Dukhi was not so encumbered. Again his voice was measured, easily discerned, piercing in its clarity as it sang past my ear, heavy with its own gravid portent.

"So, Professor Rosenbaum, you think that because the German Army, this evil spawned out of the pit of hell, is so powerful, that it cannot, that it *should* not be opposed? You think that we should not lift a finger to help the Jews before the onslaught of this demonic filth?"

"There is no Scriptural reference for in any way trying to hide from this massive oppression to come," he replied testily, shifting his shoulders in his coat with a dark and confrontational confidence. "I have done extensive Scriptural research."

"So you will sit and write books and debate with fools and tell the world that Jews are in great danger and do nothing to save them? You will let them die?" Dukhi was becoming more agitated.

"Nothing can be done. You do not know the awesome power of the Germans; nothing will stand in their way. You cannot hide from them." Bogdan chose this moment to lift his tail and mark the road with the remains of yesterday's foraging.

By now some of the Jews we had evacuated from the village the night before had come up to where the Professor sat on the log and were listening to the exchange. One of them, a younger man in a thin black coat and a long wispy beard, with the tallit under his shirt and a broad black hat upon his head, leaned slightly forward. I recognized a yeshiva student poised for a kill.

"So, Professor Rosenbaum, this Yeshua you claim to be the Messiah; you say we should just wait for him to come and strike dead all the Germans, no matter what they might do before he shows up?"

"There are...there are no references whatsoever in Scripture which indicate that we are to...to hide Jews. Putting them all in one place would be ludicrous. The German Air Force would find them instantly and, since they would be all gathered in one place, they would be easily bombed, or the Wermacht would gather them up as a group. You do not know the technologies they have today."

"So your solution then is to let them be gathered up separately?"

The Professor shifted on the log, uncomfortable now. "You do not understand," he said. "A Jew's best defense is to know the Word of God. If they search the Scriptures and feed on them and get beyond the milk and seek out the meat of the word of God, why then, this is their hope. The Word will keep them from being deceived about the times in which we live. Fighting, fleeing...it is all foolishness." He swept his hand out and away from his chest, palm flat out toward the ground, a very Jewish gesture of finality. "There will be no defense against this brutality. You cannot fight it."

"So for a Jew to be killed as long as he knows the truth is okay with you; this is better for the Jew than being killed while he is deceived?"

A woman came up; she had been riding in the wagon behind ours and had caught just snatches of the argument, but had quickly gathered the spirit of it. Her face was contorted in a mask of pain I hope I will never see again, and there were tears running down her face. She marched through the snow by the side of our wagon and went up to the self-satisfied professor on the log.

"*What do you know?*" she hissed, pain etching the words. Her hands flailed the air about his face, and he drew back in distaste. "What do *you* know of what the Germans will do? My mother was in Minsk...my mother and my brothers and their wives and their children! They were put in a ghetto and they were starved and they were shot because they were Jews! My sister—" she sobbed, and she looked upward to let the water run from her eyes, but continued, dark brown eyes flashing, "My sister escaped from Minsk, did you know? She escaped from this all-powerful German monster you are so afraid of, Mister Professor. She ran into the woods and hid for ten months, by herself, in the forest. She stumbled into our village as thin as a stick, dying, after walking a hundred kilometers through the swamps, through dozens of villages and towns that were afraid to hide her. They were afraid of what the all-powerful Germans would do. Maybe they did not see in your precious book there anything that may have specifically told them to hide my sister, my Lyebi." She leaned forward then and with biting sarcasm asked, "Is there anything in your Scriptures that says to give a woman coming out of Minsk named Lyebi a piece of bread, Professor? Is there? Look it up; maybe her name is in there. Maybe it isn't...it must not be, Mister Famous Professor, because she died. No one would help her... no one would help one solitary Jewish girl who needed a place to sleep and some bread to eat." She was shouting now, angry, grief-stricken. The professor looked as though something distasteful had been cast down at his feet. The woman was sobbing now, gasping for breath to get the words out. "And let me ask you something else, Mister Fancy Professor who writes so many books. Is there anything there in your book that says that you should be schlepping around debating, or writing books of your own, or even that you should be sitting there on that log?" Her shoulders slumped, but then she lifted up her head and leaned forward and stabbed her words at him. "Is there anything in your precious new testament that says that someone should lift a finger to help a Professor Rosenbaum when the Germans come for *him*? Is *your* name in that book?" She put her face in her hands then and fell to her knees in the snow with a wailing cry. Her shoulders shook in great wracking sobs for her sister and her family, and the young man with the wispy beard put his arms around her shoulders, helped her to stand, and led her back to the wagon.

Dukhi came out from the back of the wagon, stepped between you and me, and hopped down into the snow. I felt then as if a deeply ominous thunder cloud bristling with lightning had brushed past my spirit. The horses had been remarkably compliant up to this point, but as Dukhi came out of the wagon and hit the ground, they began to tremble, and I thought I saw again just a remnant of that luminosity which had so enthralled and entranced me that day under the white curtain of dancing, joyous snow, although there was then, when Dukhi stepped down that day to confront the professor, more of a sense, a feeling, a *spirit* of deep, righteous anger, a threatening mien of disapproval. Afanasy and Bogdan seemed to grow larger and more fierce; for some reason you did not notice this morphing. You sat there placidly with the reins gathered together in one strong hand, the other clenched tightly into a fist, eyes burning into the man whose arrogance bore deafening testimony to the fact that while he may have possessed all the knowledge it was possible to possess about the words in a book, he had never once experienced God or seen His wonders; that while he may have known *about* God, that while he perhaps may have been persecuted as a Jew who believed Yeshua to be the Messiah, while he may have taught in Yeshua's name or even cast out demons in Yeshua's name, he possessed not one true shred of experiential knowledge attendant to the One who is Goodness and Truth and Beauty—what was the most terrifying to you was your certainty that Yeshua did not know him.

Dukhi walked up to the professor on the log. The crowd of Jews pressing angrily about Rosenbaum parted, standing aside for Dukhi as he approached. The forest grew suddenly very quiet. He hobbled slowly, boots crunching in the snow until he stood before the distinguished professor, an old man in a tattered Russian greatcoat confronting a very distinguished-looking, younger, healthier, more vibrant personage. Dukhi drew himself up and stood, clasping his hands behind his back, and in that piercing and sibilant voice that he had, among the many in his repertoire, said, "Draw yourself up now, Professor Rosenbaum, and answer me."

I saw the professor struggling. He tried in vain to dismiss the visage before him; he looked around at the woods, up at the trees, anywhere he could to give the impression that there was not a thin old man standing before him, about to put him to the test. Dukhi was accustomed to this; many people never noticed him, many others intentionally ignored him, and less paid any attention to what he said, though he was always speaking to them. Perhaps they could not hear because he spoke with such a soft voice. Though Dukhi's voice may have at times been soft, it was like silken steel there that day in the snow before the learned professor, and the educated man heard every word.

Dukhi suddenly snapped his fingers, and it was as if someone had taken the man's head and yanked it so that he was compelled to turn and look directly into Dukhi's eyes. The struggle on the professor's face was evident; beads of perspiration revealed a fearsome and passionate internal conflict.

The old man stood before the proud scholar, threw his head back, lifted up his hands, and spoke in a ringing cry that rose above the trees and down into the depths of snows. "Deliver those who are being taken away to death, and those who are staggering to slaughter, O hold them back. If you say, 'See, we did not know this,' does He not consider it who weighs the hearts? And does He not know it who keeps your soul? And will He not render to man according to his work?"

Dukhi stood there for a breath of time as stars and moons and trees and our hearts stood still, looked directly at the trembling professor, and said, "Go and find what this means, Professor Rosenbaum ..."

Dukhi turned and walked back to the wagon. We had to help him up, and the entire train—horses and humans—in response to some unspoken, intangible signal, stepped up and moved along again through the crossroads and down the road, leaving the professor sitting on his log, red-faced, searching with antagonism and an argumentative spirit through his duffel bag of books for some shred of wisdom with which to refute the decrepit old man in the ill-fitting Russian greatcoat. Not one Jew even deigned to look at him.

Dukhi, grieving, curled into his pile of rags and wept as the wagon rocked slowly along the way. I had never seen Dukhi grieving, even in the midst of all the fear and terror and death that made up so much of the backdrop in our lives then, and it frightened me. I turned to you, and I saw you staring straight ahead with the sunlight flickering through the trees and reflecting upon your face, which appeared as washed stone.

Some kilometers later, as the silence drew on longer than I could bear, with the soft voice of Dukhi in the back of the wagon subdued even more so than normal, I touched your arm. You seemed to awake and turned to face me.

"Stasy," you said, as if you had just noticed me sitting next to you. "I am sorry; I have been thinking about too many things."

"Pyotr...Pyotr, why is Dukhi so heartbroken? And why are you...why has this foolish man sitting on a log in the middle of the forest, in the middle of nowhere, upset you so?"

You held the reins loosely in your hands for a few more minutes before you spoke, and when you did, it was with a curious, searching quality, reflective, wondering. "Stasy, I...I cannot say what has so grieved Dukhi, although I have a thought what it might be. For me, I can say that to see a man—a Jew who *knows* that Yeshua is Israel's true Messiah, who *knows* what horror is descending upon his people—sit and do nothing about it, who would not be bothered to lift a finger to help those through whom God has made Himself known to the world, shakes me to my very soul. He has read so much and studied so much and can argue rings around fools like me, but...but Stasy, where is his *heart*? Where is even a smattering, a morsel of compassion? If I saw an injured squirrel in the road I would go out of my way to lift it up and set it back in the forest. If my ox or my lamb fell into a well, even on Shabbat, I would lift it out again. There it would be," you said, and you held out a hand as if pointing to an ox stuck in a well right before our eyes, "and what man with even a shred of compassion would not act to pull it out? If he *knows* that Yeshua is the Messiah, shouldn't he go forth and do likewise? Stasy, you should read...you should read in the Bible I have about how many times Yeshua would heal people; he would heal them on Shabbat even, right in the face of the religious leaders. Everywhere he went he had compassion on those who were sick, helpless, or broken-hearted." Your voice trailed off into the distance, and you looked to the left and to the right, watching the lines of Jews who were accompanying the wagons walk along the road. Some were talking together, others looking pensive as everything in their lives was disrupted, the threat of dislocation or financial ruin paling before the fact that Germans were coming through the forest to kill them. Faces were long, hearts heavy. "They are like sheep without a shepherd," you said to yourself, but I heard you nonetheless.

"Perhaps," I said quietly, wondering myself, "he just wants to be right, and cares nothing for those things about which he argues. Perhaps he has never given a moment's thought to the actions that any man of good conscience would see as necessary should the events he champions come to pass. Perhaps he just likes to argue."

"I think you are right, Stasy," you said. "And yet, even so, he is a very smart man. Perhaps he knows that there really is no chance at all to save any of them, and to try and hide them is simply a quick way to get oneself killed. Maybe there is no chance."

I drew my head back and slapped your arm. It was like hitting an iron banister. "What are you saying, Pyotr? Look around you; look to the left, look to the right." I waved my hands in my emotion. My long white hair was flying out and around my head like some crazed forest fairy; I must have been a sight. "The forest parts before us like the Red Sea, and you, a Moses leading a wagon of fools through the Russian desert, and you talk such foolishness?"

"Stasy, I am only saying..."

"Be quiet, Pyotr, and let me say something." I felt then, my love, that I had to explain something that was more important than life itself, or my heart would burst. "I have watched my parents murdered and left to lie in a field for the birds. My brothers have been devoured in the killing machine that is this war, and another brother and his family have been butchered like pigs by the Nazis in Minsk. I...I saw something in the forest, Pyotr, that I cannot speak of, but it was such an evil that I do not think I will ever be the same. When you found me by the side of the road, Pyotr, do you know what it was that had driven me mad? It was a *word*...a word was spoken to me by...by what I encountered there, a dark and powerful word that formed a reality in my mind that God was not all-powerful, that God wanted to deceive me about goodness, that God wanted to keep me from wisdom and wanted to hide from me truth and sought to blind me to beauty. All these thoughts, Pyotr, were spoken to me in an instant through a word that had such power that it began to make that reality in my mind. And as those thoughts began to form even the first tinges of such a reality in my mind, it drove me mad.

"But then you and your wagon of fools found me. Dukhi spoke to me constantly, and his words beat down the iron walls of the fearsome reality that was growing in my mind. And then," and I remember here that tears began to slide across my cheeks, for I felt their moist passing in the chilly wind. "And then I watched as the horses would keep you and your...your men from all manner of dangers. I watched as...oh, Pyotr, as God himself in power and beauty and majesty kept us safe with a miracle that will break my heart for the rest of my life when I recall the sweetness of it. These fools of yours have become great and powerful warrior kings who risk their lives so that the innocent and defenseless might live to see and know that God does indeed want for us all goodness and wisdom and truth and beauty. All of you are out here so that God's chosen people can see His face in the wilderness." Mooskov was just then walking by, carrying a little girl on his shoulders; she was tugging at his cap and pulling the strings of his parka like the reins on a horse, and Mooskov would turn one way and then the other, and the little girl looked up at the horses and down at Mooskov and opened her mouth in silent laughter.

"My God, Pyotr, who cares about the speculations of one foolish old professor? Though I would not have believed it when you found me, I have seen the God of All Creation take us by the hand and walk us through the valleys and roads and pits and mountains and forests of death and hell and He has kept us safe, ordering every turn of the wagon wheel. If this God that you trust and love wants a remnant of Jews to be rescued, and He wants to use a wagon of fools to do so, then who are we to worry about it? So maybe this Yeshua is the Messiah; I will have to think more about this." I shook my finger at him then. "But who is this professor that knows so much? This professor may know what God has to say about things, but I am thinking that he hasn't even *begun* to learn about what God wants done. That *horse*," and I pointed to Afanasy then, "knows more about what God wants than that meshugganah professor." Of course Afanasy and Bogdan both lifted their heads and tossed their manes and blew air through their noses at that moment to let me know that I was right.

You smiled at me then…a slow, peaceful, thoughtful, thankful smile, and then you reached up and touched my face and wiped away a tear with your thumb, and there in the woods on a wagon I lost my heart forever. You leaned your head close and kissed me, and we drove on into Russia to find a place to hide our Jews.

* * *

All lovers should have the experience of driving a team of horses, my dear. We spent many months there together on that wagon seat, fraught with rich symbolism. At the time I had never driven a car, but I have since then. With a car, one simply opens a door and, only consulting or considering one's own will, turns a mechanical switch and lo, the car immediately responds to one's every direction; it goes where one wills it, when, and how. But to drive a horse, or a team of horses, is to be in partnership with another living creature that possesses a will of its own; flesh and blood and mind and will and spirit that possesses its own hopes and desires and fears, that sees things differently, that perceives life and truth and danger so much differently than we do. A true meshing of wills must be accomplished, and to do so a man must span the almost insurmountable bridge that exists between species—somehow a man and a horse must communicate so that together they might accomplish something. I learned from you, my love, there in the forest, that so too must there be that same intuitive, flashing blend of wills between a man and his wife, which also involves spanning a bridge across a truly formidable gap—a man and a woman must bridge the difficulties and differences that are inherent in the differences between man and woman and together work to bring about the accomplishment of a task, the raising of a family, or true love. And finally there is that meshing of wills that must be accomplished between a man and his God across a bridge that spans the infinite distance between flesh and blood and Spirit and Truth.

In each case two must work in concert—a man and a horse; a man and a wife; a man and his God. A man who has never partnered with a living creature to jointly accomplish a goal—be it to plow a field or raise a family—is a man who has not yet learned what he must about life, love, and serving the God of All Creation.

Dukhi married us under two large oak trees in the twilight, when the stars smiled upon the snow and fifty-eight ragged, starving, care-worn Jews snatched from death near a village north of Minsk stood around the canopy that Arkady and Mooskov and Svoboda had hastily erected. Isay even dredged up a glass that he had liberated from a village—'for just such an occasion', he said. "You have been looking at the Lieutenant for so long with stars in your eyes, you should have just painted a sign!" and everyone laughed when I blushed.

Dukhi said the words of the ceremony in his soft voice which I recall was as soft as ever but, like so many strange things which occurred in the forest that winter, everyone there heard every word, and each word sank down peacefully into their spirits and nestled like glowing embers of hope, as love will light even the darkest night, the darkest heart.

Oh, Pyotr, do you remember the dancing? Svoboda and Kazimir stood forth bathed in the firelight, Svoboda flicked his fingers across the body near the bridge, and then they were both off into a swirling, passionate mélange of rhythm and pounding synchronicity as each played a melody that twirled and flirted with the other; my breath fled upward with my soul. Then one of the elders from the village lifted a battered clarinet from a cardboard suitcase and began at first a slow, measured klezmer tune that traced through at first shyness and then timidity and on through boldness to pure joy. I do not know if it was the music that night that spoke such things to my heart, dearest Pyotr, or if my heart, so full of love and joy, had finally come to the point where I was able to hear such things in the music.

The most wondrous thing to me throughout all of that winter, even considering the miracles and the rescues and the times when God miraculously kept us out of danger, was that my heart, poisoned by a powerful and noxious word, could go from a sickened well from which only the water of despair, ruin, and mourning could be drawn, and a mind in which a reality without God was being formed, to a heart that could sense and rejoice in the sweetness of life again. Oh, Pyotr, He worked through your wagon of fools to rescue me from such blackness, such fear, such a horrible fate! Amos was right: I did see His face in the wilderness, my love. How sweet and fitting I felt our endeavors to be then, going about in the bitter cold and snow and rescuing Jews from just such blackness and fears and fates. Sometimes the complexity of our God makes my head spin.

I remember during our wedding celebration, as Svoboda and Kazimir began to play a tempestuous piece, that you took up a stool, and then grabbed the cap from Mooskov's head, a spoon from Silvestovic who was cooking that night, and finally an ice-covered rock. You tossed the stool in the air, and then the cap, and then the spoon, and then up went the rock and everyone gasped and then clapped and laughed as you juggled all these things with wondrous skill, all the more amazing in that it was so unexpected. The men smiled at each other to see such a surprising skill in their lieutenant, the discovery of which unlocked to them another dimension of your personality, which made them feel that they knew you better, which in turn helped them to have more confidence in you—as if they needed more. Oh no...there had been too many impossible escapes, too many successes against astounding odds, for them to doubt that God had put

His hand upon you. Even Svoboda forgot himself and became impassioned when he would speak of the amazing impossibilities of what was happening to the unit. Arkady would stand stock still and open his mouth in silent wonder; Mooskov would simply hang his head, overwhelmed; and Kazimir would cry with joy and Isay would laugh and Berestichslovski was smiling and complimenting Silvestovic and Dukhi would just whisper quietly and smile and you would shake your head at the wondrous beauty of it all. This is what I so loved about you, my dearest Pyotr. You would always see the beauty of things.

* * *

And so we went, you and I and our wagon of fools, moving behind the German lines through the winter of 1941 and on into the spring of 1942, finding Jews before the Einsatzgruppen got to them, or at times, mercifully not often, coming upon villages that had been savaged. At each of these Isay would descend from his wagon and find a boot or sometimes just a child's shoe and a cloak, soak it in blood—which was never hard to find in Russia in those years—wrap them together, and burn them.

With the spring came the rains and with the rains came the mud; this was good for the Russians, bad for the Germans, good for the Jews. Only the Wermacht had tanks; the Germans gave the Einsatzgruppen wheeled vehicles—these Einsatzgruppen were brutish, ignorant police and volunteers, mixed with a few SS—and the vehicles were utterly useless in the sea of mud that Russia had become that spring.

We came into a wood that sat atop a hill one morning in September of 1942. There were thick trees but near the edge of the hill the wood thinned and we could see down into a valley where smoke rose; men and women were working in a field, and children worked closely or played, running here and there. Dogs barked. We could see the unmistakable shape of a synagogue in the center of the village.

Coming up the hill, a strange thing happened; Afanasy went lame. It was probably the mud, you said, for sometimes a horse would put a foot wrong or wrench a knee in the unsteady footing; nothing to worry about. I stepped out of the wagon and helped you unhitch him and remove his harness, listening as you spoke words of soft encouragement while he snorted and grunted and blew and pawed gently with his lame foot in reply. You were able to lead him, limping badly, to a spot under a tree just at the edge of the wood, where he found some soft grass and promptly settled down to take the weight from his foot. You set Silvestovic to making a poultice and Dukhi came and spoke some soft words to the horse, who whinnied and nuzzled the old man gently. Bogdan came to stand next to him as well, to keep him company I suppose.

The sun was just past its zenith in the sky, and I saw you standing there at the edge of the wood, consulting with Dukhi, both looking down at the village. Afanasy gave a low rumbling grunt, and I placed my hand on his withers to comfort him.

"Dukhi, let's hitch Bogdan and we can take the wagons down to get them before dark and bring them back here. I...I am not comfortable leaving them down there. The Germans are shifting the front and they could come through this valley at any time."

Dukhi nodded, talking softly, and went to give directions to the men. You came over to me where I sat next to Afanasy.

"Stasy, my love, may I ask you to stay here and watch our horse? He will need some company." This was not a disappointment for me since I was not feeling well at the time. There was a surprising sensation of nausea and nothing that Silvestovic cooked was appealing. This had been the case for a number of days. I suspect you knew how I felt and this is why you were kind enough to let me rest. I smiled at you and you kissed me and caressed my face with your strong hand and touched the top of my head.

"Here," you said, and you handed me your worn, leather-covered Bible— the one Dukhi had given you so long ago in the pit. "Here is something for you to read while you wait." And then you hitched Bogdan to the wagon and you and the wagons and the fools turned around and went back down the road and soon I watched as your train emerged from the woods and moved along the road toward the village.

The dogs came first, and then the children, running and shouting with curiosity and pleasure, and the adults followed more cautiously. I watched as you and Dukhi got down from the wagon and spoke with some of the men in the field. You gestured, pointing over your shoulder toward the south, from where you expected the Germans to come, and then pointed up to our hill, where I waited with Afanasy.

The men nodded, and then the children were running back toward the village, and in a few hours they had loaded what valuables they possessed; their clothes, their silver, their family heirlooms, the Rabbi coming out of the tiny wooden synagogue in the center of town carrying a Torah wrapped in beautiful blue velvet—all that the horses and the wagons could carry— and you turned the wagons around and began to head back into the woods. This was when the first Panzers came onto the road.

The wagons could not move, and then infantry appeared from the tree lines on both sides and surrounded the wagons. They had dirty gray uniforms and those sinister-looking helmets and I knew they were Germans. My heart had stopped and I could not breathe. I looked more closely; yes, this was the Wermacht, the German Army. These were not units from one of the Einsatzgruppen.

A soldier pointed his submachine gun at you and yelled and I watched as you dropped the reins and stepped down from the wagon. Other soldiers were rounding up the villagers. I saw as they separated the Jews from your men. They were laughing derisively, but I sensed that they were frightened as well. Some looked over their shoulders. They pushed the Jews into a circle in the grass, and they put you and your men near the wagons. I could see Arkady, standing there very still, watching the mothers try to keep the children from becoming frightened. I saw Mooskov help a little boy who had fallen in the dirt to rise until a German came and struck him with a rifle butt, clubbing him back toward your group next to the wagons.

I watched as most of the soldiers stood in a line facing the circle of Jews, and then there was a crack, and then a rushing torrent of firing. I could see the faces of the Germans, since they stood facing the hill, and I could see the faces of the Jews as well, since for some reason when Germans would shoot Jews they made them turn their backs.

Some of the Germans were just boys, some were frightened at what they were doing, some clearly found it possessing in the way drink can be, or lust. All of them, however they felt, pulled their triggers. The Germans shot all the Jews in the field, and then an officer with a pistol walked through the supine forms to do his part to make that place in Russia Judenfrei.

And then...and then they turned toward you and your men at the wagons. I watched as you turned and put your arm around Bogdan and laid your head on his shoulder and kissed his nose, and as you put your hands over the horse's eyes a shot rang out. You fell against the horse, and they shot Bogdan, and then they shot all the fools and the horses—they shot Arkady, and Mooskov, and Silvestovic, and Berestichslovski, and Kazimir and Isay and Svoboda and the rest.

I was in shock. I had seen my parents murdered and now I watched as Germans shot and killed the only man I would ever love. I gasped as though a great fist had struck me in the chest, and I fell to my knees and wept there on the hill, moaning in pure agony, almost out of my mind with misery and despair, and then...and I do not know how long I wept there, literally on the back of that huge gray horse...then I heard a still small voice and looked up to see a thin old man in a too-large Russian greatcoat. Dukhi stood there, coat spattered and stained with blood. I had no idea how he had escaped or how he had gotten up the hill to me. I gasped for air and groaned and sobbed and leapt into his arms, and he held me as I bled my heart out from my eyes.

It was the one time that Dukhi could not calm my spirit. No, it is not correct to write this...I should not write such a thing. It would be more accurate instead to say that if he had not been there, I would have died in the wood next to Afanasy; died of a broken heart. But Dukhi began to speak to me with that soft and tender voice of his and a truth broke forth into my heart. I realized that once before I had seen the demonic power of evil walk in the forest, and the word it had spoken had blackened and almost destroyed my soul. And yet, my dear Pyotr, I can tell you that as I knelt on that hill next to Afanasy and cried and cried and Dukhi spoke with me, it was as if his words removed the power of that evil to take away my sanity. Oh, there would be pain and there would be loss and there would be heartache and sorrow and agony and grief, but after what I had experienced—or better, after seeing the face of God there in the Russian forests that winter, the power of evil to destroy my sanity was itself destroyed.

While my heart broke and my eyes filled with tears and my soul cried out in agony, I knew that I would see you again and I knew the God whom you served would prevail. There was within me, even then, collapsed as I was upon the hilltop under a tree, a dim but steady and unquenchable awareness that no amount of evil or darkness could ever take away the love that I have for you, my dear, and just so, no amount of evil or darkness will ever extinguish the light and love and power and goodness and truth and beauty in which and with which God weaves the very threads of our lives. It was with this knowledge that the great bedrock of hope that has sustained me from that day to this was formed in my own soul, my love. I know we will see each other again after what has truly proven to be only a brief time apart. I consider what happened that day in September outside that village to be something which taught me, as nothing else could, what it is truly to hope in eternal life, and what a true and good and beautiful thing hope can be, a true and righteous and good and beautiful blessing.

Dukhi spoke to me then, and I was comforted, and without words he helped me to know that there was a safe place in the very depth of my heart that He had made and had filled and that would not be overcome.

* * *

And so, my dear Pyotr, this is the story that I had wanted to tell you. Perhaps you know, perhaps you do not, but in case you do not, you should know that Dukhi and I and Afanasy made our way back out from behind the German lines and we kept going, down through the Ukraine and down further and eventually we came to Palestine, where I found my brother Yurik. I raised our daughter under his roof, my love, and she grew to be a fine and wonderful woman who married a wonderful man and they had very many fine children, all of whom have their own stories to be told. And one of those wonderful children brought forth little Areli who is now not so little and will soon come to visit and fuss over me and tell me that I should not sit near the window and look out at the ocean without my shawl. But my love, when I look out at the sea and behold the marvelous complexity and beauty and power of its constant poesis, and as I hold your handkerchief that you gave me so very long ago, I know that

23 Ya'ir Stern
Haifa, Israel
June, 2009

Mr Yurik Bereshenko
4781 Sderot Yerushalayim
Suite 103
Ramat Gan, Israel

Uncle Yurik;

Attached please find a copy of a letter from your sister to her husband, a man named Pyotr Federoskiya. I hope you do not mind but I made a copy of the letter so that I may have something that will help me remember who she was and what she did. She passed away in its very making.

Please accept my condolences. As you know, she has left me her house, but I have enclosed by separate post her shawl.

Yours;

Areli Nitzan

p.s. I loved her very much. She was very brave.

The young girl locked the door to the house, pocketed the key, drove down the hill to the beach, and parked her little car. She walked out to the edge of the cliffs where Haifa overlooks the sea and sat down on a rock and read every word of her great grandmother's letter again. When she finished, she put the letter into her knapsack and wrapped her hands around her knees and looked out at the sea and thought about love, and evil, and God. She thought about her future and about those in the world who sought to take that future from her.

There on the rocks overlooking the miraculous and constantly-changing, ever-constant sea, a burning resolve formed in her own young and tender heart, and with it came a gentle but powerful epiphany—there, on that rock, she suddenly came to understand why she had been born. An awareness of her life's calling flashed in her heart as quickly and clearly as light sparkles in a diamond. She determined—with whatever strength was given her, with whatever power or wisdom or goodness she could or ever would possess—that she would fight against that word which brought forth evil in men's hearts; that she would fight against that evil which still stalked the earth and killed the souls of men with cold cynicism or isolation or pride or the lust for power. She made a covenant with herself to continue that fight in the face of fear, or terror, or discouragement, or the loss of all hope. But this last thought frightened her, for there on the rocks, the deepest and most intense desire of her heart rose up and made itself a present to her consciousness—she realized that what she wanted most in life was to discover how, beyond a shadow of a doubt, hope could be kept alive when everything stood against it. This desire rose up so intently that it brought tears to her eyes. Her great-grandmother had known this secret; she had learned how to keep hope alive.

She raised an old worn handkerchief to her eyes as the wind blew the ocean spray over the rocks, opened a very old book with a much-worn brown leather cover, and began to read.

About the Author

Samuel Benjamin Gray is a pen name. Comments or questions would be welcomed, and may be sent through the publisher, *The Wild Olive Press* (www.thewildolivepress. com.). Address your comments or questions to manager@thewildolivepress.com.

3719490

Made in the USA